Managing
End User Computing

Houston H. Carr
University of Georgia

PRENTICE HALL, Englewood Cliffs, New Jersey 07632

LIBRARY OF CONGRESS
Library of Congress Cataloging-in-Publication Data

Carr, Houston H.
    Managing end user computing / Houston H. Carr.
      p.   cm.
    Includes bibliographies and index.
    ISBN 0-13-551458-4 :
    1. Management information systems. 2. Electronic data processing
departments.   I. Title.
    T58.6.C366 1988
    658.4'038--dc19   88-7292
                                                         CIP

Editorial/production supervision
and interior design: Rob DeGeorge
Cover design: Photo Plus Art
Manufacturing buyer: Margaret Rizzi

 © 1988 by Prentice-Hall, Inc.
A Division of Simon & Schuster
Englewood Cliffs, New Jersey 07632

Printed in the United States of America

10 9 8 7 6 5 4 3 2 1

ISBN 0-13-551458-4

PRENTICE-HALL INTERNATIONAL (UK) LIMITED, London
PRENTICE-HALL OF AUSTRALIA PTY. LIMITED, Sydney
PRENTICE-HALL CANADA INC., Toronto
PRENTICE-HALL HISPANOAMERICANA, S.A., Mexico
PRENTICE-HALL OF INDIA PRIVATE LIMITED, New Delhi
PRENTICE-HALL OF JAPAN, INC., Tokyo
SIMON & SCHUSTER ASIA PTE. LTD., Singapore
EDITORA PRENTICE-HALL DO BRASIL, LTDA., Rio de Janeiro

To my wife, Linda, and children, Steven and Roslyn, for giving me the time and support to translate my knowledge and experience.

To my colleagues, for encouraging and supporting the effort.

To my students, for using the interim manuscripts and kindly noting areas that could stand further attention.

To my mentors and managers over the years, who have trusted my judgment and given me the freedom to achieve.

To William Leon Evans.

Contents

PREFACE   *xi*

1 A PRELUDE   *1*

Introduction   *2*
Definitions   *2*
Historical Perspective   *6*
Formal Development   *7*
Research   *8*
Summary   *9*
Discussion Questions   *10*
References   *11*

APPENDIX A   DATA SERVICES: A BUSINESS WITHIN A BUSINESS   *11*

Introduction   *11*
A Production Organization   *11*
Data Services   *13*
> *Director of Data Services   14, Application Development
> 14, Computer Operations   15, Technical Services   16,
> Administration   16, User Support   16*
Data Services As a Separate Division,   *17*
Summary,   *7*

APPENDIX B   THE CONCEPT OF FORMAL
DEVELOPMENT   *17*

Introduction   *17*
The Formal Information Systems Development Process   *18*
   Problem Definition   18, Feasibility Analysis   19,
   Systems Analysis   21, Design   24, Programming   25,
   Testing   26, Implementation   27, Maintenance and
   Change   29
Summary   *30*
References   *31*

APPENDIX C   THE FORMAL REQUEST FOR
CREATION OF A COMPUTER APPLICATION   *32*

   End of Scenario   37
Summary   *37*
Case Study   *38*
Reference   *38*

2 ALTERNATIVES TO FORMAL DEVELOPMENT   *39*

Informal End User Development   *40*
Personal Computers   *42*
Outside Timeshare   *47*
Outside Procurement   *49*
Prototyping   *52*
Supported End User Computing   *54*
Summary   *58*
Discussion Questions   *59*
References   *59*

3 END USER COMPUTING   *61*

Who Are the Users?   *61*
   A More Detailed Description of End User Computing
   63
Basic End User Computing Tasks   *65*
   Task 1   65, Task 2   67, Task 3   67, Task 4   68,
   Task 5   68, Task 6   69, Task 7   69, Task 8   70

How Does an End User Use EUC?   *71*
How Do You Know If You Need EUC?   71, *How Do You
Determine the Product You Need?   72*, *How Do You Get
Started?   73*, *What Must You Do and What Will Some-
one Else Do?   73*
Supported End User Computing   *76*
Management Support   76, *Data Services Support   77*,
Data Services Alternatives   78, *A Support Environment
for the End User   79*
From the User Viewpoint   *79*
Conclusion   *80*
Research   81
Summary   *81*
Discussion Questions   *82*
Case Studies   *83*
References   *87*

4 THE INFORMATION CENTER: STAFF AND PREMISES   *88*

Beginning of the Idea   *88*
Organization and Issues   *94*
The Staff and Its Charter   94
Premises   *100*
Training   100, *Technical Support   103*, *Tools   105*,
Data Availability   109, *System Access   110*
Conclusion   *111*
Summary   *112*
Discussion Questions   *112*
Case Studies   *114*
References   *117*

5 THE INFORMATION CENTER CONCEPT: OPTIONS
AND ISSUES   *119*

Data Services Options   *119*
Data Access   119, *Hardware Options   122*
Management Issues   *124*
Security and Control   125, *Data Proliferation   128*,
Data Integrity   129, *Cost Accounting and Chargeback
129*, *Relations between End Users and Data Services
130*, *Promotion and Marketing of the IC   131*, *Computer
Efficiency   132*, *Benefits   134*

Summary   *134*
Discussion Questions   *135*
Case Studies   *137*
References   *142*

6 THE INFORMATION CENTER CONCEPT: BENEFITS   *143*

Expected IC Benefits   *143*
    *Reduction of the Backlog   143, Reduced Cost of Appli-
cation Creation and More Timely Results   144, Better
Requirements   145, Better Relations   145, Increased
Productivity   146, Improved Quality of Information
147, Better Use of Limited Resources   147, User
Literacy   147, User Enthusiasm   148*
Conclusion   *148*
Summary   *149*
Discussion Questions   *150*
References   *150*
Case Studies   *151*

7 IMPLICATION OF THE INFORMATION CENTER   *157*

Implementation of an Information Center   *157*
    *Signs of Need for an IC   157, Nature of the Company
158, Initiation of an IC   158, Information Center Style
159*
Premises   *159*
    *IC Manager   159, IC Staff   160, IC Capabilities   161,
Training   161, Data Availability   162*
DP Options   *162*
    *Growth   162, Computer Environment   163, Data
Administration and Access   163, Effect of the IC on
Computer Resources   164*
Management Issues   *164*
    *DP Contact Point   164, Data Access   164, Chargeback
for Services   165, Security   165, Marketing and
Promoting of the IC   165, Change in the Nature of Jobs
166*
Benefits   *166*
    *Primary Objective: End User Support   167, Future of
Existing Information Centers   167*
Summary   *167*
    *Premises   168, DP Options   168, Management issues
169, Benefits   170*

Discussion Questions   *170*
Case Studies   *171*

8 PROBLEMS ADDRESSED BY AN INFORMATION CENTER

179

Resources   *179*
    Mainframe   179, Microcomputer   180
Data   *181*
    Mainframe   182, Microcomputer   182
Tools   *183*
AT-Hand Support   *184*
    *Telephone Hotline Service   184, Walk-in Service in the
    IC   185, User Group Meetings   185, Chat Sessions and
    Lunchtime Seminars   186*
Quick Reaction Capability (QRC)   *186*
    *1. Urgent Request   187, 2. Description and Solution
    Model   187, 3. Data Acquisition, Preliminary Analysis,
    and Report   187, Changes and Final Report   187*
Variety of Solutions   *188*
    *Assistance with Reports   188, Assistance with Output
    Media   188, Alternative Systems   189*
Long-term Solution   *190*
    *Training   190, Software and Hardware Evaluation
    190, Technology Infusion   190*
Summary   *191*
Discussion Questions   *192*
Case Studies   *193*

9 BUILDING (OR REBUILDING) AN INFORMATION

198

Considerations for Creating an Information Center   *199*
    *Reactive Support Model for Data Services   199,
    Management Approval of the Information Center   199,
    Organizing the Team   202, Planning for the IC   203,
    Continuous Review of the Concept   206, IC Creation
    Checklist   207, Building a Centralized Information
    Center   208, Characteristics of a Successful IC   209*
Summary   *212*
Discussion Questions   *213*
Case Study   *214*
Reference   *215*

10 CONTROL IN THE INFORMATION CENTER   *216*

Information Center Models   *216*
  Reactive-Support Model   217, Orderly Organization,
  Minimum-Control Model   217, Formal-Organization,
  High-Control Model   217, A Compromise Model   218
Information Center Structures   *219*
  IC Documentation   219, Evaluation of User Projects
  after Completion   223, Security Training for IC Users
  225
Differences Between Formal and User Development   *226*
  Characteristics   228, Methodology   228
Conclusion   *229*
Summary   *229*
Discussion Questions   *230*
Case Studies   *231*

11 THE FUTURE: DATA SERVICES, END USER DEVELOPMENT, AND THE IC   *236*

The Past: Formal Development   *236*
The Present: Formal Development Versus User Development   *237*
  Formal Development versus User Development   237,
  An Alternate View of the Information Center   241
The Future: Formal Development and User Development   *243*
  Provision of Data Services: Methods and Capabilities
  243, The DP Organization: Data Services   245
The Future of the Information Center   *246*
  Stages of Growth   247, Reporting Level   250,
  Distribution of the Information Center Concept   251
Summary   *251*
Discussion Questions   *251*
Case Studies   *253*
References   *255*

INDEX   *257*

Preface

This book is directed at company and DP managers who are wrestling with the question of how to provide computer services to an ever increasing audience with an ever increasing demand. The need to address this issue is the result of success. The success of the use of the computer has created a demand for more use, and the success of the corporation has caused a need to be more successful. Past practices of providing computer services are wearing thin. The department that once (long ago) invited management to give it new challenges is now pleading for more time and, if they can get them, more people. Meanwhile, users impatiently wait for the official DP task list to shrink to below two years in length and for someone to recognize the need for computer-based tasks that until now were not considered appropriate to be added to the official list.

Though it would appear that all is awry, remember that business is being accomplished and computer services are being provided without bankrupting the firm. The relevant questions are "Is this the best way to provide this service called data processing (or management information systems)?" and "Can't we do something about the time and money it takes to get a report?" This book addresses more the answer than the questions. We will review how we arrived at this point in history and show one method of resolving the problem without trying to cover the waterfront of solutions. We will show how one solution set has been installed, operationalized, and applied, but will not attempt to show that it is the best solution or even the only one. It is simply one solution that has been tried and seems to work well.

We will show that it is not only possible but preferable that the end users who want computer services be the ones to provide them—if a support environment is provided. It seems to be a common trend that what was once provided by specialized operators becomes the tasks of the masses. For example, the first time I used Ditto® and Xerox® services, it was through a specialized clerk or operator. Now the plain paper copier is at the disposal of most people to use as they see fit because the dedicated operator has become one of the most significant costs of document reproduction. Thus it is with the use of the computer. We have reached a point of price and performance that the cost of use of dedicated labor (programmers) is a significant portion of the cost of systems development and is more costly than the use of the requesters' labor.

This book is the result of extensive personal interviews with members of DP management in companies with sales ranging from $400 million to over $10 billion, employing 400 to 80,000 people, and with DP departments ranging from 40 to over 1,000 members. The experiences of these managers are relayed to show how successful firms have addressed the shortage of time and trained personnel in the same way that the Allies did in World War II—with the best resources available, supported by training and encouragement. The resource of World War II was the "common soldier"; the present resources are the financial, accounting, marketing, and production analysts, managers, and staff members of the organization. The experiences are those of men and women who were involved in the beginning and have seen the success grow. From the perspective of the provider of services, this is both a "how it was done" and "how to do it" book. From the experiences, a methodology evolves, a profile of the participants arises, and a scenario is presented that can be adapted to a number of environments. Common tactics, applicable in a variety of circumstances, are cited.

It is hoped that this book will be used in planning and will be kept at hand for day-to-day operations. It is intended to help organizations meet the challenge of computer use by applying the best resource they have—their people, all of them.

The information center concept was developed by a profit-making firm (IBM). However, the concept of end user computing and the support environment of the information center are not unique to such an environment. Any organization—educational, governmental, private, public, profit-making, or nonprofit—can find great advantage in supporting users in their individual address of computer-based resources. Thus the concepts of this book are equally appropriate for a military command, a university, a church, a nonprofit corporation, a state government, the IRS, or any organization in which the use of computer and informational resources is appropriate.

A second use of this book is to prepare students for the DP environment of a firm. With this exposure to computer access, business and computer science students should be better prepared to understand the possibilities available and be more effective in their new jobs. To provide greater understanding of the options available, current problems with the formal request for service and the formal systems development life-cycle methodology are discussed. These are followed by discussions of end user computing, information center concerns and practices, and cautions involved with end user computing support.

The book has two perspectives, managerial and practical. One view of end-user computing and the information center is the concern for managing the technology, use, and users of computer resources. This view addresses the support environment for the users, the information center, security, cost, and managers' becoming programmers. Practical information concerns the form of the information center, how to organize one, the content of an IC user's guide, and preliminary descriptions of the tasks that users perform and the technology that supports these tasks. Thus the thrust of the text is to mix management and use to enhance the productivity of the users while protecting the data and computer resources of the organization.

The introduction of end user computing has created new positions in the DP/MIS field. As information centers are created and expand, IC managers and staff members are needed. Because programmers and systems analysts are already in short supply, new sources are necessary, and recommended, for the IC staff. This book describes the environment and positions that these employees will occupy. Case studies show that there are many alternatives in filling these positions and that the IC has the potential to be very effective in enhancing the productivity of the MIS department and user organizations.

1

A Prelude

[Information systems] technology, at least in its modern form (with high-speed computers), has had a very short life. Its earliest commercial application occurred in 1952. Thirty years is a very short time for the distilled outline of a new management profession to develop. Fields like marketing, accounting, finance, and production had a thriving body of literature and know-how in place in 1920. An incredible amount of knowledge and change in thinking have occurred in these fields in this century, but it has been able to be assimilated within an organized field of thought. Evolution, not revolution, has been the challenge in these fields. [1-1]

The computer is both a tool and a perspective. Firms, large and small, have adopted the computer and computer-based methodologies as a way to reduce their costs and improve their productivity and their competitive position. Applications range from recording of facts to decision support and include a wide variety of capabilities in between. What was once a subdepartment of accounting is now an organization on at least the same level as its former master. Data processing (DP) now accounts for a sizable portion of operating and capital budgets. In fact, DP is now referred to as a "business within a business," with all the functions of the parent.

This is a book about one view of data services, end user development. It omits, by design, a lengthy historical development of the computer and its software, leaving this subject to classical MIS and computer science works. In doing this, we will often discuss specific aspects of MIS/DP and uses of the computer that are artificial and sometimes confusing departmentalizations of the total concept. For example, we will discuss topics such as end user computing, decision support systems, and prototyping as if they were separate and distinct areas of thought, when in reality they overlap and are often simply different views of the same concept. Someone said that nature doesn't really have separate areas of interest, such as zoology, biology, and botany; nature just is, and humans separate

1

it into categories for study. Thus it is with the computer and computer-based systems. Therefore, when we discuss a topic as if in isolation, remember that it is always a part of the total topic and we separate only for convenience.

> *The topic of end user development requires a discussion of several areas to provide perspective: (1) hardware and software history, (2) the DP organization, (3) formal development, and (4) the administrative process for requests for data services. These are presented in this chapter and its appendixes.*

INTRODUCTION

This book focuses on one aspect of computer-based systems, end user development and its support. Because of the complex nature of the primary area, we will review or discuss a number of allied topics:

1. Historical development of the physical computer—the evolution of the present-day micro and mainframe computer environment
2. Formal development of systems—as a point of reference
3. Evolution of the data processing organization—changes in organization and technology
4. Use of computer-based applications—the tools by which the user addresses the computer and information resource
5. Concept of end user computing—direct approach by the person with the problem for which computer-based systems and information are appropriate
6. Management of end user computing—through the support environment called the information center

DEFINITIONS

In the process of developing the basis for utilizing an organization's greatest resource, its people, to address solutions via computer-based systems, we will consider the responsibilities of the user and the data processing organization, the authority of each, and their views of organizational power. The subject of this book has significant potential to affect the way jobs are performed, who performs specific jobs, and the relations between suborganizations. The potential exists to increase productivity, creativity, and even the competitive posture of the organization. To do this, the participants must understand the nature of the environment, the use of the capabilities, and the management of human, machine, and information resources. For us to discuss these concepts in context, some definitions, by way of a quick review, are in order. The concepts are summarized in Table 1-1.

TABLE 1-1 CHARACTERISTICS OF INFORMATION SYSTEMS CAPABILITIES

Capability	Orientation	Level	Focus	Nature
TPS	Data	Operational	Task, efficiency	Structured
MIS	Information	Management control	Resource	Structured
DSS	Decision	All, strategic	Alternatives	Unstructured
OAS	Productivity	Operational	Task, efficiency	Structured
EIS	Problem	Executive	Status, problem	Flexible, easy
AI/ES	Knowledge	Operational, tactical	Problem	Structured

A **system** is a group of interrelated parts working together to achieve a common goal. This is as true for a manual system as it is for one that is computer-based. Thus when we refer to systems we created on the computer or that use computer-based capabilities and information, we are addressing not a single entity but a collection of interrelated parts that work together to achieve an objective or goal. The system of interest contains those things over which we have control that are related to the goal and other parts of the system. If there are items of interest that affect the system but are beyond its control, those items are, by definition, in the environment, that is, outside the system.

TPS (transaction processing systems) are capabilities designed to capture and store data on the activities of the organization. These were the first systems to be computerized. Initially this was done to save clerical effort and cost of collection and to improve data accuracy. With the expansion of computer-based systems, TPS are installed to store the basic activity of the organization in a way that is readily accessible by individuals and other systems. The focus of TPS is data and short-term events of the organization. For example, the payroll system is used to collect labor hours expended by person and by project. This is the basic data of the system, which is generally used at the operational level of management to direct the day-to-day operations of the organization. From this storage of data comes summary reports and the information needed to produce paychecks and W-2 forms. This same data might also be used by another system to determine charges for the products created.

MIS (management information systems) take data from TPS and transform it into information to support the basically structured decision process. These capabilities produce scheduled reports and provide the basis of information used by middle and upper management for the management control function. Where the focus of TPS was data, the focus of MIS is information. An example is an MIS that uses the payroll system data to produce a report for each department showing the costs by project, indicating overruns and schedule slippages. The report has summary data on top, potentially only exceptional data (falling outside of specified bounds), and only shows detail upon a special request.

MIS tend to produce structured reports that are consistent and change only over long time periods. The focus is on information content to support the management control function of the organization. As we will indicate in the discussion for decision support systems,

MIS support the structured control function of the organization, often at the tactical or resource planning level.

> A final definition of MIS, by Ralph Sprague, is the entire set of systems and activities required to manage, process, and use information as a resource in the organization.
>
>   In the same light, Data Services is characterized as dedicated to improving the performance of knowledge workers in organizations through the application of information technology. [1-2]

DSS (decision support systems) may be any capabilities that aid or assist the decision process, but more specifically they provide access to data and models to support unstructured problems. The focus here is on the decision process involving planning and trouble-shooting. It is often believed that DSS are used most at the executive levels for strategic planning. In reality, decision support is of significant value in any situation and at any management level where the problem being addressed is not well defined and where the answer to one question may prompt other questions.

In the payroll example, it may have been suggested that department 10 is undeservedly paid more than department 18. A DSS would provide ready access to the data from payroll to display a mean and a standard deviation of the pay rates of each department and even a statistical analysis to determine if indeed one department was higher paid. Once this question was answered, the user could query the same data to determine if one department has greater overtime, absenteeism, or missed schedules. None of these questions were expected at the time that the present MIS were created, and some questions are the result of previous answers. Thus DSS are decision-oriented and are designed to answer impromptu questions in a style suiting the user.

OAS (office automation systems) bring technology to the office and to knowledge workers. As drill presses and cutting machines have aided factory workers and increased their productivity, word processing, facsimile, and electronic mail increase the productivity of knowledge workers. These technologies affect not only the way jobs are done but also what is done. The emphasis is on support in the use of information. One classic example of the purpose of such technology is to increase the efficiency of office tasks while producing a paperless office. For example, instead of an individual creating a memo, giving it to a secretary to type on a typewriter, making changes, retyping it, and putting it in the mail, an organization using OAS would have the originator create the memo on a word processor and distribute it over telephone lines via electronic mail. Even quicker for a single recipient, the creator could write the memo by hand and send it over facsimile, much like a copy machine with output at a remote location, with no further support.

EIS (executive information systems) are designed with the executive in mind in that they provide very easy access to current information needed by these managers. The presentations may be used in planning or in following progress. Information content is high and data content is low. Such managers are interested in up-to-date information with a minimum of effort. Data from our payroll example might be used in one EIS screen to show progress on one program, total cost in another, and overtime by department in another.

AI/ES (artificial intelligence/expert systems) add the personal knowledge of an expert to computer systems, thereby allowing nonexperts access to this same capability. Where TPS and MIS might provide the publicly available data required for a problem, the knowledge base of the AI/ES capability and its inferencing ability allow wide use of expertise not available through other means. The emphasis is on privately held knowledge and heuristics. Such systems tend to be difficult and expensive to build, and many people are hesitant to rely on them due to the critical nature of some problems. For example, medical diagnostic expert systems are just now being accepted by doctors, although the ability is not new. With such a system, a doctor in a small town can have access to diagnostic expertise and counseling that would generally be beyond his knowledge, without requiring travel or the presence of a specialist.

As noted in Appendix A at the end of this chapter, I contend that the **data processing organization** has evolved from a group that once spoke in strange tongues, behind locked doors, and worried mostly about keeping the computer busy so as to be cost-effective. It is now characterized by analysts as opposed to coders, data administrators and managers as opposed to card sorter technicians, and concern for program quality and data integrity as opposed to tight code and fast processes. The extent of this change has created, in my domain, a new title for this organization that better describes what the individuals and sections do in the modern world. The title is **data services,** indicating the impact of the organization on the total organization entity. Thus I will use *data services* to refer to the evolved data processing organization.

Though this may seem like a simple substitution of words to refer to the "DP shop," it is important to realize that this entity is not a shop but a service organization with significant resources and extensive influence. Where DP used to create vertical systems for vertical organizational structures, they now create systems that cut across all parts of the organization and provide information support to the total organizational structure. Data services provides data and information services and is changing the way business is conducted.

The **firm** in this book is intended to mean any formal organization, either educational, governmental, private, public, profit-making, or nonprofit. Generally, it is understood that a firm or company is a recognized entity. It may have subdivisions, such as personnel or engineering, which might be called *organizations*. To avoid confusion between the part and the whole, I will use *organization* or *department* for the part and *firm* or *company* for the whole. Please realize, however, that the concepts of this book are equally appropriate for other setups: a military command, a university, a church, a nonprofit corporation, a state government, the IRS, or any other unit of any size in which the use of computer and informational resources is appropriate.

HISTORICAL PERSPECTIVE

A standard, or classical, review of the history of the introduction and use of computers might use the hardware generations as a point of reference. This would begin in the 1950s with vacuum tube technology and continues at the present time with generation 4 VLSI (very large scale integration), with a quick mention of artificial intelligence (generation 5). Another view would be that of developing software. Initially there was only machine language, then symbolic languages like Assembler, then high-level languages that were really direct-link compilers and interpreters (like COBOL and BASIC), and finally fourth-generation software capabilities. These later capabilities are frequently referred to as user-friendly and nonprocedural, which is meant to say that the language must be given less structured instructions to achieve the same result as earlier capabilities. Stated another way, the new software must be told what to do, not how to do it.

As hardware has increased in capability, its cost has decreased. The investment in a mainframe computer was once a major part of the capital budget; it is still an important outlay, but of relatively reasonable size. Today, software is more complex, exceeded in cost only by the salaries of the employees that tend the machine and software and others affected by data services.

Three events during this span of more than three decades that are not as obvious as the evolution of hardware and software are responsible for the evolution of data processing and end user development. One was the success that engineering personnel had with personal use of the computer as opposed to requiring that data services be an intermediary. Engineers were willing and able to take on the development of capabilities that would otherwise be the responsibility of systems analysts and programmers in data services. These engineers carried out the same tasks as the analysts and programmers, in the defined area of engineering problems.

The second event was the change of training received in college. Business graduates are now significantly more computer-literate. They are ready, willing, and able to address their own needs. With less fear of the computer and an eagerness to acquire computer-based support, these employees are less willing to wait for service and more willing to accept the challenge.

The third force was the evolution of the use of computers and computer-based information. The 1950s and early 1960s was the time of transaction processing systems (TPS), which replaced clerical effort and captured the events of the firm's activity. The focus was storage and use of data, efficiency of machine processing, and concern for proper use of the new resource. From the mid-1960s to the mid-1970s the advent of management information systems (MIS) created a new environment. The focus changed to information to support management, effective use of data as well as computer resources, and a view that the computer was an important element in the company's tactical and strategic, as well as operational, plans. After the MIS view came the evolution to decision support systems (DSS), with a focus on the decision-making process, addressing underspecified and unstructured problems, and a view that the computer was a vital part of the firm's existence. As the view of the computer changed from data to decision, from efficiency to effectiveness, and from tolerated to vital, the mind set of users and management alike evolved. Now the

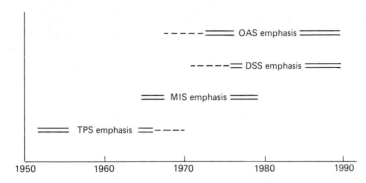

Figure 1-1 Relative emphasis of TPS, MIS, DSS, and OAS

computer was an available, usable asset, not an expensive liability. Figure 1-1 illustrates the periods of relative emphasis of these areas of computer-based support.

While the TPS-MIS-DSS evolution would be apparent, a fourth area of computer support has developed in the office. The effect of office automation systems (OAS) has been felt as technology arrived in the office in the form of word processing, electronic mail, and facsimile services. As was the case in financial and accounting systems, as the office workers evidenced success, more was sought. Familiarity bred contentment, and pressures developed in the office to better apply technology to enhance productivity.

FORMAL DEVELOPMENT

Formal development is an approach to satisfying users' information requirements that relies predominantly on data services' supplying the tools, resources, and expertise required. Typically, it is implemented using a life cycle approach; development is *partitioned* into activities with defined roles and responsibilities for users and data services personnel. Activities will have *specified end products*, and the life cycle is subject to frequent formal *review*. Formality may ease political problems because roles and responsibilities are defined. Partitioning facilitates management of development, though there is a tendency to meet schedules as opposed to managing development.

The stages of the systems development life cycle (SDLC) comprise the phases during the life of a computer application. Definite actions take place, and specific and often visible outcomes are produced. The phases of formal development are (1) problem definition, (2) feasibility analysis, (3) systems analysis, (4) design, (5) programming, (6) testing, (7) implementation, and (8) maintenance and change. These phases of the SDLC are addressed in more detail in Appendix B at the end of this chapter.

In and of itself, formal development is a good thing. Through structured analysis and design, structured programming, and planned testing, complex programs are able to be maintained through their long lifetime. The objective of formal development is to define the problem adequately and design the solution system so that it meets the needs of the ultimate users and can be maintained and upgraded by people other than its creators. This formal methodology takes time, effort, and significant resources, but the complexity of modern systems requires such. Formal development is addressed in some detail at the end of this chapter. It is important to understand this methodology because of its universal appeal and use in development of any and all systems. Whether you are creating a new payroll system, building a bridge, or developing a system for delivering welfare services, the phases of formal development (systems development life cycle) are appropriate, even if the names of some phases must be changed to match the task.

However, the formal development process causes problems associated with timeliness of delivery, effectiveness of the final result, and cost of creation. These traits have created a backlog of work that is, in many companies, in excess of two years. This is the official queue, or backlog, of work that has formally been presented to the review committee and officially accepted for later action. Meanwhile, there is another backlog of work that is never presented, an unofficial queue of work five times as large as the official backlog that has received management review and approval. The inability of data services to respond adequately to the official backlog of requests and the failure of the company to address the smaller needs of the users have spurred users to seek alternative ways to get their jobs done.

This is a book about the alternatives available to resolve the problem of the backlogs, both of them. The chapters that follow will address these alternatives and the consequence of each. The point at which we will aim is that there are two ways to address the power of the computer and computer-resident data, and each is valid under given circumstances. Until now, it has been assumed in many instances that there was only one method, formal development. History has shown this view to be limiting. We believe there is at least one very acceptable and complementary alternative that has support in many firms.

RESEARCH

The discussion in this chapter has been designed to introduce the reader to ideas, definitions, and a brief historical perspective. The appendices that follow this chapter discuss the nature of the data processing organization, formal development, and the administration of data processing requests for service. At the end of appendix C we have included the first of a number of case studies that demonstrate and support the central theme of the book and the ideas presented in specific chapters. To appreciate the value of such cases, consider the following.

Firms that wish to achieve the user productivity potential discussed here have two sources of information. The first is the advice of consultants and writers as presented in the trade journals. Subscribing to computer and MIS publications is vital to keeping abreast of the changes in a field that is evolving like the discipline of MIS. While often important in the furthering of the field, such articles and advice are often general, opinionated, and incomplete. Reading of weekly, monthly, and quarterly publications is important to maintain a level of knowledge. However, it is often not sufficient to reach an adequate level with minimal background.

The other way to gain insight into solutions is by knowing what other firms are doing in the area of interest. This means reading the results of research done in the field. This book is the result of field research in firms that have adopted formal support for end user computing and are being successful in enhancing user productivity. This book is the result of extensive interviews with data services managers in 20 firms in the Dallas–Fort Worth, Texas metropolitan area. Table 1-2 lists the firms that participated in the research.

FIGURE 1-2 FIRMS INTERVIEWED FOR INFORMATION CENTER RESEARCH

Nr	Company name	Industry	Chapter
1	FMC Corporation	Machinery, chemicals	6
2	Texas Instruments	Semiconductors, electronics, computers	7
3	Federal Reserve Bank of Dallas	Services to banks	10
4	American Airlines	Air transportation	10
5	MOSTEK-Thomson Components	Semiconductors, electronics	4
6	Electo-Tex Services*	Computer services, facility management	6
7	Potato-Tex*	Packaged food products	9
8	Soutex Company*	Oilfield services	11
9	General Dynamics—FWD	Defense contractor: aircraft, systems	3
10	Middle-Texas*	Construction materials	5
11	NorTex Services*	Oilfield supplies and services	
12	Texas Electric Service Company	Electric utility	1 Ap C
13	Otis Engineering	Oilfield engineering and services	3
14	Eastexas Industries*	Oilfield supplies and services	4
15	J. C. Penney Life Insurance Company	Insurance	6
16	City of Dallas, Texas	City government agency	7
17	Quick-Tex Corporation*	Convenience stores	5
18	Zale Corporation	Retail jewelry stores	8
19	Southland Royalty	Oil exploration and production	5
20	Pier 1 Imports, Inc.	Retail sales	8

* Name has been changed at the request of the company.

As noted in Figure 1-2, this group of companies is a diverse community. Included are firms recognized as successful, innovative, and having traits of excellence. The firms have a wide range of size, product, and environment. The one thing they have in common is success in supporting end user computing.

SUMMARY

- The importance of the use of computers has evolved from a concern for efficiency to a view of effectiveness.
- As computer hardware has increased in capability, it has decreased in cost. A dissimilar relation has been true for software, with an increase in cost accompanying increases in capability.

- Three events have added to the increase by business end users to have personal access to the computers: (1) the success achieved by engineers in this regard, (2) training in computer skills in college, and (3) the evolution of computer applications from data gathering to information reporting to decision supporting.
- Office automation systems have had reasonable success in supporting productivity increases in the office through the introduction of technology.
- Formal development is an approach to development wherein data services supplies the tools, resources, and expertise. It is implemented using a life cycle approach, with a partitioning of activities and responsibilities, and is accompanied with frequent formal reviews.
- The inability of data services to satisfy the requests for service has caused significant pressure for end users to find alternative ways to meet their needs. The formal backlog of requests for service is less than one-fifth of the total demand.
- There are alternatives to waiting for formal development.

Key Terms

Organization	Hardware
Computer generation	Information
Data processing	Mainframe computer
Data services	Microcomputer
Decision	Management
Computer	System
DP organization	Formal development
End user computing	Transaction
Support	Software
Transaction processing systems (TPS)	Expert systems (AI/ES)
Management information systems (MIS)	Decision support systems (DSS)
Executive information systems (EIS)	Office automation systems (OAS)

DISCUSSION QUESTIONS

1. Discuss the concept of a system without reference to the computer. Note the parts of a specific system, such as a fast-food restaurant, and the elements of the environment.

2. Discuss a computer-based system with which you are familiar, such as the registration system at school, food inventory at a fast-food restaurant, point of sale at a department store, or traffic ticket inventory at the local police station. How is the computer-based system different from the non-computer-based system?

3. Describe a TPS and an MIS and discuss how they are similar and how they are different. Is it difficult to separate any given system specifically into the category of TPS or MIS?

4. Describe a decision support system with which you are familiar. Was the problem it was designed to support structured or unstructured, strategic or operational, at the executive level or for day-to-day operations?

5. What generation level of hardware is the IBM personal computer model AT? How do the capabilities of this machine compare with those of previous generations?

6. What careers are open to an MIS student?

REFERENCES

1-1. McFarlan, F. Warren, and James L. McKenney, *Corporate Information Systems Management— The Issues Facing Senior Executives*, Homewood, Ill: Richard D. Irwin, Inc., (1983).

1-2. Sprague, Ralph H. Jr., "A Framework for the Development of Decision Support Systems," *MIS Quarterly*, Volume 4, Number 4, June 1980, pp. 1–26.

1 Appendix A

DATA SERVICES: A BUSINESS WITHIN A BUSINESS

INTRODUCTION

When the computer was introduced into organizations, it was placed under the charge of a group that came to be called **data processing.** The title was appropriate, as that was what the organization did, process data. Since that time the organization and its function have evolved, and now it provides service to the entire firm. Thus it is appropriate to refer to this entity as **data services** and realize that it has become a "business within a business." The discussion to follow will endeavor to show that data services has all of the functions of an operating production company and has analogous management positions. Thus we should expect data services to be performing not a mysterious series of activities but a classical set of operations.

A PRODUCTION ORGANIZATION

Figure A-1 represents an organization chart for a classical production company. At the head is a president, general manager, chief executive, or chief operations officer. Reporting to this person and supporting all levels of the company is a staff group. This includes department-specific tasks such as planning and companywide support such as personnel. Functional departments reporting to the top position carry out the role of discovery, production, selling, money management, and customer support. These functions exist in almost any organization that deals with a product or service and sells to a customer. This can be as true of a governmental organization, military unit, educational entity, or hospital as it is for a profit-oriented production company. The point is that these functions are required.

Product development strives to find and/or create products that can be produced and marketed by the firm. This entails development of new products and refinement and

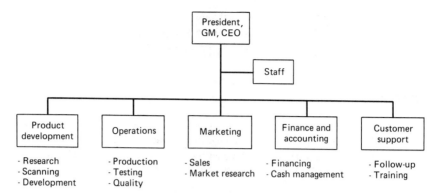

Figure A-1 General production company organization structure

extension of existing items. There are two ways to do this: (1) primary research and (2) scanning the environment.

Primary research deals with new items and concepts that have potential commercial application. This can range from laboratory experiments in solid-state theory and computer design of new circuitry such as that which produced Dolby noise reduction for audio sound and the audio compact disk to the library-based development of a classroom course outline.

On the other end is the process of *scanning the environment* for ideas. This includes response from market research, feedback from customer support, and tracking the industry and, especially, competitors. The point is to detect opportunities and problems for which a product can provide a solution.

A third aspect of product development is when a client comes to the organization to request the design of a new product. The request would generally be based on a demonstrated ability to design and produce the entity or the organization's having a unique, or even monopolistic, ability in the requested area. In this case the client provides most of the marketing data in that the production will normally be for just that client.

Once products have been developed to where they can be produced in appropriate quantities and a market has been identified, **operations** sets up to produce the entities. Items suitable for mass production will require high-volume operations where items of a unique nature will be produced in small quantities, even one of a kind. *Testing* and *quality control* are vital activities to ensure that the result is what was desired.

As noted, prior to production of the products, **marketing** must have determined that a market exists in sufficient quantity to warrant the expense of operations setup and repayment of development costs. Through *market research,* the areas of product, place, promotion, and price must be identified and matched to ensure that the production effort is viable. As appropriate, the *sales* force must be trained and supplied to sell the product.

Supporting the product development, operations, and marketing departments is **customer support.** This group effects *follow-up* with the customer for *training* and to ensure that products perform as advertised. This function, even when handled by the sales force, is vital in its capture of feedback from the ultimate user of the products. Often this feedback will indicate new uses for the product or ways that product development can extend the life or value of the item.

The **finance and accounting** organization budgets, invoices, collects, and finances the development, manufacture, and sales of products. This organization supports all areas of the business and provides periodic report cards on operations.

DATA SERVICES

Figure A-2 lists the departments and functions provided by a data services organization, and Figure A-3 illustrates these functions in the same manner as done for the production company. As we will show, all of the generic functions performed by a production company

---

1. Application development
   A. Systems development
      i. New applications
      ii. Maintenance
   B. Data administration
      i. Data management
      ii. Database administration
      iii. Quality control
      iv. Security
2. Technical services
   A. Operating systems
   B. Telecommunications
   C. Maintenance and upgrade
3. Computer operations
   A. Data entry and library
   B. Machine room
   C. Scheduling
   D. Output distribution
4. Administration
   A. Personnel
   B. Purchasing and inventory
   C. Finance and accounting
   D. Budgets and forecasting
   E. Request for services management
5. User support
   A. End user services
      i. Consulting and trouble-shooting
      ii. Data access
      iii. Training
      iv. Equipment acquisition and support
   B. Decision support systems
   C. Executive information systems
   D. Expert systems

Figure A-2 Typical organizational structure of data services

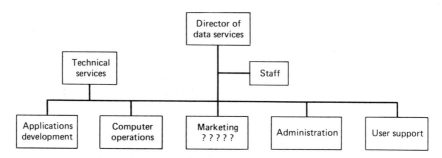

Figure A-3   Organization chart for data services

are performed by data services. We are accustomed to using different names for departments and functions within the DP industry and therefore do not always make the connection with production activities. Even so, all of the functions do exist.

Director of Data Services   President, GM, CEO

This person is the executive manager of the organization. He or she provides guidance to the technically oriented personnel of data services while communicating with the executive and middle-management levels of the firm. The director addresses the strategic planning of the organization, sets global goals and objectives for data services in concert with the parent company, and resolves exceptional problems. Due to the nature of the product, data services, the director is generally involved in tactical planning for hardware and software to provide processing power, data and program storage, timesharing facilities, and output capability. The director is a member or chairperson of the MIS review committee, which examines all requests for data services and sets priorities.

The director, along with the managers of application programming and user support, is the primary interface with the firm's management and must develop the ability to listen to and sell ideas. Generally, the director comes from within the data services organization and therefore has a technical background. To be effective, he or she must suppress this technical inclination in favor of a generalist attitude and business traits. Many leaders of data services find this a difficult transition to make and never evolve to the level of executive management equal to that of directors in the firm.

Application Development   Product Development

Marketing

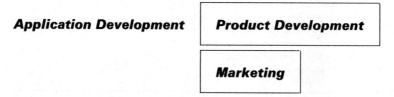

Often called systems and programming, this section develops and maintains computer-based applications and organizes and maintains the data resource. The function has evolved from pure programming to include a thrust for application quality, data integrity, and information resource management. For this reason the section is shown as having the two primary tasks of the analysis and development of systems (akin to product development) and administration of the data resource.

Application development, specifically *systems development*, has generally been the primary contact with users of computer capabilities. It is responsible for the formal development of computer-based applications, maintenance of and changes to existing applications, software problem resolution, and, in general, customer support. Department members interface with other functional areas within data services for the users and manage the total capability.

Data administration addresses the logical and physical storage of the corporate data resource. It is concerned with the storage (database technology), security, quality, and administration (presence and characteristics) of all data. This function is rapidly rising to the same level as application development, as data is recognized as vital to the organization. Thus it is *information resource management* that is being recognized as vital, not creation of applications.

There tends to be a shortage of qualified and experienced people for both groups, a condition that has been noted in causing the formal development backlog of requests for new applications. This has caused severe pressures on systems development and has been a factor in the emergence of end user computing and the evolution of the data services organization.

Marketing and market research are areas new to data services. During their short lifetime, most DP organizations have had little time or need for seeking additional work. Overload has been the order of the day. Since the equipment was very costly and development complex and expensive, only selected applications were initially allowed. Thus systems development did not seek new customers or research the market to determine new areas of need. However, as DP shops mature into data services organizations and the view of the organization changes from one of tolerated expense to a vital investment, this function will gain importance. Though systems development programmers continue to address the backlog of existing work, the new customer service organization (user support) is working with users to effect productivity. It is at this juncture that market research takes place.

Computer Operations | Operations |

The *machine room* is the part of data services in charge of the day-to-day running of the computer, scheduling of jobs, obtaining supplies for the computer, and organizing the entry of production data outside the timeshare environment. This function has diminished in size and importance as the operating systems have computerized many functions previously performed by the computer operators. Unlike many jobs in data services, positions are filled by high school graduates and people with junior college and trade school training.

The primary interface between users and computer operations is when mainframe problems develop. Then the user or customer support person of data services works with technical services and computer operations to resolve the problem. In a microcomputer environment, the function of computer operations is performed by the user.

Technical Services   Operations

This group is responsible for the care of the computer and the general welfare of the hardware and software resources. Duties include hardware maintenance, updating of operating systems, and trouble-shooting of processing. In addition, department members are concerned with telecommunications between the mainframe and remote terminals, PCs, and other devices. This is where the most technically trained personnel are found, those that can speak to the computer in its own terms. Whereas programmers may come from business or computer science backgrounds, tech services people tend to be from only the latter.

As noted, the primary occasion when the user interfaces with technical services is when a problem exists that is not in the domain of systems development. However, when a new capability is being obtained, possibly under a make-or-buy decision, tech service personnel review the requirements to ensure that the system can support the new capability.

Administration   Finance and Accounting

The functions of data services administration are akin to the functions of any firm's accounting, finance, personnel, and procurement operations. This department often duplicates these functions carried on by the parent firm because of the specialized nature of the people and products. However, there is great similarity with the parent firm and a need for business majors who understand the nature of the tasks in a computer-oriented environment.

The administration section processes requests for services from users; aids in the acquisition of PC hardware, software, and supplies; forecasts budgets; and apportions computer charges, as appropriate. It works behind the scenes, and the user has little contact with it.

User Support   Customer Support

Though the customer support function might be included as part of application development, its charter and responsibilities are changing and evolving to such an extent as to warrant a level equal to other departments within data services and a direct line of communications to the director. The staff directly supports the user community, end user computing, and the personal use of the computer and data resource. User support personnel will come less and less from computer science and application development and more from business backgrounds and the user community.

The advent of end user computing is changing the way data services are provided to the organization. Instead of waiting for formal development, the support of the user by user support allows rapid development of capabilities, using mainframes and microcomputers, aided by user-friendly software. Thus, due to the evolution of the technology, changing characteristics and demands of the users, and a new support methodology, a new resource is being used for decision support: the users themselves.

DATA SERVICES AS A SEPARATE DIVISION

Some firms have found data services to represent the "business within a business" so well that they have separated that organization as an autonomous division or operating entity. This allows the organization to solicit business from outside of the firm and to operate as a profit center. Not many firms have succeeded in this venture. Thus most data services organizations tend to support only the firm's needs. Even this goal is no small task, and the changing nature of providing data services is making it even more complex.

SUMMARY

The organization responsible for managing and processing the data of the firm has evolved over its short lifetime to become a service-oriented group with functions and responsibilities like that of a classical production company. With this expanded view of what was once the DP shop, the activities provide change to support the total operation and objective of the firm as a whole.

1 Appendix B

THE CONCEPT OF FORMAL DEVELOPMENT

INTRODUCTION

The word *formal* in the term *formal development* may be new to the reader, but it is not a stranger. When an individual or group wishes some new thing, such as a new machine for the factory or a computer application for financial analysis, the individual or group goes through a formal process to obtain it. A formal process is required, especially in large organizations and companies, because many people are involved and often a significant amount of money is needed. To acquire the money, one must complete the required paperwork. In this process, the applicant defines the objective, the cost, and the benefits. Again, whether it is an expansion of the parking lot or a new inventory management program, the processes are similar—and formal. They have been formalized in organizational directives, they require following a formalized routine, and they necessitate the filling out of forms.

There are two formal processes to be followed in the creation of a computer-based program, application, or system. One is the process required to administer the program and the funds. This is the responsibility of both the administration section and applications development as a new request for service is created and followed. This formal process is discussed in Appendix C to show the nature and complexity of the administrative task.

The other part of formal development is described here. It is the process by which something is created.

THE FORMAL INFORMATION SYSTEMS DEVELOPMENT PROCESS

The process of formal development includes the members of data services in interaction with requesters and users as well as a significant amount of work that does not involve them. This second method of formal development, the process of creating and maintaining a computer-based application, is called the *systems development life cycle* (SDLC). It is composed of eight stages and is equally applicable to any system (computer-based or otherwise), with the exception of the stage of programming, which is the "build it" stage and would have a different name in any given profession.

Formal development is an approach to satisfying users' information requirements that relies predominately on data services to supply the tools, resources, and expertise required. Typically, it is implemented using a life cycle approach; development is *partitioned* into activities with defined roles and responsibilities for users and data services personnel. Activities have *specified end products*, and the life cycle is subject to frequent formal *review*. Formality may ease political problems because roles and responsibilities are defined. Partitioning facilitates management of development, though there is a tendency to meet schedules as opposed to managing development.

Figure B-1 shows the phases of the systems development life cycle and the relative amount of time or effort required for each. These areas of interest comprise the stages during the life of a computer application where specific actions take place and specific and often visible outcomes are produced.

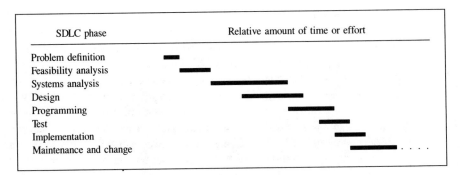

SDLC phase	Relative amount of time or effort
Problem definition	
Feasibility analysis	
Systems analysis	
Design	
Programming	
Test	
Implementation	
Maintenance and change	

Figure B-1   Phases and effort of SDLC

Problem Definition

It should go without saying that the problem in question will be identified and defined before any other effort is undertaken in systems development. All too often it is assumed that the problem is understood or that it will be uncovered during feasibility and analysis stages. It should not be up to the systems analyst or designer to discover what the problem is. The users should be able to describe the problem that led them to request a solution, which is what the data services team will address. Given that the details of the problem and the level of complexity will indeed be defined during feasibility and analysis, the nature of the problem should be delineated before any other tasks are pursued.

Problem definition can be effected by the *white paper* technique, derived from a method used by television network news teams. When news teams wish to research and discuss a topic without taking sides, they create a white paper in which they describe the situation at hand and the available facts. Some opinions may be stated, but the point is to remain unbiased where possible and set the stage for further investigation. Thus it should be with problem definition: Write a white paper stating the facts of the problem and providing guidelines for solution. The paper should be agreed on by the major parties requesting the new application and will be the starting point of the investigation by data services.

Deliverable output	*Definition of problem to be solved by computer-based capability or system*
Problem definition	

Feasibility Analysis

This is the time when a preliminary solution is composed in order to determine if it is technically, economically, and behaviorally feasible to accomplish the task. This stage is often overlooked because it is assumed that the task can and will be accomplished.

Technical feasibility is the analysis performed to determine if the existing computer facilities can accommodate the solution. This would concern processing power for mainframe computers, size of main memory or the existence of a virtual system, availability of appropriate software, access to secondary disk storage, and people to operate this environment. It also means that printed output can be achieved within the desired time frame and in the volume required. It concerns the availability of terminals and local printers in the users' area, plus communication lines and electrical receptacles in the case of new equipment. Technical feasibility is the most obvious and probably the easiest analysis to perform.

Another aspect of technical feasibility is the availability of human resources. It has been indicated that 50 to 70 percent of the programming force in many firms is fully utilized in maintaining existing applications. Given this, the question arises as to the availability of sufficient programmers of the necessary experience level to create new applications. The supply of hirable programmers is low, so often application development will have to use what is available. This may mean employing recent college graduates who have a primary computer science or MIS education but lack experience, especially in operational situations. For example, if you are trying to create an IMS* application, do the programmers to be used have IMS and DL/1 language experience? If the analysis and programming experience and background of the data services team is limited, thought should be given to the alternatives of outside procurement of software, development services, and contract programmers.

Economic feasibility considers the question "Can we afford the application?" If the technical analysis indicated that the present facilities are adequate, the only cost will be the time of the programmers. However, if additional facilities are required because those present are inadequate or the new application will press resources to an undesirable limit, additional out-of-pocket costs must be incurred. A combination of technical and economic feasibility might involve the ongoing cost of operation. Overtaxing of the mainframe may occur, or reports may become so voluminous that they result in significant variable costs and time delays. Time-share versus batch processing is a technical and economic issue; which environment best serves the need?

Realizing that the cost of the application development section is a fixed cost—that is, the expense incurred for the year will generally be the same regardless of what the analysts and programmers do—the main consideration is whether programmers can be better utilized on the task in question or on some other task. The consideration may involve one versus many applications. "Can we afford the application?" may be asked not so much in terms of dollars as in relation to other tasks. In an environment of scarce resources, it involves making a judgment call on resource utilization.

Behavioral feasibility refers to the impact of the application on users. The computer is a harbinger of change and is often viewed as a replacer of jobs. The change of people's jobs is an important behavioral issue, and questions such as these must be addressed: Are the users able to adapt to the change brought on by the computer-based application? How will the application change the flow of work, the nature of work, the interactions of the people, and the ability to serve the customer? Fear of replacement of personnel, real or imaginary, is a management issue that must be addressed if disruption is to be avoided.

Before one can determine the feasibility in all three areas, one must understand the computer-based task to be performed. This implies an analysis of the problem and the task. This will be done in great detail during the systems analysis phase (which follows feasibility), but a reasonable analysis must be done during feasibility to ensure that the task is indeed technically, economically, and behaviorally feasible. At the end of the feasibility analysis stage, the reviewing analyst or team will most likely be required to give a preliminary cost estimate, if not a fixed cost figure for the project, to indicate or update a cost-benefit ratio or a return-on-investment value. Again, the team will have only a basic idea of the task but will be required to give an accurate estimate of cost. As unfair as this may be, it is a reality. Another reality is that the range of this estimate should be considered good to only plus or minus 50 percent. Thus management should realize that a $100,000 project will cost somewhere between $50,000 and $150,000. It will not be until the completion of the systems analysis stage that the range will drop to 20 percent in either direction, and

* Information Management System by IBM.

even in design the range will likely remain at 10 percent. (This is an optimistic range assuming less than experienced people in normal circumstances involving honest scheduling and work practices.)

Deliverable output	*Report on technical, economic, and behavioral feasibility of developing and utilizing the proposed capability.*
Feasibility analysis	

Systems Analysis

This stage has gained greater importance as programmers, users, and management alike have realized that the more we know about the task, up front, the better the application can be designed, created, and maintained. Management agrees only hesitantly with this view, because the more time spent in analysis, the later the "real work" (programming) begins. Thus there is conflict over the level of analytical detail and effort and the time until something is produced.

Systems analysis picks up where feasibility analysis left off and has the specific objective of providing sufficient information so that a correct and complete design can be created and maintained. This involves extensive interaction with the user to determine what is achieved now, what new system or change in procedure is desired, and what the end result should be. Here computer science majors must converse with business people to achieve communications. This is not an easy or trivial task, because each of the participants uses a different point of reference and often a different form of communication. Users are looking for the end result, while programmers are considering the means of the solution. The two approaches do not necessarily communicate well or produce the same outcome.

Add to the difference in nature of the participants the fact that the users may not know exactly what they hope to achieve, let alone how to achieve it. This creates additional problems. How does the analyst determine the problem and provide a solution if the user cannot indicate what they are? It is not that users are illiterate or lacking in talent; they just may not be able to verbalize the problem or its resolution. With this limitation, how does the analyst determine what is really required? Davis [B-1] indicates that there are four methods of gaining this information: (1) asking, (2) looking at the existing or similar systems, (3) looking at other user systems, and (4) building a prototype. This contingency view means that the analyst must be alert to communication problems and use different methods as appropriate.

Given that the analyst is aware of the communication problems, what does he or she hope to achieve in the systems analysis phase? The outcome of this phase should be a specification of the existing system as well as the requirements of the new system in such detail that a new system can be created and maintained from the document. In addition, the data gathered must be in such a form that it can be shown to the user to determine if understanding has been achieved. DeMarco and Yourdon [B-2] have introduced the idea of data flow diagrams that show the flow of information in a vertical hierarchical form, IBM [B-3] has vertical hierarchical input–process–output (HIPO) forms, Orr-Warnier [B-

4] has horizontal diagrams, and over 90 other authors have suggested methods to capture and present the information gathered in systems or business analysis. Regardless of the method used for data gathering, two questions must be answered in the affirmative: (1) Have I gathered and captured the relevant data? (2) Is the capture form suitable for communications among data services and user personnel?

The understanding, or lack thereof, achieved in this stage will last for years, perhaps decades. The documentation will be used for system design, testing, training, operation, maintenance, and change. The adage "Sin in haste, repent at leisure" is appropriate here. If users become too eager to get on with creation of the system at the expense of analysis and documentation, they will pay in the end by change after change after change. Though many feel that change is inevitable, it is nevertheless cheaper to do (in analysis and design) than redo (in maintenance and change). The cost of creation is significantly less than the cost of change and re-creation. Another adage, "An ounce of prevention is worth a pound of cure," emphasizes the relation between the analysis and change stages.

So what we are looking for out of the systems analysis stage is (1) a document of understanding and (2) requirements that (3) the users and programmers understand and (4) can use for system design and maintenance. Unfortunately, the specification document tends to be large, not too interesting, and not widely read. An overt attempt must be made to avoid this situation, by means of a supplemental user summary, a set of diagrams, or other format that communicates well.

Prototyping.   This brings us to a technique that can do just what we want. It is called *prototyping*. If the project were the creation of a new radio by engineers, the designers would create an engineering model or prototype to show what was happening. It would be a "lash-up," "breadboard," "mockup," or Tinkertoy model that had the required features and could be used to communicate, demonstrate, and "specificate." So it is with business systems; analysts can construct a prototype model to demonstrate to the users what is understood. This model can range anywhere from paper reports to a fully operational system. Examples of prototypes are input formats, output reports, terminal screens that show form and format, make-believe terminal activity that demonstrates system dynamics and decision points, and a capability created in special high-level languages to show system operations. All of these model forms are designed to be (1) quick to create, (2) easy to change, (3) inexpensive to build, and (4) inexpensive to discard. In this environment, analysts and users can evolve the system concept, trying several ideas without being constrained to the first because of time or cost. With an operational prototype, users can work with the model and see if it does what they expected. If not, the model is changed, and users try again. The result is significantly better communication and understanding of what is desired. As users work with the evolving model, their concept of the system evolves, matures, and solidifies. Although users may be very unsure as to their desires at the beginning of the prototype phase, they will tend to have stabilized to a single design concept by the end of prototyping. This means not only that analysts and users have a better understanding of the requirements but also that the requirements have stabilized and later change is less likely.

In cases of small, noncomplex system, the prototype can become the final application.

In most instances, the prototype is the model for the specification. It is used for communication and then discarded. The model has a finite useful lifetime and can be abandoned or kept without great concern for cost.

Make-or-buy decision.   A specific reason for a comprehensive systems analysis is so that a decision can rationally be made at the end of the stage. That decision has to do with where the system is created. For example, suppose the requirements call for what appeared to be a very specific, unusual, user-oriented cash management system. After the systems analysis stage it is found that 95 percent of the requirements are not so unusual after all and can be met with a commercially available product. Not only does the off-the-shelf product cost only 20 percent of the projected cost of the task if created in house, but the software can be installed by the end of the month, training can start at the vendor's facility next Monday, and the total capability can be operational by the middle of next month. The program has already been tested and is used by 26 other firms with good success. The idiosyncrasies required can be designed quickly outside of the vendor's package by application development for 1 percent of the total task cost or they will be incorporated by the vendor at 4 percent of total cost.

There are two points to be made here. First, a thorough analysis is required regardless of where the final system is developed. Without determining what you need, no product purchased or developed will likely satisfy the real requirement. Second, new systems do not have to be invented over again, in house. Products that have been developed and time-tested can be significantly cheaper in the short and long run for both application development and users. Taking advantage of others' development cost, and mistakes, can save large amounts of money and time. The major stumbling block to outside purchase seems to be spending the money. It was stated previously that the applications development section is a fixed charge regardless of what is achieved during the year. Therefore, in-house development appears to be very low in cost because the money would be spent anyway. However, also remember that there are many projects to be completed, and these people can be effectively used on other projects if this project can be satisfied with a commercially available package. Thus purchase of software permits both the satisfaction of this need and the application of the resources to another project, all for the purchase price of the package. The only problem is that the funds for the purchase are visible, whereas the salaries of application development personnel are not as visible.

One of the objectives of the systems analysis phase is to determine the *architecture* of the ultimate product. This refers to several aspects of the specific application or system and to entities that appear outside of its realm. Bob Katchmar [B-5], IBM Director of I/S support and operations in Bethesda, Maryland, describes architecture as follows:

> *Architecture is a specification which determines how something is constructed, defining functional modularity as well as the protocols and interfaces which allow communications and cooperations among modules.*

Specifically, we are concerned with (1) application architecture, (2) data architecture, (3) network architecture, and (4) support system architecture. These portions of architecture are effected after the strategy of the capability or system is set, in relation to the objectives and strategy of the firm, and before planning for its design and use take place.

> Strategy *leads to* architecture *leads to* planning *leads to* development.

Application architecture specifies structure descriptions and relationships of the application and their components to support the business processes. This will guide the design of application programs and modular construction of functions. It will determine the technology used and the way the user's conceptual frame will be implemented.

Data architecture specifies the structure and relationships of the data and its components to support the enterprise. This should identify the sharing, standardizing, controlling, auditability, and security of the data of the system. If the new capability uses database technology, it will rely on existing data and control measures. However, if the capability is totally autonomous, it most likely will be designed to stand alone in each of these areas, resulting in significantly more effort on the designer's part.

Nowadays, *network architecture* can be as important as any other part of the system because of distributed departments, processing, and data storage. This portion of the total architecture specifies structure descriptions, relationships of network senders, and receivers, logical paths, and communication functions that manage and support the transfer of information. A normal information system developer might consider the transfer of computer digital data, but today the consideration of networks must include voice, images, text, and data.

The *support systems architecture* specifies the structure of relationships of system interfaces and functions that provide access and interface management of the application, data, system software, hardware, and network facilities. Not only does this address how the capability and users will be supported during normal use, but it also addresses how to protect the application investment from changes in technology, data, and operating systems.

Deliverable output	*Specification of requirements, defined strategy and architecture,*
Systems analysis	*and, where practical, a prototype of the system.*

Technology support for systems analysis.   The objective in addressing the phases of the SDLC is to consider how computer-based capabilities are created. The analysis phase is the most important because the phases that follow build on the results of analysis. It is the most difficult phase because determining what the users want and creating a specification tend to be more of an art than a science.

Over 100 manual and computer-based methodologies and tools have been developed to aid the analyst. These range from textbooks on how to draw a variety of diagrams to keep the process straight to $8,000 software packages to draw the diagrams, hold the data dictionaries, and create the resultant code. Although the software packages do not gather the data or set the architecture, they do aid the analyst in conceptualizing the system and communicating it to others.

Design

The design of the new system, based on the requirements gathered during the systems analysis stage, involves the creation, on paper, of the system parts and interactions. If the system were a bridge, design would entail the creation of engineering drawings from which the parts would later be made and the bridge constructed. For a computer application, the design stage produces a detailed layout of the total task that can be programmed, tested, and maintained.

One way to describe the design process is to consider the output. A successful design should create something that can, of itself, be translated into a product. For a computer-based application, the output of design should be sufficient documentation so that programming can produce the ultimate system. What makes design difficult, and so important, is not just the process of translating the requirements of analysis but the process of breaking the total system into manageable, doable parts. Thus one output from design is a module diagram. This is a diagram that shows the total system broken down into small, specific, identifiable stand-alone tasks (modules) that can be created and tested in isolation. Yourdon and Constantine [B-6] and Paige-Jones [B-7] give excellent narratives on the considerations of design, the main point of which is that the modules should be as autonomous as possible. When modules are autonomous and do specific, singular tasks, they will be small and understandable and will not interfere with each other.

Consider for a moment the importance of a well-thought-out modular design, consisting of autonomous parts that have very limited interaction with each other. (Limited interaction means that the data required by the module enters it by one door only and the results leave by the same door and that there are no side doors. Also, the processing inside the module does not affect other modules except by way of output data.) Such a design will be a programmer's dream during programming, testing, and debugging as well as during maintenance and change. It is very likely that any given problem can be isolated to a specific module. If that module is so badly written as to be of little continuing value, it can be discarded with little cost and a new one created in its place. The effect of a change to a module should have no surprising consequences in other modules or areas of the program. A fix or change is simple and noninteracting.

Design deals with how the software will handle the data, where it will store it, and how input will be received and output generated, physically. Databases are designed, communications are considered, and languages are selected. It is at this stage that the ideas of analysis are translated into the realities that will be used in implementation.

Deliverable output	*Diagram showing the components and hierarchy of the modules to be programmed.*
Design	

Programming

This is the stage that user management has been waiting for. It is only here that they believe that progress is made. Here the design is translated into machine-usable code and the application takes form. Now the analyst can report to data services management and to user management that code is being created, databases established, and test data prepared for system checkout. In other words, the fun has begun, and there is something to talk about that everyone thinks they understand. However, this is one of the easiest stages and the one that may be of least significance.

To say that computer code creation is the easiest and least significant stage seems harsh. However, consider that creation, or programming, can only take place after analysis and design have been accomplished. The better the analysis and design, the easier the programming. The more thorough the analysis and design, the easier to program in isolation, the less interaction required, and the less creativity required of the programmers. In fact, low creativity, based on sound analysis and design, is precisely what is desired in order to keep testing, debugging, maintenance, and change simple.

To help make programming clear and to increase the probability that someone other than the original author can follow the flow, a structure must be included. The programmer must follow guidelines and conventions and use specific methods, while avoiding others. This is called *structured programming* and, as noted, makes the end result easier to follow at the time of any change.

Given that a thorough analysis has taken place and has produced a modular design product, the analyst team takes the design and programs the pieces. With the total task described in the form of hierarchical modules, the analyst has two choices, top-down or bottom-up programming. Bottom-up programming starts at the lowest level of modules and programs and tests them individually. Then modules are grouped together up the hierarchical chain and tested at a higher level. This continues, grouping and testing, until the top module is reached. Top-down programming is the reverse. The top modules are programmed, with stubs created for the next lower level of modules. The programmed modules are tested, using the stubs for receivers and responses from the lower modules. Then the next level of modules are created and the system is tested to that point. The result is conceptually the same, a programmed system. Each module and group of modules is tested, and the whole system exists at the end.

Deliverable output	*Coded and tested modules that perform the tasks indicated in the specification.*
Programming	

Testing

During this stage, the system is tested as an entity. Where parts and groups of parts were tested in the programming stage, the intent of the testing stage is to exercise the system as the users will do later. To do this, a test plan and test data are required.

During design, the analyst should be determining what system testing will be required, a schedule for this, and what test data will be needed. The data should be a simple enough to produce understandable and traceable output but complex enough, eventually, to test all of the important parts of the system. Notice that I did not say to test *all* parts of the system. The testing phase is to find the *major* flaws prior to turning the system over to the users, who will find more flaws in usage than formal testing can ever do.

Consider for a minute the magnitude of testing *all* parts of a system. Let us assume that you have a moderate size system with, say, 30,000 lines of COBOL code. In the system, there are 500 conditional statements (IF THEN, ELSE, or the equivalent). Now, how much data will be required to test the results of placing all 500 statements in all combinations of settings? Taking the example of flipping one coin five times and getting 32 possible combinations, the number of combinations is large with only part of the 500 conditional statements dependent on each other. Thus the amount of data and the time to test all possible combinations in even this moderate-sized program is large. So the practical thing to do is test the major junctions of the modular design and let the users test the rest in operation.

The test plan should show a schedule for exercising the paths of the system, in progressively more rigorous form. Initially, small quantities of concise, familiar data should be introduced into the system in the way that users ultimately will do. The outputs should be checked to see that nothing unusual has happened. Given this success, a more complex and comprehensive group of data should be introduced. The increase in data content should be kept to increments that can be checked for accuracy and reliability. Although this sounds simple and logical, there is a tendency to jump from the first to the most complex form, without a finite path of progression.

During the testing period, the system should be isolated from other operational systems so as to not damage them. This may mean the creation of responses that appear to have originated from these outside systems until the new system is considered "safe." At that point, the connection to operational systems can be made direct and usable.

Deliverable output	*A working system that performs in accordance with the specifi-*
Testing	*cation, tested using representative system data.*

Implementation

Once the system has been programmed and tested, it is turned over to the users. There is much that should have been done up to now to prepare for this stage, such as user documentation, preparation for training, placement of new equipment, and plans for switching over to the new system after an appropriate period of use.

In the feasibility study, the technical and behavioral impact of this system were analyzed. Now is the time to implement the created capability and to see these effects firsthand. The users have been hearing about the system for some time, especially since testing began. It is likely that some of the users were involved in the testing stage. Now, in implementation, all users will become familiar with the capabilities and impact of the system. New equipment must be installed and explained. The terminals and printers will be the most visible and produce the most concern to the ill-informed. The manner in which the system is introduced and how the switchover occurs will have a great deal of influence on the behavioral aspects of this new capability.

A new capability can be introduced in a number of ways. As a pilot installation, the total capability can be used by a select group or department before the entire system is brought up to full speed. Meanwhile, the old method is used by the rest of the users. An alternative is to use the entire new system in parallel operation with the old system. As with the pilot installation, this method has the safety, but also the redundancy, of dual capabilities. Alternatively, phasing the new capability in avoids some redundancy as parts of the system are tried and stabilized before additions are made. The last and most dramatic method is to have a sudden switchover to the new system with no pilot, parallel, or phased introduction. This is the quickest method but has the greatest risk.

Each of these implementation options has different effects on the users, different appearances of change and technology, and different responses. If the user community is accustomed to technology and change, less preparation is required, and a sudden switchover is possible. However, with a user group that is not computer-literate and views the system as threatening, parallel and pilot operations have much to offer. In any case, the programmers must provide ready and visible support to avoid a negative response on the part of the users. This support must take the form of personal availability, training, and user documentation.

The documentation (diagrams, pictures, and narrative) that meets the needs of the programming team will be of little use to the users. Therefore, written material must be prepared that communicate at the level of the average user. The documentation must be comprehensive without being patronizing, complete without being too lengthy, sufficient without being too technical, and informative at several levels of use. Training sessions that provide hands-on experience with the system and the documentation may well be the most efficient and effective use of all persons involved.

With the increased power and lower cost of computers, it is reasonable to include a "help" capability in interactive systems whereby the user can request assistance and information from the system while using it. For example, at different points in the program, the user can press a function key or type in "help" at the terminal and receive an explanation of the feature being used at that time. Several levels of help can be programmed, giving new users greater information while not annoying seasoned users. Another training method, computer-aided instruction, can guide the user through a new system, with testing accomplished along the way to see at what rate the user is progressing. Both of these methods can be quite friendly, with help being only a key away.

Another method of reducing the fear of introduction and use of a new system is to establish user specialists, users who seem to relate well to the system and can become points of contact within the user community. As any new capability is introduced in an organization, some users grasp the workings and potential of the capability more quickly than others. These people are natural aids and trainers of other users and can relate to them on a readily available, nonthreatening basis. Since they already are the user community, no special effort is required to discuss problems and new features.

It must be remembered that the implementation phase does not last forever. The process of turning the system over to the users and making them competent in its use will be a specified portion of time on the system plan. Although the maintenance and change phase does follow, there must be a time when the users see the project as complete and installed, even though they realize that it will evolve over time.

One way to ease the end of the formal development project is to show the users the timing of the implementation phase and include a system warranty during this time. This will state a specific time during which the development team will have close contact with the user community in order to train them in system use but will indicate when the concentrated aid will end. The warranty period that is coincidental with the implementation phase, and possibly extends a small amount of time beyond it, is a time when the team will fix problems without additional charge. However, at the end of the warranty period, the usual charges of the maintenance and change phase will begin.

At the end of the project, which is the end of the implementation phase, the development team should take time to evaluate the project. The question to be answered is whether or not the intent of the project was met and whether the team was effective and productive in its efforts. It is most likely that the final system is only an approximation of that described during the feasibility analysis and has evolved since systems analysis. However, the end result should be quite recognizable, and the team and users should be able to define the level of success in meeting the users' needs. The project team should also be able to evaluate the project development methodology and its ability to produce a well-defined product in an orderly and coordinated manner.

Deliverable output	*Installation of capability, education and training, user docu-*
Implementation	*mentation, and evaluation of task and system.*

Maintenance and Change

This stage follows the implementation and acceptance of the system by the users. As users operate a new capability, problems are uncovered, new views of the system's intent become apparent, and new possibilities are realized. The problems require quick correction, and the changes and extensions need to be considered. If the system ran into problems in the testing phase, or even as early as programming, many problems may have been left for resolution during maintenance. Thus this stage may be very obvious, lengthy, and costly.

One cause of high maintenance is rushing through feasibility, analysis, and design so that programming and testing can get under way. With ill-defined systems, rushed design of less than total modularity, and poor documentation, maintenance becomes more difficult. This means that the maintenance stage becomes more resource-demanding. Again, "Sin in haste, repent at leisure."

The other view of this stage is that it is a natural part of a system's growth and evolution. When an improvement or addition is required, it must, itself, go through the stages of feasibility, analysis, design, programming, testing, and implementation. Thus the change stage contains numerous small system developments, each of which must work within the total system. The problem, however, is that the change can be larger than the system. If the system was constrained in analysis, it must be completed in the change stage. If the schedule was too tight and some features were omitted and problems not solved, they must be resolved in the maintenance and change stage. The stage that should have a legitimate position, becomes a make-up, make-right, fix-all hodgepodge.

Several issues must be faced by data services, the users, and management if maintenance and change are to be reduced to a reasonable level. First, application development management must realize that the scheduling done in feasibility was a first look and will have to be updated as new information is received in analysis and design. Second, user management must become more patient as the feasibility and analysis stages are in progress. They must learn that there is more valid work in these stages, as well as in design, than in the visible stages of programming and testing. Third, the users must take an active part in the system during all of its development. Somehow, the users must learn to communicate with the development team, and vice versa. This means that the user department must attract or develop talented personnel that can understand system development and computer application. These senior, special users must be given the task of being part of the development team so that they are planning for implementation from the beginning of the project. Fourth, data services must see the need for programmers and analysts to have an understanding of the users' business and be able to converse and communicate with all levels of users. Last (maybe), both firm and data services management must realize the evolving nature of information systems and be willing to adopt new software, methods, and techniques. Higher-level software, computer-assisted structured methodologies, and database technology cost money to acquire but are the only hope for an organization (data services) short on personnel, time, and funds and long on requests. When all of this happens, new systems can be developed that better meet the needs of the user and thus have a shorter and less costly maintenance and change stage.

Deliverable output	Corrections of errors, changes, and enhancements. Continues during life of system.
Maintenance and change	

SUMMARY

This appendix has been a lengthy discussion of what is necessary in large system development. However, the time and cost of this type of methodology have been the roadblock to development for small systems, impromptu analyses, and ad hoc reports. If the capability to be developed is complex, will affect many people, and will have a long life, the use of the systems development life cycle methodology should be considered. However, if the time for development is likely to be longer than the life of the application, losses in communication will be detrimental, and the nature of the application is likely to evolve during development, other methods should be considered. Even with nonformal development methods, the stages described will be followed, though they will not be as costly or as time-consuming as in formal development.

An advantage of formal development is that in large data services organizations, groups of expertise can be formed in the various phases of development and applied to their area of concentration. Analysis is an art, and an expertise must be developed to ensure that the analysis function is carried out correctly. Of more obvious merit is the expertise in the areas of programming, database design and DBMS use, and testing. Formal development provides for partitioning of tasks and, potentially, the use of experts in each phase. At a minimum, these experts are on call in large organizations to assist the development group. Formal development also supports the establishment and use of standards by which applications are made more uniform, quality standards are required, and maintenance is made more possible. In formal development, data is treated as a centrally available corporate resource. This means that the tendency to know about and use existing data is higher in a formal process than when achieved by the end user.

The systems development life cycle has advantages in that (1) systems are developed by professionals and contain appropriate control and security functions, and (2) systems may be developed in keeping with overall organizational goals rather than strictly departmental goals. In contrast, the disadvantages noted in the SDLC are (1) a long system development process, (2) the development of systems that do not meet user needs because users may not be able to identify their needs adequately without experiencing the system, and (3) the fact that user needs may change during the development process. The last disadvantage is especially expensive in the final stages when specifications have been essentially "frozen."

In contrast, end user computing will be shown to have the advantages of (1) users designing the systems to meet their needs rather than have their needs interpreted, (2) working systems are usually available more quickly, (3) users can change systems to meet changing needs as they use their systems, (4) users can independently meet their unexpected need for information, and (5) the risk of completed systems not meeting user needs is reduced. End user computing also has disadvantages in that (1) the data resource can get out of control, (2) there is a potential for data and application redundancy, (3) users may not ensure adequate security and control measures, (4) there are potential problems with auditability, (5) there is a potential failure to ensure adequate testing, and (6) there is a probable lack of documentation, making maintenance difficult.

The stages of the systems development life cycle show the progression of the development of a computer-based application. It is the purpose of these stages in formal development to capture, monitor, and effect all tasks required. However, it is the very nature of the stages that causes scheduling, cost, and time problems. As noted, the same stage progression is appropriate for any development, but it is hoped that other, less formal methodologies will avoid the penalties while keeping the intent.

REFERENCES

B-1. Davis, Gordon B. "Strategies for Information Requirements Determination." *IBM Systems Journal* 21:1(1982):4–30.

B-2. DeMarco, Tom, *Structured Analysis and System Specification*, Englewood Cliffs, NJ: Prentice Hall, (1979).

B-3. "A Design Aid and Documentation Technique," *IBM GC20-1851-0 (1974)*

B-4. Orr, Ken, *Structured Requirements Definition* Topeka, KS: Ken Orr and Associates, Inc., (1981).

B-5. "Information System Architecture for the Enterprise," presentation by Robert L. Katchmar, Director I/S Support and Operations, IBM, Bethesda, Maryland.

B-6. Yourdon, Edward and Larry L. Constantine, *Structured Design* New, NY: Yourdon Press (1978).

B-7. Page-Jones, Meilir, *The Practical Guide to Structured Systems Design* New, NY: Yourdon Press (1980).

1 Appendix C

THE FORMAL REQUEST PROCESS FOR CREATION OF A COMPUTER APPLICATION

The following story illustrates the tasks involved in getting a computer-based application developed. This discussion addresses only the administrative process, not the systems development life cycle, which is covered in Appendix B. Here I am trying to give a flavor of the task to administer and coordinate the request for service from the user of data services. As with many difficult situations, humor sometimes helps relieve the tension. Thus it is here, in that the intent is never to criticize but to narrate to show tension, complexity, and human nature.

1. *Manager determines that he or she wants a problem solved.* This is akin to the first phase of Herbert Simon's [C-1] three phases of decision making, intelligence. The manager "scans the environment" and determines that a problem has arisen that requires solution via a computer-based system. The manager does not necessarily know what the form of the solution is but does have an analytical or intuitive belief that the computer can be well applied in this situation. It could be a change to an existing application or a new program. In either case, some new feature is required to meet a new or evolving problem.

2. *Manager assigns problem resolution to a staff member.* It would be unusual for a manager to follow through with the request to data services, but it can happen. More often the manager assigns the problem resolution to a staff member. The point is to assign someone to work with the problem definition, data services, and the ultimate application.

3. *Staff member fills out DP request for service form.* The staff member, after making a preliminary investigation of the problem, determines what paperwork is required by the company and by data services in order to request a new computer-based application

and to allow the expenditures. The staff member writes a description of the problem, as he or she understands it, and sends it to data services. Companies vary widely on the content of this form. Some want only an authorization to begin charging time in order to determine the nature of the request. Others require a fairly detailed description of the problem and the system desired. Either is acceptable because any description at this point will be completely revised in the data services development phases.

4. *Request for service form is sent to data services for logging.* The administrative branch of data services receives the request for service form and logs it into the unofficial work queue. This simply acknowledges the existence of a request by the user without committing data services to any effort. The request will be put into the queue with any other requests received at the same time. Often a formal work authorization is created in order to charge time expended against this request, even in the definition and feasibility stages. The authorization may be a common task authorization, or it may ultimately include the cost of the total system.

The notation

>>> Delay <<<

is an indication of a time delay, the passage of time during which little or nothing happens, as far as the user is concerned. The reason or nature of the delay is listed to the side.

>>> Delay <<< Administrative

5. *Programmer-analyst receives request for service and determines scope.* The data services administrative branch forwards the request to the manager of application development, who probably logs in the request again. The manager most likely reviews the request so that he or she can be aware of the level of requests and then forwards it to the appropriate section within application development. The request arrives at the desk of a senior analyst or programmer-analyst (P-A), who is to review the request for generalized scope. The P-A reviews the request, in time, and makes plans to talk with the staff member noted on the form.

>>> Delay <<< Other work requiring attention of P-A

6. *P-A meets with staff member to discuss request.* The P-A calls a meeting with the staff member (and possibly the manager to add prestige to the need). The parties discuss the (real) intent of the request, and the P-A tries to determine the scope of the task. The user describes the task in user terms, and the P-A responds in DP terms. Both think they know what is needed or desired and leave the meeting with a confident feeling of understanding.

7. *P-A estimates scope and cost of request for service.* As we discussed in Appendix B, the first part of the development of a new capability (after problem definition) is a feasibility analysis. This is the phase where the P-A determines that it is economically, technically, and behaviorally feasible to do the task. In some cases, the meeting that has just transpired will be called the feasibility analysis and the P-A will attempt to create a document for committee review and approval. In most cases, the output of this meeting is just a better description of the task that will make some sense to the review committee.

The P-A performs any additional feasibility analysis required, determines the cost, describes the intent of the request, and sends it to his or her manager for approval. This informs the manager of application development of the real intent of the request and places this manager in a position of power, with the ability to delay or even reject the request. The manager will also be informed of the task so as to appear knowledgeable at the time of formal committee review.

>>> Delay <<< Other work and lack of personnel

8. *Request sent to review committee for approval and priority.* The manager of application development forwards the request through the administrative branch of data services to the review committee for formal review. The review committee (often referred to as the steering committee) is composed of high-level managers of various departments and has the responsibility of reviewing all requests for service sent to data services that are not immediately rejected in data services. Although the head of data services is a member of the review committee, and possibly the coordinator or chairperson, the committee is intended to provide a review authority outside of data services to give all users a fair and equal chance for service. This gives the members visibility as to the demand placed on data services and an apparent voice in the setting of priorities of data services efforts. The authority of the committee is also of value to data services because it removes the total judgmental burden from their shoulders but still gives them a large voice in the actions. However, often the non–data services members have little interest in projects other than their own and are afraid that asking questions will demonstrate their ignorance of data processing. Thus the data services member has disproportionate power and can often apply his or her will and make it appear as committee action.

>>> Delay <<< Review committee meets only periodically

9. *Request for service is approved and added to backlog of requests.* This request will likely be one of many presented for review, whether the cycle of review is weekly or quarterly. There are four considerations of the request before the committee: (1) the appropriateness of the work for formal development, (2) the cost-benefit ratio or return on investment, (3) the existing backlog of requests, and (4) the relation of this request, other requests, and the backlog.

Companies are finding that the cost of data services is in the range of 2 to 10 percent of sales, depending on how the cost is measured. In a firm with only $100 million in revenue, this amounts to an annual data services budget of between $2 million and $10 million, a sizable figure for what some consider bookkeeping activities. As to the availability of programmers, often 50 to 70 percent of those working for the company are employed full-time in maintaining and changing existing applications. In addition, there is a shortage of experienced programmers, making the hiring of new talent both difficult and expensive. Thus the review committee is in a quandary, the demand is high, existing supply of experienced programmers is limited, and the supply of new programmers is small and in high demand. This requires the committee to weigh carefully the applications added for formal development, for two reasons. First, without careful review of requests, the backlog will grow even greater, and second, the longer the queue, the longer the wait by the users, and the more the customers complain. Due to this environment, fewer than 2 out of 10 needs that the users recognize reach approval status.

To give the committee a methodology for approval or rejection, other than the subjective view of appropriateness, companies will often use the same criteria for new computer investment and applications as they do for physical plant-and-equipment capital improvements. This is the relation of cost and benefit and the return on investment. The criteria for cost-benefit ratio or return as a percent of investment can be based on the total dollars available for application development for that year or can be established as a value that must be met to be accepted. Cost-benefit ratios of 1 to 3 (3 to 1 for benefit over cost) are usual and often exclude certain cost avoidance figures and expenditures in the calculations. Return on investment can be figured by any of the usual financial methods, such as Net Present Value (NPV), Internal Rate of Return (IRR), or years for payback, and will usually be in line with returns for other capital expenditures.

Of great interest at the time of review are the total cost and the benefits of the application. What makes these of such interest is that the task has had only limited analysis, often no more than a preliminary feasibility study, and decisions are made as to timing, schedule, levels of effort, benefit, and total cost. In reality, these values will not be determinable with any level of certainty until much later in the application's development lifetime. Not until the P-A has completed the formal systems analysis stage can the cost of the application be specified within as narrow a range as 20 percent in each direction. However, it is likely that cost and benefit figures must be presented with apparent confidence to the review committee. Unknown to the members present is that the estimate of costs and benefits made at this point in time is, at best, accurate within a range of plus or minus 50 percent.

Once the item is considered appropriate for formal development and meets the financial considerations, the task is added to the formal backlog of requests. At this point, the requesting department would make a plea for a high priority. Thus the importance of the task would be considered in light of others in the backlog, and a time or priority number would be set for this task. In large firms, a wait of one to three years is not unusual.

$$>>> \text{Delay} <<< \text{Backlog of other tasks}$$

10. *Request is assigned to a P-A, who works on the program in isolation.* When the time has come for the task to be worked out, it is assigned to a single P-A or a P-A team to begin the formal chain of development. These tasks (or phases), described in

Appendix B, often involve users to only a limited degree. It is the lack of user involvement that has such far-reaching effects. The users often feels, or are made to feel, that the computer solution is the domain of data services and that users are involved only peripherally. The P-A asks the users to tell or write down all they know about the problem, including possible solutions, and translates this into a specification. After a required signoff of the specification, the P-A goes off into seclusion to do the job, returning only when the task is complete.

>>> Delay <<< Program analysis, design, development, and testing

Since a feasibility analysis has taken place, the next step is a complete analysis of the task to be undertaken to determine all aspects of the problem and solution. Once completed, a design will be created for the new computer-based system or an existing system will be changed, thus making the solution operational. After design completion and signoff, the programming begins. Once programming is complete, testing of the total capability is accomplished, and the new capability is turned over to the users.

11. *"Finished" program is shown to the staff member.* This is the program that the P-A has developed without the involvement of the user. It works efficiently and does what the P-A understands the user needed and wanted, as stated in the specification. The P-A is pleased with his or her work and calls a meeting with the staff member to give instructions as to the working of the program.

12. *Staff member says the program does not meet the need.* The P-A shows the staff member how to use the application, with great excitement. At the end, the staff member informs the P-A that the program is nice but does not meet the need because it is not what was requested, and besides, the problem has changed during the ensuing time, resulting in changes to the specification. The P-A says he or she did what the specification asked for and feels that the staff member is being unkind. The P-A adds that changes are to be handled later and that all efforts should concentrate on the original requirements, which were supposed to be stated completely in the specification. The staff member has not even looked at the specification for many months because of the delay involved and feels that the P-A should have understood the need better.

After much disagreement, the staff member agrees to try to use the system, in spite of the limited documentation, and write down the changes needed to meet the original intent. The P-A reluctantly agrees to make changes to the program to meet the real original intent but refuses to add what appear to be enhancements. Both parties leave the meeting with little optimism and no confidence in the other party.

>>> Delay <<< Program changes and testing

13. *New program is given to the staff member, who shows it to his or her (new) manager.* During the time of waiting for the project to start and for development to be completed, a new manager has been assigned to the user organization. Thus when the P-A and the staff member bring the application on which they have finally agreed, the

manager does not see it as a valid solution because the problem is viewed differently. Not only have the personnel changed over time, but the problem has changed as well.

There are several alternatives at this point. (1) The manager can scrap the project and try to define the real problem and a new solution. This will entail a loss of face due to the cost incurred that will be a sunk cost, so the manager sees that as not a very viable alternative. (2) The manager describes the problem as he or she sees it to the staff member and directs him or her to redefine the system requirements in light of the new need. A compromise is reached as to the new version of requirements, and the old system is accepted with the proviso that the system will be changed to meet the new needs during the maintenance and change stage. This means that a drastic change will be made to the application to meet a different need.

14. *The P-A considers a position in another company.*

End of Scenario

The above description is not intended to be facetious or frivolous but tries to show the timing and frustrations involved with formal application development. Several individuals, personalities, egos, and power structures are involved in using computers, each with specific goals and objectives. Even when dedicated people work on a new application, honest differences of opinion develop, and honest variance of viewpoints evolve. Application programmers are considered specialists in their field and seldom have experience in the business of their customers. The users are business specialists and have had limited interest in the technology of the computer. Each understands a different view of the problem and most likely speaks with a different vocabulary. The P-A sees and seeks the beauty of the computer solution, whereas the user sees and seeks an effective solution to the business problem, at the same time pleasing their bosses. Each of these participants is rewarded by different organizations of the firm and for different performances. There is no pat on the back for either party for cooperation, just results as seen through the eyes of the individual managers. These differences in view, objectives, and rewards create misunderstanding, conflict, delays, and cost. The question is whether there is an alternative.

SUMMARY

The process by which formal development is administered and controlled is important to the total MIS effort. This discussion attempted to show that such administration takes time and effort. We also know that the development process takes time and effort to ensure that the system or capability is complete and correct to the extent possible. The two control mechanisms working together attempt to ensure that the final result is what was desired and that it can be maintained and evolved over its lifetime.

CASE STUDY

Texas Electric Service Company

Texas Utilities Electric Company (TUEC) was incorporated in September 1982. On January 1, 1984, Dallas Power & Light Company, Texas Electric Service Company, and Texas Power & Light Company—formerly the electric utility subsidiaries of Texas Utilities Company—merged into and became operating divisions of the Electric Company along with a fourth division, Texas Utilities Generating Company. The Electric Company is engaged in the generation, purchase, transmission, distribution and sale of electricity. Operating revenues for 1983 for the Electric Company were $3,488 million. Texas Electric Service Company provides service in 48 counties in north central and west Texas.

TUEC Annual Report

Texas Electric (TESCO) is a customer-oriented company that presently has in excess of 700,000 customers, serviced by 2,800 employees based in Fort Worth, Texas, and 31 outlying offices. The computer came into use in 1957. Like any firm operating with a large number of retail and commercial customers, TESCO relies heavily on the computer and its customer information system (CIS).

In early 1980, TESCO became aware of the IBM marketing thrust concerning the support of users. Management indicated a strong need to reduce the applications development backlog, which contained a large number of one-time user requests and small systems that the user should do. In late 1982, TESCO formed a committee to pursue the end user support concept. At that time, there was no informal end user computing and thus no user base to form the core for training and support. However, the engineering groups had acquired their own Data General minicomputer for specialized work. The result of four months of planning by this committee was a formal, justified information center (IC) that began operations in February 1983. The benefits expected centered on (1) the users' being able to answer their own questions and improve their decision making, and (2) reducing the workload on DP. A minor consideration was an increase in productivity for the end users.

Prior to the initiation of the IC, the scenario of a user request in the CIS area started with the creation of a formal request document for data services containing a description of the task to be performed. This document went first to application programming. If approved at this point, it went further in DP for approval, budgeting, and scheduling. A programmer was assigned who would visit the user to confirm the intent of the request. The program would be written in COBOL and passed to the user, usually weeks or months after the initial request. Now, with the IC capabilities, more than 70 people have been trained to use Model 204 with the CIS database and provide their own reports on a routine basis.

REFERENCE

C-1.   Simon, Herbert A., *Models of Man*, New York: John Wiley & Sons, Inc. (1957).

2

Alternatives to Formal Development

Alternatives are different ways to achieve a given end result. When an individual wishes to create a new computer-based application, the question of alternatives quickly rises. The first response to this impulse may well be that there are no alternatives because data services is charged with all computer-based development. But what about purchasing the application instead of inventing it? That would be a lot faster than the wait in the backlog.

Upon investigation, there are indeed alternatives when you look around. Where the users were once non-computer-literate, they now are trained in college to address the computer resource personally, or at least to understand the process of seeking out possibilities. In this chapter we will address the alternatives that are possible, without trying to relate these alternatives to the specific area of supported end user development. That is, we will see that there are ways of getting the application running with the present resources and not have to look for personal aid and support.

To do this, we must realize that we are separating concepts and defining them in order to study them. You will realize as you read later chapters that I am covering subjects here and there by different names and directions. Accept for the minute that the alternatives presented are possible with little aid and support. Later we will see what the addition of aid and support can mean.

There are, basically, seven ways to develop or acquire a new computer-based capability. The first is via formal development by data services. Since the subject of this book is to consider alternatives to this method, there are six alternatives available to the user of computer services: (1) informal end user development, (2) use of personal computers, (3) outside timeshare, (4) outside procurement, (5) prototyping, and (6) supported end user computing.

> *End user computing (EUC) is the direct hands-on use of computers by people with problems for which computer-based solutions are appropriate.*

INFORMAL END USER DEVELOPMENT

Informal end user development refers to mainframe computer access. It means doing work on the computer in an unofficial, unsupported, and sometimes illegal manner. In the case in point, the user wishes to get a report from existing data but believes that data services is too busy to get the task done within the time frame required. Lacking other alternatives in this case, the user decides to take matters in his or her own hands and seek a solution without help or even asking anyone, especially data services.

Access means getting the computer to acknowledge you as a legitimate customer and allowing you to do things. Development means that you create something by which the things accomplished can be done. For example, once the user has gained access, he or she might create a file, use a word processor, write a BASIC program, or use a fourth-generation language to query a database and create the report. (Please accept for a moment that these are all possible methods. We will explore what each means in detail later.) The user develops a routine, capability, or file that can be exercised on the computer to provide a capability or service that would be time-consuming, tedious, or impossible manually. It involves using technology for the performance of a task.

The user sees a need for computer services and/or computer-resident data and no way to meet it, so he or she goes around official channels to get the job done. This can mean anything from a borrowed account number and password to a discovered secret way into the mainframe computer. The advantage to the user of informal services is getting the job done. The official disadvantage to data services is that the user is not authorized to access the computer and there is no budgeted computer time. The latter comment means that if there is significant informal computer usage, actual utilization will be recorded as it happens, but the level will be outside of the predicted bounds; this would imply that control is lost and charges to departments may be incorrect. The advantage cited is valid, as the whole point of informal access is to thwart and bypass control. If data services is pressing the limit of its ability to provide computer resources, additional usage may be of concern. However, the incorrectness of charging is of little concern because research has shown that only one firm in three holds user departments accountable for computer forecasts and budgets. Of greater importance than either of these views is that the informal users are alone in their use of the computer and are generally denied access to computer-resident data. Since the intent of informal use is to remain invisible to data services, the user is without support except as he or she can gain it from other users. The expertise, consulting, and training of data services are out of bounds. Access to company data that is resident in computer files and databases is out of reach when protected by the security of data services. Thus the user has access where it was previously denied but is severely restricted as to resources.

Several factors have spurred the desire of users to take advantage of informal access and development. The first is impatience; the users want a response within a short time frame and view data services as unable or unwilling to provide service due to a lack of resources. (There is nothing quite so motivating as a "no" answer.) The second factor has been business users' seeing engineers with computer access providing their own service and capabilities. These users think, "If the engineers can do it, why can't we?" The third factor has been the increased emphasis on computers in college. Engineering schools were the first to introduce computer applications into their curricula. More than a decade later, business schools followed suit. Like hand-held and desktop calculators, the use and expected use of computers was ingrained in the students since the mid- to late 1970s. The fourth factor has been advertisements on TV and the implication that if you are competent, you should be using a computer.

Not all employees are candidates for informal end user access and development. Not all are computer-trained or even want to use the machine. But those that do will—this is a trait of motivated individuals. Another trait of these same competent people, however, may well be having more tasks to accomplish than can be done with grace and rigor. That is to say, when one application is developed to solve the problem at hand, the user moves on to the next problem, without ensuring that the prior task is documented so as to be usable and maintainable by others. Thus the two main problems with informal end user-developed programs are (1) inadequacy of testing and (2) incomplete documentation. Problems are most likely to occur in these two areas, which are specifically addressed by the systems development life cycle methodology.

The practice of informal end user access and development should not be confused with the modern practice of "hacking." Hackers are individuals, outside of the firm, who gain totally unauthorized access to the computer and computer data. The usual profile of a hacker is a talented teenage boy with a terminal or a personal computer, a communications package, and a MODEM. The individual or group has the objective of gaining access to computers and data "for the fun of it." They relish breaking password codes and perusing files in defiance of security attempts. This is not informal end user access and development; it is breaking and entering, and it is illegal, the computer-based equivalent of shoplifting. Of note, hacking is possible only where the computer connects with the "outside world" via communication lines, (the telephone). Hacking occurs infrequently and is far from the most significant security risk of the firm. It is new and newsy, especially since the motion picture *War Games*. However, it can be defended against, but usually at the expense of legal use and user-friendliness.

The existence, or suspected existence, of informal end user access and development should be a signal to management and data services that change is in progress and changes by data services are in order if control is to be maintained. It should be received as a sign that pressure is building. Management and data services should take the sign as an indication that a number of users are ready, willing, and able to be trained to take on greater computer-based development responsibilities.

The following is a story, in parts, about John Bartharamew. The point is to illustrate how the various alternatives of end user computing might be applied. These stories are fictitious but are based on the author's experience.

John Bartharamew is a pricing analyst at General Western Company. The company designs and manufactures spare parts for the oil-drilling industry. John creates estimates of the prices of the parts and assembles a catalog from which the oil companies order the required spare parts. John has been with General Western for four years, during which time he has developed a recognized skill in his ability to produce the parts estimates rapidly. John has not been able to obtain any computer support, even though he has talked with his manager on many occasions as to how fast and accurate a computer-based pricing and cataloging system would be. The catalog could in fact be developed on a dial-in capability, and terminals could be placed in the offices of the larger customers. The customers could place their orders directly from the catalog, and the order-shipping process would be expedited.

One day, John was walking through data services and noticed what looked like a very special typewriter. When he asked its purpose, he was told that it was a little-used dial-up timeshare terminal. He asked if it would be possible for him to try it out; he was given an old account number and an instruction manual and was told that he was on his own. After hours during the next two weeks, John learned how to use the terminal and created a parts catalog. He had only the manual for support and could not even get any of the programmers to talk with him. Even so, he created a capability that would (1) allow him to create and keep updated entries on all spare parts, (2) make a request for an order of parts and have an invoice printed, showing total cost, and (3) print out a complete catalog.

John printed out a catalog and slipped it into the folder that contained the normally typed catalog. The next day, John's manager asked him about the new form of the catalog. John first asked if it seemed to be acceptable and received a very positive response. It seemed that John's manager finally realized that somehow a computer-based catalog had been created and that it would eliminate the need to update by typing new pages. John indicated that he had created the catalog on his own time and with no support and that he would be glad to demonstrate the system to his manager. John was immediately given this chance and, at that time, showed his manager how orders for parts could be placed in the same system. With this, John's manager went to the director of data services and strongly suggested that his department be given the terminal John was using and plan on supporting this new venture.

PERSONAL COMPUTERS

Microcomputers appeared as new potential in the home and business with the introduction of the Radio Shack TRS-80 and Apple II in 1976 and 1977. However it was not until September 1981, when IBM introduced its Personal Computer, that the use of microcomputers was accepted as a genuine business force and the "computerization" of American business took a mere 30 years. Figure 2-1 shows the evolution of mainframe hardware and the introduction of the mini- and microcomputers. This shows a scant 20 years between the first uses of mainframe computers and the minicomputer and only another decade until the

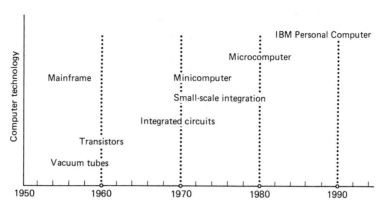

Figure 2-1   Evolution of computer technology

beginning of the proliferations of desktop microcomputers. Figure 2-2 adds the development history of the IBM PC onto the time line of Figure 2-1 to show the advances in this microcomputer technology. Again, the rate of advancement of this technology is quite apparent.

The introduction of the microcomputer in the late 1970s was an evolution of what had been the computer mainframe. Size decreased with each year, electrical energy required and heat generated by the computer diminished, and the processing power available increased. As technology improved, prices declined, and technology familiarity grew. The Tandy Corporation and Apple Computers produced the first seemingly stable microcomputers. With a few false starts, the microcomputer gained a firm stand. However, it was not until IBM introduced its Personal Computer (PC) in late 1981 that anyone realized that a new force had entered the workplace. Since that time, literally dozens of foreign and domestic companies have developed microcomputers, with prices ranging from $4,000 to $6,000 for IBM's PC/AT to $39 for the Timex/Sinclair.

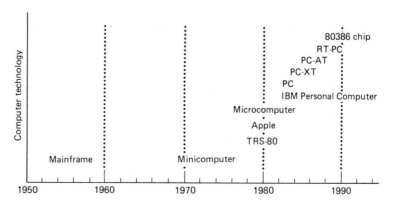

Figure 2-2   Evolution of small computer technology

The personal computer (PC) is a stand-alone, fully capable, internal-program digital computer. It contains many of the same features of mainframe computers and competes with some in speed. PCs are designed to be user-friendly and have application software that is reasonably inexpensive. Most can accommodate the BASIC language, and a large number accommodate operating systems that emulate compatibility with the IBM PC so as to be a substitute for that brand and its PC-DOS operating system. Software vendors have developed a wide variety of applications for these devices, ranging from games to artificial intelligence, from home accounting to general ledger accounting, from music to mind probing. Millions of PCs have been sold, with the early models becoming obsolete and reaching the pawnshops. The acceptance of the PC is so great that software piracy (copyright infringement) is a major problem.

Statistics gathered by InfoCorp indicate that as of the end of 1985 there were over 21 million microcomputers installed, of which about 45 percent were in the home. This indicates there are some 12 million microcomputers in industry, education, and government [2-1]. If these computers averaged only $1,000 each, this is an installed base of over $10 billion.

User-friendly Skies

Chicago, Ill.   **What's cooking?** In United Airlines Food Service kitchens, the answer is routinely dished up by IBM Personal Computers. For kitchen managers nationwide, the PCs also answer questions like: "Who's cooking?" and "At what cost?" Reed Deemer, information systems administrator, Food Service, explains his group has placed nine of its 14 PCs in the kitchen where some 20 million passenger meals are prepared annually. One of the PCs' major tasks is the production of labels to ensure special-meal orders are delivered to the right passenger. Spreadsheets help determine whether it's more economical to buy meals from outside vendors or prepare them in-house. [2-2]

The PC is a major factor in the office. A complete PC capability can be purchased for as little as $2,000, and provide an alternative to formal development. Many reliable applications exist by which repetitive solutions can be run (accounting) and new problems can be investigated (spreadsheet). The PC is far less intimidating than mainframe access, since passwords are generally nonexistent and operating systems are designed with the user in mind. Flexible (floppy) disk storage is inexpensive, and the PC and its applications allow the user to be creative on his or her own terms. Many engineering and business schools are using PCs as part of the curricula, and some even require them of entering students. It is the embodiment of technology, and new business employees who are not computer-literate are considered at a disadvantage.

If the user can get to a PC and get the job done, what is the problem? First, most of the firm's data is resident on the mainframe computer and is not addressable by the PC unless data services provides the capability and permission for access. Second, users and PCs operating in isolation can be redundant, costly, and sloppy, may use old data, have resources that cannot be exchanged or used by others, and generally lack control. Control is part of the value of the PC and part of the problem. A number of data service departments have created mainframe alternatives in order to stop the proliferation of PCs. They see the PC as a problem of security, cost, and eventual support and believe having the user in the mainframe environment is the better alternative. If nothing else, the PC has made data services aware that its clients are more willing and able than suspected to take on computer-based tasks, so a different form of service is needed.

PCs are not necessarily good or bad for the user department. They appear inexpensive but can reach a cost of $20,000 each when a full complement of software, attachments, and training is acquired [2-3]. Managers have been seen as programmers as they try to learn the PC and its capabilities. Thus the PC must be viewed as another resource that is part of a complement of resources.

John Bartharamew developed quite a spare-parts catalog. However, due to funding constraints and a lack of mainframe capability in data services, he was not able to convince his manager to put terminals in the major firms that placed orders for spare parts. John kept thinking about this opportunity along with a new problem. With the exposure to the mainframe on the parts catalog projects, John realized the value of computer resources. However, he was unable to convince his manager or data services that he had tasks important enough to warrant additional computer services. One day John saw an advertisement for a Commodore 64 home computer. When he investigated the $200 computer, he realized that it was indeed low-priced computer power but lacked a significant amount of the resource he had found in the terminal at General Western. However, he found that there was an IBM office nearby and asked them what they had between the Commodore 64 and a mainframe with a terminal. The response was a $3,450 Personal Computer with disk storage and printer. From what John could see from the demonstration, here was a device he could get for less than $4,500 after he added some software. He knew this was a magic number because his manager had approval authority for projects of less than $5,000. In addition, he knew if he could learn to use the mainframe computer with only a terminal and a manual, he could surely learn the Personal Computer with all of the documentation that it and the PC software had to offer.

John convinced his manager to purchase the personal computer, spreadsheet software, and a microcomputer database program. It was not long until John had developed a program on the machine, using the database, that would hold his parts catalog and let customers access any part they wished. Then John developed a database program that allowed customers to create orders based on the catalog. John went to his manager, showed him the programs, and announced that it was now possible to give these programs to their customers at no cost to those firms. The customers could use their own machines, create the orders, and send disk and paper copies of the orders to John for processing. It was not an on-line mainframe capability, but it did place the spare-parts catalog and ordering capability in the hands of the customers and give John's firm a decided advantage over the competition, all for less than $5,000.

CORPORATE ADOPTION OF PCs: A SHORT HISTORY
BY JIM SEYMOUR

How long have PCs been a force in your company? Three years? Four? Five?

This is a business with short memories and little sense of history. Year's end may be a good time for a little reflection on how we got where we are, and where the still-growing importance of PCs may take us.

It seems to me there have been four stages in the adoption of PCs by American business. Stage One was the Guerilla Warfare era, when microcomputer buffs were sneaking Apple IIs, Radio Shack Model 2s and the occasional Northstar into their offices. You couldn't tell DP you were buying computers; that was their turf. So these early micros appeared in budgets as calculators, desks and dictating machines.

Some visionary managers bought micros for their departments out of their own pockets, then got reimbursed in devious manners. One common ploy was to keep track of how much you'd spent, then get that money back as bogus cab fares over the next few months.

Even better was the retirement-party game. Using one of the bennies most managers are allowed to hand out, the PC guerillas would claim retirement-party expenses—for employees who had no plans to leave—then apply the $500–$700 to micros.

Stage Two was the DP/MIS world's Thou Shalt Not response, characterized usually by fire-breathing memos, approved-equipment lists and 40-page cost justifications to acquire PCs.

Alien Software

My favorite relic from this craziness is a memo from a DP boss at a Fortune 500 company. In harsh terms it warns readers that no equipment or software not listed in the memo may be bought. In a stirring coda, it adds that "any alien software found on the premises will be confiscated." I'm not sure exactly what "alien software" is, but I love the phrase.

Stage Three was the If You Can't Beat 'Em, Throw 'Em a Micro Manager era. Whether more enlightened or simply exhausted, DP management decided to work with the people who were becoming so attached to PCs, and began establishing PC-support departments. Under intelligent, resourceful micro managers, these tiny shops began an era of good feelings, and bridged the gap between DP and PC users.

No development in the adoption of PCs by American business has been more important than the rise of the micro manager, for his or her appointment had both symbolic and practical significance. Not only was the corporation endorsing PCs as business tools, validating the good judgment of those who had been screaming for them; corporations were saying PCs were so important that they'd put extra dough, beyond acquisition costs, behind the idea, to build a PC-support infrastructure.

Corporate PC users quickly became accustomed to training classes, telephone help, "outcall" visits from an expert when they had a problem, fast repairs or exchanges, quick acquisition of machines for new employees, and good advice on new hardware and software. Which has led us to Stage Four today: the What Have You Done For Me Lately? era. Accustomed to that level of service, corporate PC users are now getting more demanding about how the PC support shop helps them.

With DP budget cuts, and Info Centers sometimes being eliminated or crippled, some micro managers have tried reducing or eliminating outcall help. When a user calls in with a problem, he can no longer count on someone appearing at his door within a few minutes. Instead, micro managers have been trying to push users into undeniably more cost-efficient classes, at scheduled intervals.

But when Jane Doe calls in with a Lotus problem as she's preparing the department budget she has to have to her boss tomorrow morning, she doesn't want an invitation to a class three weeks hence. She wants help now. And she ought to get help. Users' new assertiveness seems to me a healthy evolution in the role of PCs in corporations, but it's a difficult and threatening stage for micro managers caught between angry users and budget cuts.

The bottom line is that you can never retreat from a given level of support. "What have you done for me lately?" is an eminently fair question, and demands an honest "Not enough" at some companies, and an open-minded "What would you like us to do?" at many others. [2-4]

OUTSIDE TIMESHARE

Outside timeshare refers to computer access, often on-line, provided by a firm other than the one employing the individual. It generally means using a video display or typewriter-type terminal and a telephone with modem to connect to a remote computer. With this access, the user has the power and resources of the timeshare service, which include computational power, data and program storage, output printed and mailed to an address or printed to a terminal, and even programming support. All the user needs is money.

The main premise of a timeshare contract is that the person on the terminal end will either use procedures and capabilities available on the system or will provide his or her own programming. Although contract programming support is available, it is not the primary reason for gaining access to the timeshare service. A user who wants a program developed outside the company would do best to negotiate with a software development firm. Thus the assumption is that the timeshare service provides the user with access to the computer for hardware, software, and processing considerations.

As noted, outside timeshare services are, by definition, not part of the user's firm and therefore lack the computer-resident internal data of the firm. There is usually a concern for security in placing the data on the computer of an outside company, even though such companies are adamant about the extreme quality of their security measures and practices. Thus the computer power is not the same environment as internal resources. If the user is proficient in the language or application desired, has little need for in-house data, and can work in an isolated environment, outside timeshare is a good alternative for the work at hand. However, its main use is to bypass constraints or lack of data services machine resources, not programming resources. The use of outside, or in-house, timeshare (official or informal) does not address the problem of supported development.

MEETING ALL YOUR INFORMATION NEEDS REQUIRES TOTAL SYSTEMS INTEGRATION KNOWLEDGE AND EXPERIENCE.

Meeting information needs has become a major international concern. One in which maintaining compatibility and unity is a difficult task. That's why Boeing Computer Services offers a

An additional problem with the use of outside timeshare is the perspective of management and data services as to the expenditure of funds. Specifically, "real" monies are flowing out of the firm to pay for the services of the timeshare firm, whereas budgets expended on in-house timeshare or other data services resources appear to be from a pool of fixed costs and do not cause additional out-of-pocket or out-of-firm expenses. More succinctly, data services will most likely believe it can better use the funds that are going to the outside timeshare firm, and management will wonder why this often significant expenditure is necessary in light of the large data services budget. Although the use of outside timeshare can be valuable in times of severe hardware constraints, its acceptance will most likely be short-lived as the cost incurred grows.

John was quite pleased with his success with do-it-yourself mainframe access and the personal computer. However, he knew that if he wanted to continue his career path, he must show his manager that the parts catalog was really just a small part of what could be accomplished with proper computer support. However, John quickly realized that he was moving out of the area of personal computers, as his new idea of an integrated ordering and shop assignment system would require very sophisticated programs and a large amount of storage space and processing power. Data services was very clear as to its lack of storage and processing power and had little hope of convincing upper management to add resources for new projects at this time. John knew he was fighting against the inertia of the status quo and had to find a way to demonstrate the system to prove his point.

John told his manager that he wanted to spend $5,000 with an outside timeshare computer firm. (You will remember that his manager could personally approve this amount.) He told his manager that this expenditure would allow demonstration of a capability even better than the catalog and that the manager would have to trust John as to the rest. The manager did just that, and John signed an agreement with Boeing Computer Services (BCS) the next week. BCS provided John with a video display terminal, a modem, a small printer, and an account number. The fixed cost of the service, mainly for equipment, was $150 per month. John had access to all of the applications on BCS, most of which carried a small royalty fee, and could program in any of six programming languages or five fourth-generation languages.

During the next six months, John learned the RAMIS system by Mathematica, Inc., and created a database system that (1) contained his entire catalog, (2) would allow access and query of parts, (3) allowed the customer to place an order on the basis of either specific parts or contingency lists of generally used parts for a specific system, and (4) scheduled the manufacture of the parts ordered based on known orders and sequencing of tasks to make the parts. To create this capability, John had first to learn the basics of RAMIS via a tutorial on the computer. Realizing that this was not really enough, he attended a three-day course in RAMIS at the BCS training facility. This was adequate to allow John to create a significant system.

After lengthy testing of the system based on historical data captured in the personal-computer-based system, John presented and demonstrated the new system to his manager. Due to the available processing power of the BCS installation, the program ran rapidly. The presentation duly impressed John's manager, who presented the system, with a demonstration, to upper management. The president was impressed with the system, but even more with the ability to get one created. Even though it had cost $4,700 in funds that were paid to an outside firm, a capability had been created without affecting existing operations in data services. The president called the data services director and asked him to provide an estimate of continued use of the system on BCS timeshare or bringing the capability in house. John had created a capability with resources outside of data services but realized the financial implications of leaving the system there.

OUTSIDE PROCUREMENT

Outside procurement is the purchase of anything that you use in the conduct of business that you could potentially create yourself. It is the *buy* option in the make-or-buy decision. The practice of buying a complete software application from someone outside the firm is quite apparent to the user of a personal computer. The application might be generic in the form of spreadsheet, database, or graphics programs, or it might be as specific as an accounting capability, personnel information system, or parts cataloging package. However, the use of a PC would generally not seem appropriate for major applications. A large company would not feel comfortable establishing its total payroll or accounts receivable capabilities on a microcomputer. It is in this type of environment that outside procurement for mainframe applications is appropriate.

The question being addressed in the make-or-buy decision is (1) how to get an application that meets the users needs while (2) reducing the time and cost associated with in-house formal development. Thus some form of analysis must be conducted to determine the users' requirements so that they can be compared with offerings of the software vendors. Then the software industry must be investigated to determine if the package exists, its success rate, the cost, and available support. Once the software package is found, the requirements of the application to be purchased are compared with the resources of the firm's computer and the methods of the organization. If these match, purchase approval is required. Once a contract is negotiated, preplanning can start, and training can be scheduled. Although this sounds very complicated, all of these actions can be accomplished in a four- to ten-week time span.

Outside procurement is a substitute for the systems development life cycle stages of design, programming, and testing. As indicated, some form of analysis of the need must be made prior to package purchase. The systems analysis stage that developed the package should have been much more extensive than the one to purchase it, as the package will likely be designed to encompass more than the needs of one user. The software vendor will have accomplished the design, programming, and testing phases that will ensure a reliable, maintainable, workable application. The vendor has, by definition, resources available to ensure that problems are resolved within a reasonable time frame. The vendor can provide training and even operation support and may have on-call assistance in the form of a help hotline.

The advantages of outside procurement for major, often used applications should be obvious. Why develop your own payroll system when payroll is one function that all firms must perform and it is likely that there are systems available from several sources that will meet most of your needs? In cases where the firm has unique requirements, the first inclination should be to get the package that meets most of them and create an add-on application to complement the main package. This latter package can be purchased from the application vendor or developed by data services. In either case, the time and cost will be significantly less than for total in-house development. Indications are that outside procurement costs can be as little as one-fourth those of in-house development. Even if the final purchase price seems large, it might be small when a two-year wait can be avoided.

SAMPLE OUTSIDE PACKAGES AVAILABLE

Information Technology, Inc. Personal Accounting System (PAS) *Specification Application*: Provides general ledger accounting functions; Automatically extracts transactions from checking account. *Specific Industry*: Banking/Financial. *System Requirements*: Burroughs B90, B1000. *Operating System*: CMS. *Memory Required*: 512K Bytes. *Source Language*: Cobol. *Source Code Available*: No. *Purchase Terms*: Purchase. *Price*: $3,000 to $14,500. *Number Installed*: 35. *Date First Installed*: 1982.

Management Science America, Inc. (*MSA*) The MSA Accounts Payable and Purchase Order System. *Specific Industry*: Manufacturing, Banking/Financial, Medical, Education, Government, Nonprofit Organizations. *Systems Requirements*: IBM 370; Burroughs B2700; Honeywell 66/6000; IBM 30XX. *Operating System*: OS/VS; DOS. *Memory Required*: 65K bytes. *Source Language*: Cobol. *Source Code Available*: Yes. *Purchase Terms*: Purchase. *Number Installed*: 678. [2-5]

There seems almost no reason to avoid outside procurement of large applications. In fact, I contend that the first thought should be to purchase moderate to large applications that will have extensive use. However, this is not necessarily true of the small to medium-sized programs. The time to seek out an existing capability and bring it in house may be longer than the time allowed for providing a solution to the problem at hand. While the purchased application may have a longer useful lifetime than one developed for the problem being addressed, the pressure may be too great to wait.

The PC software market is providing answers for many of these applications, especially where generalized programs such as databases and spreadsheets can be a generator for the ultimate capability required. When this is not the case, individual development, often with a unique language, may be necessary. In these cases, the best solution may be to have the ultimate users create the desired result. It is the users' intimate knowledge of the problems and the form of the solution that is of such great value.

Suppose that a user needs a small system that cannot be created on a spreadsheet or database program. The alternatives are to (1) search in house, (2) investigate the open market, or (3) have the user develop it personally. Research indications are that in-house environments do not yet accommodate the exchange of information and programs developed by end users, so the search for programs developed in-house may be lengthy and disappointing. There are sources indicating the availability of software on the open market, but even these sources can be expensive and time-consuming and may not necessarily contain the specialized program required. If the program is one requiring one or two workerweeks of effort for development on the part of the user, the most effective and efficient use of the user's time may be personal development rather than search.

It should not be assumed that personal development is the best alternative to outside purchase or formal data services development. In each case, analysis is required before any development or procurement can be accomplished. However, there are cases when each is appropriate.

John continues to be successful with computer-based applications. He recently developed an order entry and factory scheduling capability on an outside timeshare service using a fourth-generation capability. The president has directed that the capability be brought into the company and installed on the computers in data services. However, two problems have arisen: (1) Data services does not have a fourth-generation language like RAMIS and indicates that it will be very expensive to purchase one, and (2) the director of data services is adamant that the application should be written in a general-purpose language that can be understood and maintained by his programmers. Thus the direction to bring the application in house has resulted in a potential delay of two years, during which time the program will be written.

John realizes that the impact of his program will be lost if two years' time elapses before the capability is available. Upon investigation, he learns that Hodge and Dodge, a software development firm, offer a MRP (manufacturing requirements processing) package that will handle the factory scheduling. Also, H&D indicate that they will develop the catalog and order entry capability for $10,000 and guarantee to have the total system up and running in three months for a total cost of $40,000. John believes that this is a reasonable offer and asks for a demonstration of the MRP package. He visits H&D and is impressed with the MRP package but finds that it will require a minor modification in addition to the indicated development. H&D agree to work with John to develop a complete package in accordance with the RAMIS model on Boeing Computer Services and that the total cost of the resultant capability, including training, will not exceed $55,000. In addition, H&D agreed to all maintenance responsibilities for an annual fee of $2,800. The time to completion remains at three months from contract date. John goes directly to the president of General Western with the idea of outside procurement and receives approval.

PROTOTYPING

The term *prototyping* can signify several things and is used here to refer to two basic concepts: (1) the quick creation of a small model of the real thing you want to build and (2) creating the thing with the involvement of professional developers and the ultimate user. In software development, it can mean quick-and-dirty development to present a model for discussion. It can also be assistance to the user by a programmer to speed the task, the user concentrating on what the system does and the programmer focusing on how to do it.

James Martin recommends prototyping as an alternative to formal development when the environment accommodates it. In his book *Systems Development without Programmers* [2-6], Martin recommends a systems analyst assisting the user to develop the capability. His point is that software capabilities exist that allow the analyst to develop quickly what the user wants and let the user try it, without the cost and time associated with formal development. The intent is to develop the actual capability with involvement on the part of each party. An example may best describe the process.

Back at General Western, John has procured the new order entry, catalog, and MRP system. It has been installed and operating for a year, with excellent results. One day John's manager wants a new report from the system. The task is one of those that are too small to warrant formal development by either data services or H&D and would most likely not even be accepted for consideration by the review board. Because data services has experienced a number of small requests lately, it has assigned a programmer to assist users in the prototyping methodology. John requests help from the programmer and is added to a waiting list. Since the programmer works only on small tasks, John's wait is not very long. When the task begins, the programmer and John discuss the report and the location of the data. Using a newly acquired fourth-generation language, the programmer queries the MRP database containing the data and saves it in a file, printing a copy for John to review.

John goes over the presented report and confirms that the data is correct and complete. The programmer, sitting by John at a terminal, uses the same or another language to format a report as desired. Upon inspection, John requests changes to the format of the report, which the programmer makes quickly. As they sit at the terminal, the second version of the report is processed. From the second report, John determines that some calculations and manipulation are required and that some data really is required from another file. Unfortunately, the location of the data is not known; it is just known that the data is presently on a specific scheduled report that John has seen on his manager's desk. The programmer goes off by himself to find the data and determine the process of the added programming. Two days later, the programmer returns with a new report, based on the added data and new processing. He and John review the report and find it correct and complete. But now it is obvious that a graph is in order. The programmer uses another language and produces the graph. This appears to end the task.

Martin indicates in his book that users do not know what they want until they see it and then want something else. Thus it was with the example just given. However, with prototyping, the time to completion is very rapid, a matter of hours or days. In order to have this quick reaction capability, two things must exist: (1) Data services must allocate personnel, preferably experienced analysts as opposed to programmers, to be available to users, and (2) the users and the analyst must realize that the tasks are to be small ones. An analyst who finds the originally described task to be a lengthy development should refer it to his or her manager for other considerations. Otherwise, the work on the task would be done as quickly as possible. Several tasks may be worked simultaneously in order to allow the analyst to be of service to several users and to let the users have time to think through the results.

Several points about prototyping should be obvious. First, there was no up-front feasibility study. The user simply stated the need and was admitted to the prototyping queue. In reality, the feasibility analysis was conducted at the time of the first meeting between the analyst and the user. Second, there was no requirement for a written specification. The analyst and the user discussed the need, and an output was quickly produced. The user then reviewed the output against what he or she believed was wanted. Corrections and changes were made as the user recognized and communicated them to the analyst. Even a user who has only a vague conceptual idea of the end result will realize quickly if the processing is off base. That is, the user has a reasonable conceptual model of the end result but can not usually express this, only recognize it. Third, testing is inherent in the design and development. As the process is developed, data query and reporting in this case, it is tested by the user reviewing the output. As Tom Peters, of *In Search of Excellence* fame, indicates, they are "getting the chicken test done early" [2-7]. This means that the system is tested as soon as a test is practical and failures are discovered early, not after months of design and expenditures of large amounts of time and money. Fourth, implementation takes place early and on a recurring basis, with the first report. With a continuous process of design, test, implement, redesign (Peters's "ready, fire, aim"), the user is highly involved in the activity as a contributor, not as just an onlooker.

Note that it is not necessary for a prototype model to work; it may only be important that the prototype be a realistic representation of the user's concept of the desired result. For example, it is possible to create models of printed or screen reports using a word processor. This capability readily exists and can be used to display the design intent. Changes are easy, and the ultimate meaning can be presented. Thus prototypes may be without internal processes and still have significant value.

So far we have not listed any disadvantages of prototyping. This methodology is sound and has a potential to solve many problems for the user at a reasonable cost—except for one scarce resource. One of the forms of prototyping requires the services of data services personnel to work with and assist the user. The analysts provide a valuable service in their experience in analysis and tool usage. Lack of this support, especially for the new user, can leave a void. Analysts are in short supply. Thus even though the use of these personnel for prototyping may be the most productive and cost-beneficial use of their time and talent, the pressure to keep them on maintenance and new development is very high, and prototyping suffers.

As we will discuss in later chapters, prototyping is a process that end users can use effectively without the analyst when they are supported through other means. Thus this term is used both within the supported end user computing concept and outside of it, as discussed. Both uses are valuable.

SUPPORTED END USER COMPUTING

Our discussion so far has taken a path of describing several alternatives to formal development that are available to the user and then indicating that each has disadvantages. This would lead the reader to believe that he or she is being led somewhere specific. Well, we are now at that destination, an alternative with many advantages. We will also indicate some disadvantages, but the atmosphere will be one of strong recommendation.

> *End user computing (EUC) is the direct hands-on use of computers by people with problems for which computer-based solutions are appropriate.*

Supported end user computing is an environment in which the person with the problem uses the computer and computer-resident data to solve the problem and has help doing it. Thus if you are a manager, financial analyst, secretary, inventory specialist, teacher, company first sergeant, member of the clergy, or account executive and you use computer-based resources in a way other than keying into someone else's application, you are an end user. End user computing sounds simple, and in fact it is. L. W. Hammond, of IBM, indicated that "if provided proper education, technical support, usable tools, data availability, and convenient access to the system, users may directly and rapidly satisfy a part of their business area requirements that depend on an I/S environment." [2-8]

Thus we arrive at the theme of the book: "Let the user do it!" The path here has been rather classic in that we have presented many possibilities but have always indicated that there is something better. Each of the alternatives presented in this chapter have uses. Outside procurement is an excellent method of exchanging money for time. Personal computers have a valid place, as is evident from their popularity and high sales. Outside timeshare from service bureaus is an excellent short-term solution to a lack of significant computer resources. Even informal end user computing can be condoned, under some conditions. However, each of these alternatives has some disadvantage. Another way to consider these alternatives is in a setting where you can have the best of them all and avoid the shortcomings. Thus, taking Hammond at his word and establishing an environment where users are provided proper education, technical support, usable tools, data availability, and convenient access to the system allows the firm to realize the best from its finest resource, users.

An alternate way of describing end user computing is by means of an example from everyday life. When you drive the family car into a filling station to get gas, you are confronted with two options. Since the "gas shortage" that started about 1972, most service stations that sell gasoline for motor vehicles have offered self-service and full-service capabilities. Full-service is offered for the motorist wishing to have a professional fill the gas tank and service the car. It might require waiting for the individual to perform this task and always means a higher price. There are times when these costs are worth the price, especially if trouble exists and advice is required. However, the alternative of self-service allows the motorist to pump his or her own gas and check the oil, with less waiting and at a lower cost. With less service comes a lower price tag. The potential of higher risk is also present, however.

The scenario of the self-service versus full-service gas station is analogous to the full service offered by MIS professionals and the self-service of end user computing. With full MIS service, you receive the attention of a professional that may be vital to the successful completion of the task. However, the time required is greater than with the self-service end user computing option, and the price is higher, often significantly higher. Neither full service nor self-service is right or wrong; the value of each will depend on the situation and the users. However, there is evidence that end user computing can provide the needed service in as much as 80 percent of cases [2-6].

Figure 2-3 shows the chronological path that many companies take on their way to embracing end user computing. The trip starts with the introduction of computer technology into the firm. With initial success comes the desire for more usage and more success. At this point development passes from phase 1 of a staged growth phenomenon, initiation, into phase 2, expansion. Success breeds success, and with increased levels of applications comes higher costs. This eventually comes under the view of management as high cost and marginal gain, resulting in imposition of controls (phase 3). The controls are by way of review and justification of requests for new applications. The review process, along with a shortage of data services personnel to work on applications, causes a backlog of work. The pressure builds, and users seek alternative ways of getting the application instituted or problem solved.

This chapter was intended to address three concepts: (1) who develops computer-based applications and systems, (2) where they are developed, and (3) how they are developed. We have already discussed the ''who,'' beginning with the differentiation of development between the MIS professional and the end users. This discussion will continue for many chapters because it is an important issue. Development by MIS professionals and development by end users are not mutually exclusive situations; they are on a continuum. This means that users will have different levels of involvement based on the ''who'' of development. Seen in this light, it should be apparent that both ends of this continuum are appropriate and that users' involvement is important in each, but of varying degrees.

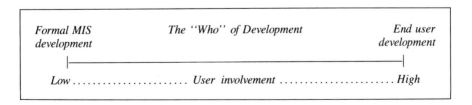

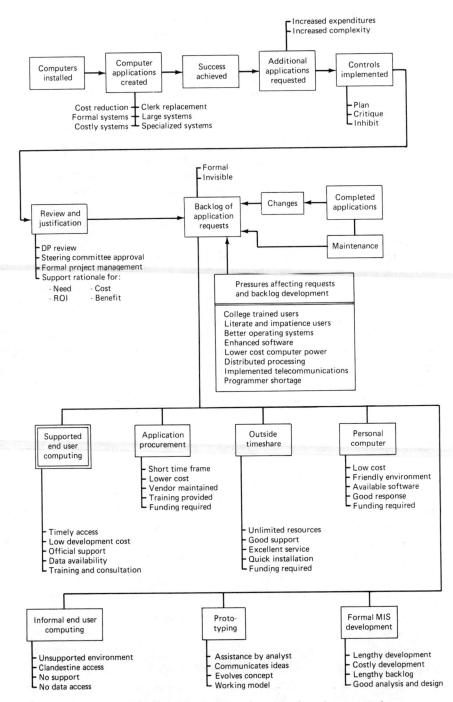

Figure 2-3 Chronological developments of pressures for end user computing

The "where" of development began in this chapter. One "where" is with an outside vendor, in outside procurement. Another "where" is in the MIS department during formal development as the user is more of a sideline observer between the systems analysis phase and the implementation phase. The last "where" is in the user's area with supported prototyping and use of personal computers and mainframe timeshare. One aspect of the importance of "where" is that of the "home field advantage." In sports, it is believed that the team playing at home, in front of the team's fans, has an advantage. This is the advantage of territory. End users would appear to have this advantage when they are performing their own development. Also, the users would appear to be at a disadvantage when the development is elsewhere and the result is brought to them or they go to the development site to see interim results. The concept of "where" should take on more meaning as we develop the support environment for the end user.

The "how" of development began in Appendix B of Chapter 1 and continues in the next chapter. In Chapter 1 we reviewed the processes of formal development. In Chapter 3 we will address the basic tasks involved in computer-supported problem solving and discuss examples of how to develop each with specific, but generic, tools.

Another way to address the questions of who, where, and how is to consider the centralization concept. Centralization generally means to concentrate resources or power. Our meaning will be that of a centralized group of professionals in a concentrated area when we address formal development. However, in end user development we generally think of distributed development; that is, each user is a decentralized point of development. Obviously, the actual development activity can take place between these two extremes, as noted previously. Also, the type of centralization practiced by data services can vary.

One model for the physical location and organization of data services is to have a dedicated place of residence in the firm's single building. All personnel of data services are located together. The mainframe resources can be either with the personnel or remote, with little consequence. MIS personnel, being in the same building, are accessible to users, and the distance between the two may be small.

However, another model of the location of MIS personnel may be quite different. If the firm has outgrown its physical facilities and some people will be relocated to another building, those people might be the MIS personnel. This is an obvious selection, since they are a homogeneous group, generally work away from other groups, and need some isolation. Also, if data services has contracts outside the firm, this separation would seem a good business practice. Thus all MIS personnel are moved to a location that is remote from their customers. Now, when a user needs MIS assistance, the options are (1) use the telephone or (2) travel.

A decentralized model for data services would also be possible. Some data services groups, such as administration and finance, could be centralized, and other groups, such as the applications development analysts and programmers, could be distributed to the functional groups they support. This would centralize groups that support all users and distribute others to have the most contact with those they uniquely serve. Figure 2-4 illustrates the alternatives open to data services.

This same process can be true of the EUC support group. We will develop the support concept in later chapters, but the idea of a centralized support group and area is like that of data services. A decentralized support group is not only also possible but is even considered the ultimate form of the concept. This will be considered in the last chapter.

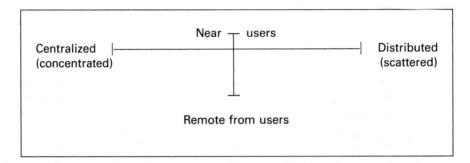

Figure 2-4   Centralization and proximity of data services

SUMMARY

- Informal end user computing is the clandestine use of existing computer resources without sponsorship or support. The practice exists where the users have the ability and willingness to address computer resources but where those resources are not provided as a matter of course.
- The existence of informal end user computing should signal the presence of strong pressure against the wait for formal development and for the support of officially supported end user computing.
- Personal computers allow the users computer resources with a high level of control, provide a user-friendly environment with significant software availability, and can be obtained with minimal funding. However, without support, the value of PCs may deteriorate over time.
- Outside timeshare services provide a cost-effective alternative to lack of in-house resources. Their use should be restricted to what cannot actually be provided by data services.
- Outside procurement of software should be the first thought for capabilities that have general appeal. The practice can save a significant amount of time and money.
- Prototyping is the use of high-level computer languages and capabilities to build new applications in a short amount of time. It may involve an MIS analyst or not, but it is based on involving the user in the creation process, even to the point to building a nonworking model of the desired result in order to communicate and evaluate.
- Supported end user computing allows the best use of MIS and user resources. It offers too many benefits to be ignored.

Key Terms

80286/80386 microprocessor	Alternatives
8088/8086 microprocessor	Annual fees
Large-scale integration	Chicken test
Maintenance contract	Modem
Outside versus in-house development	Minicomputer
Home computing versus business computing	Copyright infringement
Vendor	Personal computer
Small-scale integration	Procurement
Development	Prototyping
Do-it-yourself	Programmer
EUC	Support
End user	Systems analyst
Hacker	Timeshare
Remoteness of data services	Informal
Centralization of data services	

DISCUSSION QUESTIONS

1. Discuss when you have gained access to computer resources and/or computer-resident data without permission or support. Discuss the ''crime'' and the pressures of the situation and indicate if the end did indeed justify the means.
2. Discuss the concept of user-friendliness as it relates to computer programs. Include both mainframe and personal computers. What programs have you used that seem to lack user-friendliness?
3. Under what conditions would outside timeshare be preferable over outside procurement and vice versa? How can the cost of either be controlled?
4. What examples of prototyping have you seen? Describe a situation where you could use a word processor to prototype an interactive, database-oriented transaction processing system. How dynamic can you make this prototype, or is it just a dull discussion tool?
5. How does one become an MIS systems analyst?
6. Is it necessary to program in order to start an MIS career?
7. Who is James Martin?
8. Is IBM the only computer environment?
9. What do you think of General Western Company? Of John Bartharamew?

REFERENCES

2-1. Special Report, *Wall Street Journal*, June 16, 1986, p. 110.
2-2. ''User-friendly Skies,'' *IBM Innovation*, September 1984, p. 3.

2-3.   Edelman, Franz, "The Management of Information Resources—A Challenge for American Business." *MIS Quarterly* March 1981, p. 17–27.

2-4.   Seymour, Jim, "Corporate Adoption of PCs: A Short History," *PC Week* December 23–30, 1986, p. 37.

2-5.   "Applications: Financial-General Ledger," *Computerworld, Buyers Guide—Large Systems Software*, Volume 18, Nr 26A, June 27, 1984, p. D101.

2-6.   Martin, James, *Application Development Without Programmers* Englewood Cliffs, NJ: Prentice Hall (1982).

2-7.   Peters, Thomas J., and Robert H. Waterman, *In Search of Excellence* New York: Harper and Row (1982).

2-8.   Hammond, L. W., "Management Considerations for an Information Center." *IBM Systems Journal* 21:2 (1982), pp. 131–61.

3

End User Computing

> *End user computing (EUC) is the direct hands-on use of computers by people with problems for which computer-based solutions are appropriate.*

WHO ARE THE USERS?

> *End users are individuals who are willing to use computer resources to get their job done.*

The end users of end user computing are individuals who are willing to use computer resources to get their job done. Users come in all types and sizes: engineers, managers, secretaries, clergy, military officers, police officers, factory supervisors, and company presidents. Some are college-trained, some have a very high level of motivation and a willingness to go it alone, while others just want to get the job done. Regardless of position, end users often require support and training in using the computer in its various forms. The individuals of interest represent points on a continuum of users who are willing to use computers and data.

A study of 200 end users and 50 information systems managers [3-1] determined that end users can be classified into six categories, as follows:

1. *Nonprogramming end users'* only access to computer-stored data is through software provided by others.

2. *Command-level users* have a need to access data on their own terms. They perform simple inquiries often with a few simple calculations such as summation, and generate unique reports for their own purposes.

3. *End user programmers* use both command and procedural languages directly for their own personal information needs.

4. *Functional support personnel* are sophisticated programmers who support other end users within their particular functional areas.

5. *End user computing support personnel* are most often located in a central support organization such as an information center.

6. *DP programmers* are similar to the traditional COBOL shop programmers except that they program in end user languages.

The following conclusions can be drawn from this study:

1. End users are diverse.
2. Diversity in end user activities necessitates a variety of software tools.
3. Diversity among end users also necessitates strongly *differentiated education*, training, and support for the various classes of users.
4. Finally, and most significant, the classification highlights the existence and importance of functional support.

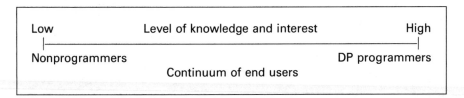

Thus we have a differentiated list of users, ranging from the programmer-analyst from data services to the data entry clerk in accounting. While all of these individuals make valid use of the computer and its resident data, we will concentrate on users in categories 3, 4, and 5. These are the individuals who will accept aid and training from a support group and use the gained ability to increase their productivity.

At this point, you should begin to realize that the ultimate aim of this text is to show the value of an EUC support group. This collection of people who are dedicated to the aid and assistance of end users is vital to the ultimate gains in user productivity. This group will be introduced in more detail in the next chapter. For the time being, it is sufficient to realize that support is vital.

When users find out about an EUC support group, they approach in three waves. These waves tend to categorize the users and give us an idea of what a support group can expect.

The first users of supported end user computing, and the ones who employed unsupported end user development, tend to be the better-trained, more technically oriented individuals who can work alone (categories 3 and 4). This first wave of users is more self-sufficient due to their background and orientation. These users do not feel threatened by mainframe or personal computers and often relate well to such highly complex issues as job control language and database query. These people require little support from data services but tend to be in short supply. With support, they quickly become specialists and act as in-area support for the other members of their department. Unfortunately, only 5 to 10 percent of the potential user population falls into this group.

The second group of users, both in number and in line for use of the computer, is eager to use technology but lacks the training and technical know-how. Thus these people require support and will tend to hold back until it is available. They will tend to work within the system and only address the computer when "allowed" and supported. This group is larger than the initial group and will require much from the support staff. However, when given training and counsel, these people will blossom and quickly become productive with technology. These people account for 10 to 20 percent of the total potential user community.

This leaves 70 to 85 percent of the potential collection of users. This final group to use the capabilities of end user computing is the mass of people who have no training and little technology orientation but who can become more productive when educated, trained, and supported. These people range from clerks to presidents and will require detailed support and patience. Secretaries who are comfortable and competent with an electric typewriter, filing system, telephone, and dictation machine often freeze at the sight of a video display terminal and the thought of computer files and electronic mail. Executives must be educated as to the appropriateness of terminal usage and the appearance of typing. All members of this group require the building of confidence in themselves in relation to technology.

It is not obvious which group will gain the most from end user computing. While the first, technically oriented group will require the least assistance and will tend to do the most with the resources, it is small in number. The second group seems to return the most output per hour of assistance, while the third group is the largest in number. The point to be made here is that the support staff needs to recognize the differences in people and address their needs appropriately. In time, each group will approach the staff for assistance, and each will have different personalities, needs, and responses. The staff must not assume homogeneity of users and likeness of support styles. Such a situation requires a support staff that can respond to changing customers and varying needs.

A More Detailed Description of End User Computing

A review of articles about end user computing should provide some insight into the subject. Literally hundreds of papers and news reports have appeared, some of which are referenced here. Even if the authors do not use the same definition of end user computing or end users, they all seem to have reached consensus on the importance of the concept.

End user computing is an environment that allows the person with the problem to have access to computer and data resources. Robert Rosenberger of IBM defines the end user as "any non-DP-trained individual who, with the right tools and support, could take advantage of the power of the computer" [3-2]. This means a marketing manager, financial staff analyst, inventory clerk, or secretary can apply the power of the computer to day-to-day problems that involve information, reports, office automation, and personal computing.

"In its simplest form, end user computing involves a straightforward query to a file, such as 'Find record X.' At the other extreme, end user programming is akin to conventional programming—but programming that uses a non-procedural language" [3-3]. *Demand processing* is both another name for end user computing and a subset of the process and constitutes "query, analysis, reporting, forecasting and 'what if . . . ?' kinds of planning activities, often using private as well as organizational data" [3-4].

The objectives and advantages of end user computing are that (1) more resources are applied to the application development backlog, (2) the user gets involved with the solution, not just the problem, and (3) action replaces waiting. Benefits of end user computing include (1) increased motivation and better use of professional talent, (2) timely availability of information, (3) the ability to analyze business problems more thoroughly, and (4) increased productivity of office staff, both professional and clerical [3-5]. Part of the thrust is that people are willing to get the job done when given the tools [3-6].

Not surprisingly, some observers feel that "end user computing is in its infancy for any other than scientific or engineering applications" [3-7]. However, one source indicates that the end user computing growth rate is estimated to be 50 to 90 percent per year [3-1], while another indicated a 400 percent increase between 1983 and 1985 alone [3-8]. This indicates that the end users are not just waiting for the formal development backlog to catch up with their needs. This growth rate is even more significant when compared with a projected data services growth rate of only 5 to 15 percent per year [3-7].

There appear to be four reasons for the high growth rate of end user computing: (1) vastly increased awareness of the potential of EUC, (2) improvements in the technical capabilities that make EUC increasingly more flexible and less costly, (3) the more difficult business conditions that prevail today, and (4) the fact that users' needs cannot be satisfied through traditional information systems organizations [3-1]. One analyst expressed the force of end user computing in this way: "End User Programming is 'inevitable' and will bring with it the need to change the data processing organization, if not the profession itself. End User Programming is coming, because it offers just too many benefits to end users" [3-9].

While it is important to recognize the growth rate of EUC, it is essential to realize that for end users, the computer is a tool, not a career; it simply assists them in their work [3-10]. This is quite different from the engineer or scientist who began programming in college and continued it in the firm via outside timeshare access or in-house resources. Business end users are a varied group, coming from many kinds of organizations. This organizational background, different college training, and lack of a well-defined power base make them quite different from the engineers and scientists.

Now that we understand the end user and end user computing better, what would a EUC support group look like? One early view is shown in Figure 3-1, which portrays the concept of an EUC support group that aids and assists the end user and interfaces with other parts of data services. The group provides consulting, education and training, and direct assistance to the users while providing services of evaluation, planning, and ad-

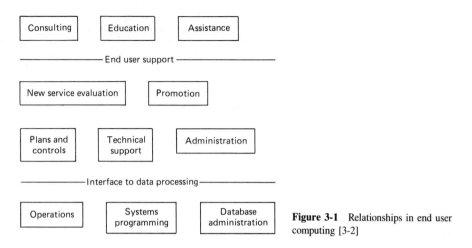

Figure 3-1 Relationships in end user computing [3-2]

ministration behind the scenes. In addition, this group is a very valuable interface link between the users and the technical areas of data services.

This support group concept will be fully pursued in the next chapter. At this point let us pursue a deeper understanding of users and their tasks.

BASIC END USER COMPUTING TASKS

We have said that end user computing exists when the person with the problem that could be solved by computer-based resources uses these resources to solve the problem directly. It is a "Let George do it" environment; data services stays out of the picture except in a support role.

But what does end user computing look like? Can one see it or go to where it is done? To see it, in this book, we need to visualize. To assist, we will describe eight basic distinct instances of end user computing, including the tasks and the tools. Figure 3-2 shows the basic task and the computer-based tool that supports it. Each of these eight tasks will be described in turn. In each case, a task will be presented without reference to technology, where possible. This task statement will be as a manager might give to a staff member, with only the basics indicated. This will be followed by a more specific description of what the result will be like, still without reference to technology where possible. Then we will give a generic statement of the task, the computer-based tool that supports this task, brand names for representative PC-based software capabilities, representative mainframe-based capabilities, and a solution for the task, using the technology.

Task 1

Create a budget for your organization, by line item, for each of the next five years. At a minimum, you will sum across years for each item and sum all items by year.

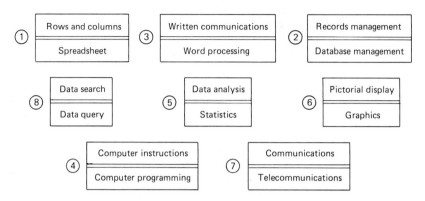

Figure 3-2   Eight basic tasks of end user computing

The task here is to make a detailed accounting sheet report that shows what items will require funding for each of the next five years. You will need a total for each item and a total for each year. The orientation is rows for expense items and columns for years.

Task: Column-and-row orientation; accounting sheet; *X–Y* matrix
Tool: Spreadsheet program
PC package: VisiCalc, Lotus 1-2-3, Symphony, IFPS/Personal, SuperCalc
Mainframe: SAS/FS-CALC, IFPS
Solution: Lay out budget items as lines in the spreadsheet program. Enter budget for each year into columns. Any given cell, the intersection of a row and column, is an item for a year. Commands/formula will cause row summary, column total, row or column percentage. The program will automatically perform the prescribed mathematics upon the entry or change of a cell. An example follows.

	A	B	C	D	E	F	G
1			*Five-Year Budget*				
2							
3							
4	*Item*	*1987*	*1988*	*1989*	*1990*	*1991*	*Total*
5							
6	Labor	32,400	10,030	15,000	4,000	3,000	54,430
7							
8	Machinery	100,500	50,000	0	0	10,000	160,500
9							
10	Supplies	500	1,300	100	4,050	200	6,150
11							
12	Computer usage	2,300	3,000	4,000	4,500	5,000	18,880
13							
14	Total	135,700	64,330	9,100	12,550	18,200	239,880
15							

Task 2

> *Create a client information file by which you can store data on your clients (customers, companies, inventory) and be able to ask questions about individual items or groups of individuals.*

The task here is to track a group or series of entities and create reports on the status of the individual entries or groups of entries. The orientation is record-based, and each entity has a record of data. This is similar to keeping the data in a notebook or on file cards where each page or card relates to a single item. The ultimate aim is to produce reports on the items, taking data from the pages or cards.

Task: Equivalence to a box of file cards, cardex file, notebook
Tool: Database management system (DBMS)
PC package: dBase II and III, Lotus 1-2-3, PC-File III, AppleWorks
Mainframe: RAMIS, FOCUS, SAS
Solution: Create a database in the DBMS. Each record will contain data on a single client. The record has fields for individual data elements, such as name, telephone number, age, amount purchased this month, and ZIP code. List generally or in a report for the entire file or for clients meeting a specific qualification. The DBMS can count entries by ZIP code, calculate total amount purchased in current month, and show client age per ZIP code. A sample database follows.

Client name	Telephone	Age	Purchased this month	ZIP	Family size	Occupation code
Jones, Mary	(404) 435-3321	45	$34.51	30303	4	93-221
Smith, Thomas	(303) 445-2232	34	$3,556.34	20500	2	23-331
Johnson, Ted	(817) 292-2590	24	$100.00	76133	1	43-776

Unlike the spreadsheet solution, the report output does not necessarily take the form of the database. A simple listing of the clients based on selection criteria would look like the sample data presented. However, a formatted report could look completely different.

Task 3

> *Write a memo, white paper, or to-do list, or organize your thoughts. The object is to communicate your thoughts to yourself or to another person.*

The task is simply to write down thoughts in an organized way. You want to begin with a list of thoughts, then move into categories or prioritize them, and finally fill in the thoughts with words to form complete communications. Your product must be neat and changeable.

Task: Written communications as on a typewriter
Tool: Word processing package
PC package: AppleWriter, Display Write IV, WordStar, PC-Write, PC-OUTLINE
Mainframe: Script, PROFS
Solution: Write the narrative text into a word processing package where it is permanently stored on a disk or tape. Make additions and corrections, run a spelling check, and print a copy. Retrieve it months later, change, and print.

This task description is an example.

Task 4

> *Gather a special set of data, manipulate it, and produce a report.*

The orientation here is data gathering, data manipulation, number crunching, and report production, but not in a row-and-column or database form. Though tasks such as this may be waning in importance, they are still performed by large systems. The object is data capture, manipulation, and report generation.

Task: Computer programming
Tool: BASIC, FORTRAN, COBOL
PC package: IBM BASIC, AppleSoft BASIC, MicroSoft BASIC, BetterBasic
Mainframe: IBM VSPC BASIC
Solution: Learn the syntax of the language and create a unique program that asks the user questions and records the answers. Then create a report in the same or another program to print the results.

As with database, the outward form of this task is totally dependent on the user. The program will be in a file where the report will be on paper.

Task 5

> *Perform analysis of data on sales.*

The task here is to transform the potentially large amount of data gathered by another task into usable information. You may need the descriptive statistics of mean, standard deviation, median, or a trend line created by regression. The focus is to transform a large amount of data into a small amount of information.

Task:	Similiar to a (programmable) calculator
Tool:	Statistics package
PC package:	SPSS/PC, SAS/PC, Mini-Tabs, EQUISTAT, RATS
Mainframe:	SAS, SPSS, BMDP
Solution:	Create a file of data and process it in the statistics package. Receive mean and standard deviation, regression, or other results upon demand.

The form of the output will be dependent on the package—a simple listing of results or a formatted report.

Task 6

> *Display data as pictures.*

The task here is to transform numeric data into graphic or pictorial representations. It follows the adage "A picture is worth a thousand words." Where numbers are processed sequentially by the logical left hemisphere of the brain, graphics are processed in parallel by the right hemisphere. The focus is information content, appropriate for all levels of management.

Task:	A picture is worth 1,000 words; holistic, right-brain
Tool:	Graphics package
PC package:	PC-DRAW, Lotus 1-2-3, PC-PG, GEM-Draw, ExpressGraph
Mainframe:	GDDM, Tel-a-Graf, SAS-Graph
Solution:	Using input from the keyboard or from a file, draw a graphic picture of the data and display it on the screen, print it on a printer, or send it to a plotter.

The output will be in the form of unique drawings, sketches, and charts.

Task 7

> *Communicate from your computer to others.*

The task here is to replace physical mail. Specifically technology-based, it allows electronic communications between computers to avoid delay and replace other means (paper). When combined with word processing, it is the basis of electronic mail.

Task:	Electronic communications equivalent to telephone
Tool:	Terminal software and communications hardware plus telephone lines
PC package:	Hayes Smartmodem, Apple Cat, MCI Direct, PC Network
Mainframe:	IBM's PROFS, GE's Telenet, BITNET
Solution:	Purchase hardware and load software to connect via a telephone line to another PC, communications network, or mainframe. Send electronic mail, data, or files. Send data at night and receive unattended. Download data from mainframe to PC.

An example cannot be given because the task is designed to avoid use of physical media (paper).

Task 8

> *Search through data stores to find records that match a specific search criterion.*

Task: Look up data in folders in a file cabinet
Tool: Mainframe terminal, on-line or batch program, or PC communications and terminal emulation package to connect with mainframe data
PC package: Hayes Smartmodem, or PC-3270 plus FOCUS, RAMIS, SAS on mainframe
Mainframe: FOCUS, RAMIS, SAS on mainframe
Solution: Logon to mainframe and use fourth generation to query file or database. Place data in file or download it to PC file. Use data for analysis noted in task 5 or make graphs as in task 6.

The eight tasks are for the most part distinct and separate functions. Often the tasks will be combined in the process of arriving at a decision point. This combination of tasks could be described, as follows, as three processes of effort: (1) management information system, (2) decision support system, and (3) knowledge-based (expert system) enhanced decision support.

Process: Management information
Objective: Create report for use by management
Task sequence: 1. Query a file or database or input data.
                  2. Create a (subset) file from query or input.
                  3. Organize data in various ways with interrelationships.
                  4. Analyze data with statistics. Produce a graph.
                  5. Print a report and add to white paper by user.

Process: Decision support
Objective: Use data and models to address unstructured problems
Task sequence: 1. Data-oriented capability primarily queries databases.
                  2. Model-oriented capability primarily performs analysis via various statistics and models, such as NPV.
                  3. DSS integrates both with a user dialog component.
                  4. User queries database, makes second query based on answer received in first. Sequence is unknown at beginning.
                  5. Final result is to arrive at a decision to an ill-defined problem.
                  6. Area of investigation may be very broad.

Process: Knowledge (expert) enhanced decision support
Objective: Add private knowledge of an expert with publicly available data and address problems with benefit of experience normally requiring use of expert
Task sequence: 1. Capability incorporates data from MIS and/or DSS.
                  2. Includes a knowledge base of private data from expert.
                  3. Prompt for data not in knowledge database.
                  4. Uses rules to evolve or infer an answer.

5. Where DSS aids user in arriving at an answer, the expert system provides the answer to the user.
6. Area of knowledge is small and finite.

The point is that EUC does not have to be just spreadsheet, word processing, and graphics. It can integrate data query, models, and expert knowledge to support the decision process. EUC may require a systems analyst or other support staff to assist the user. The support person may help create a prototype information or decision support system, with the user continuing its development. Technical assistance may be called upon for database access, syntax support, data access, or training. In the end, the user may have evolved the task from a simple idea to a complex system. The end result is generally known only at the end of the project.

HOW DOES AN END USER USE EUC?

End user computing occurs when the person with a problem for which computer-based resources can be applied directly addresses these resources. This means that the end user will take the action to (1) determine the nature of the problem, (2) select the appropriate computer-based tool, (3) delineate the appropriate method of solution, and (4) do the work to create the computer-based solution. For the most part, the end user will be working alone. However, when a user needs assistance, he or she can call on the staff of the EUC support group for (1) training, (2) consulting, (3) suggestion, (4) trouble-shooting, and (5) guidance. It is the end user's problem and the end user's solution, but the user is not alone in the process.

The point of knowing about end user computing is that there are technology aids that you can apply to problems as you see the structure of the solution. As you learn how to use the computer-based tools, you will determine the form of the solution and the method of solution address and apply your understanding of the problem to the solution. Thus you will not need to explain the problem to others unless you are asking for their assistance. You will work the problem in your time frame, applying as much of your effort and energy as is necessary and appropriate. You will not wait for others; you will work at your own pace.

How Do You Know If You Need EUC?

Not all problems cry out for computer-based solutions. Some will be solvable by existing manual methods. For example, it may be far better to use a calculator and add a series of numbers than to spend the time to determine how to let the computer do it for you. Simple file cards or a notebook may be an adequate database for simple situations or instances where it is quicker to find the answer than to design a computer-based solution. Some problems can be supported with computer-based capabilities that require only entry of data into existing programs and receipt of structured reports. Your organization may have an existing computer application that will aid in a solution for a new problem, requiring no new effort. Thus the first consideration is whether a present capability or manual method can suffice.

Another consideration is the need for data and its source(s). If you have the data at hand and/or the quantity is small, the pencil or calculator may be adequate. If the quantity of data is large or in a computer file, the use of computer-based tools would seem appropriate.

If it appears that the time available is adequate to apply computer-based techniques, data volume is significant or computer-resident, and the problem is sufficiently complex to warrant use of more than pencil and paper, it would seem that a computer-based tool is proper.

How Do You Determine the Product You Need?

Once you decide that you will use a computer-based tool, the first impulse is to use the tool and technique with which you are already familiar. Thus if you have already been trained in the use of a spreadsheet, and that is all, the world will seem to be filled with spreadsheet problems awaiting solution. However, referring to the eight basic tasks of end user computing in Figure 3-2 will show that the spreadsheet solution is only one view, one with potentially limited application.

Thus the first thing you should do upon recognizing or being presented with a problem is to describe the problem as *you* understand it: who the people involved are, what condition(s) must be changed, when the answer is needed, in what form, and so on. First determine a view of the problem; then select which of the eight basic tasks seems to apply. Is it written communications, an X–Y matrix with relationships, the storage and processing of records, data that needs to be transformed to information via statistical analysis, or one of the other tasks? It is important to determine the task at hand because that will establish the model of the solution.

When the task is identified, you should determine if you presently know of a tool that addresses that task. If you do, decide in your own mind if it adequately provides for the subtasks required. For example, if it is an X–Y orientation, as in a budget problem, will you need financial functions such as net present value and internal rate of return, and can the package you have or know provide these functions? If the answer is yes, you probably have an appropriate tool. If the answer is no, you need to seek advice and a new tool.

If a new tool is in order, or if you are not sure of the exact task and tool relationship, seek out members of the EUC support group for advice. They are prepared to discuss the problem with you, asking questions to be sure you and they have a common understanding, and recommend an attack and a tool. If the time to solution is short and the tool is quite new to you, the consultant may simply create a solution for you. After this occurs, the staff member will likely recommend that you sign up for training in the tool so that you can maintain and expand the solution. However, should the time to solution be adequate for you to receive training with the new tool and effect a solution, it will be appropriate for you to receive the training and address the solution yourself, with support from the staff consultant.

How Do You Get Started?

Assuming that you have a proper tool and adequate knowledge of its use, the next step is to address the problem within the domain of the tool. That is, now that the task type is defined and the tool selected, the model of the solution should be developed as appropriate for the tool.

One way to address the solution is to define the form of the answer and work backward to a solution. For example, you need a five-year forecast for your department. Mock up what such a report will look like on paper without any particular data (see Table 3-1). Get a feel for the type of data to be used and the relationships to be established, and then determine the data needed to achieve the end result. Given the form and the data, you can move the solution to, in this case, a spreadsheet on a personal computer.

Another process is to apply project management to the task, that is, to map out the process from problem to solution (see Figure 3-3). Suppose, in the case of the forecast, that you mock up the report and realize you will need data from several diverse sources. Make an outline or road map of the process by which you will receive the data, and place it into the solution mockup. The activity of defining the process is quite important in that it places limits on your actions. Start your map with a few entries and then examine the tasks and results. From this will come a definition of necessary actions and actors that will end in a fully defined solution.

A word of caution: A common mistake in end user development is to underanalyze and underspecify the problem. Make sure you define the problem at hand and all of the required parts. In our example, what parts of the budget are required, and what level of visibility is needed? Will responsible parties be noted or just their data? Will the solution devised address the problem at hand adequately?

What Must You Do and What Will Someone Else Do?

Since you are the end user who will be responsible for the solution development via computer-based resources, you must understand and define the problem and the solution model. This will include knowing who else will participate and to what extent. Given the actors, you must begin to create the solution from the solution model.

TABLE 3-1 SOLUTION MOCKUP

	Five-Year Budget					
Item	1986	1987	1988	1989	1990	Total
Labor	xxx	xxx	xxx	xxx	xxx	xxxxx
Machinery	xxx	xxx	xxx	xxx	xxx	xxxxx
Supplies	xxx	xxx	xxx	xxx	xxx	xxxxx
Computer use units	xxx	xxx	xxx	xxx	xxx	xxxxx
Total	xxxx	xxxx	xxxx	xxxx	xxxx	xxxxxx

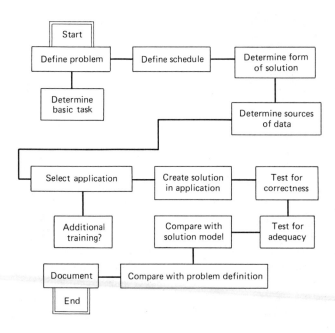

Figure 3-3   Map of problem resolution

The solution model (called a solution mockup in Table 3-1) is the form and structure of the solution to the problem at hand. The solution is the specific operationalization of the model. The model might be a bland or generic accounting sheet, whereas the solution would be the line items, cell entries, and relationships to effect a final spreadsheet result. The model was created in the mapping of the problem, making a mockup or prototype of the solution, and evolving it to a final form. The solution is effected by taking the model, placing it into the computer-based tool, and making the tool produce the desired results.

TABLE 3-2   INITIAL SOLUTION

	A	B	C	D	E	F	G
1			*Five-Year Budget*				
2							
3							
4	*Item*	*1987*	*1988*	*1989*	*1990*	*1991*	*Total*
5							
6	Labor	32,400	10,030	5,000	4,000	3,000	54,430
7							
8	Machinery	101,000	70,000	0	10,000	20,000	201,000
9							
10	Supplies	1,000	3,900	300	800	300	6,300
11							
12	Computer usage	2,300	3,000	4,000	4,500	5,000	18,800
13							
14	Total	136,700	86,930	9,300	19,300	28,300	280,530
15							

For a spreadsheet-based forecast, the solution is effected as you create the individual cell entries. Table 3-2 shows the initial model of the five-year budget in a spreadsheet package. At this point the solution contains only the major categories, which have summary numbers inserted, under the assumption that the problem is being worked from the top down. The next step is to expand the entries in the solution to include the detail that will produce the totals. Table 3-3 shows this expansion.

When the solution is created and compared with the original (definition) model you established, you are ready to test it for correctness. This requires testing of the solution with simple data, data you understand. The purpose is to exercise the solution and determine that the result is correct for the data entered. This tests the relationships established but not necessarily the degree of solution.

When the solution is tested for correctness, you are ready to test it for adequacy and completeness, comparing the solution with the solution model and the original model. Then you must enter data that will exercise the relationships again, resulting in a complete solution.

As you develop the solution model, you should document your method and intent. This entails starting a notebook or word processor file with notes about the path you are taking, the form of the solution, the rationale of the relationships, and the desired end

TABLE 3-3 EXPANDED SOLUTION

	A	B	C	D	E	F	G
1			*Five-Year Budget*				
2							
3							
4	*Item*	*1987*	*1988*	*1989*	*1990*	*1991*	*Total*
5							
6	Direct labor	12,400	5,030	2,000	2,000	1,000	22,430
6	Indirect labor	15,000	3,000	2,000	1,000	1,000	22,000
6	Other departments	5,000	2,000	1,000	1,000	1,000	10,000
5							
6	Total labor	32,400	10,030	5,000	4,000	3,000	54,430
7							
8	Heavy machinery	80,500	50,000	0	0	10,000	140,500
8	Light machinery	20,500	20,000	0	10,000	10,000	60,500
5							
6	Total machinery	101,000	70,000	0	10,000	20,000	201,000
9							
10	Direct supplies	500	1,300	100	100	100	2,100
10	Indirect supplies	400	2,300	100	100	0	2,900
10	Disposable material	100	300	100	600	200	1,300
5							
6	Total supplies	1,000	3,900	300	800	300	6,300
11							
12	Computer usage	2,300	3,000	4,000	4,500	5,000	18,880
13		———	———	———	———	———	———
14	Total	136,700	86,930	9,300	19,300	28,300	280,530
15							

result. When you create a computer-based solution, via a spreadsheet in this case, add comments in the notebook or file, or in the spreadsheet if possible, to indicate what you are doing. Why is net present value appropriate as opposed to internal rate of return? What is the source of data? What result are you achieving and what are the assumptions you used? The documentation you create will allow you or others to maintain and change the solution with a minimum of error and misunderstanding. It is likely that others will make use of the solution and will need to understand the nature of your actions.

So you have created a solution model, drawn a map to get there, found a solution, tested the model for correctness and adequacy, and added documentation for maintenance and change. This creates a package that should be registered with the EUC support group in the form of a copy of the notebook or file, a copy of the program, data, and solution reports, and commentary by you as to the success of the project. From this the EUC support group can recommend your solution model to others.

SUPPORTED END USER COMPUTING

We arrive again at the definition of end user computing: the environment in which the person who has a problem that requires access to computer resources and computer-resident data is provided an environment wherein he or she uses these resources and data personally. (This tends to rule out outside procurement, by definition, although this alternative can be an excellent choice.) End user computing allows for a variety of resources that can include personal computers, the mainframe computer, in-house or external timeshare, and proto-typing in a variety of forms. Very important in any environment is an atmosphere of approval and support. This means that management and data services recognize that end user computing is a valid use of the user's time and talent as well as a proper use of computer resources. Without support from all levels of corporate management and from data services, the result is significantly less than would be possible otherwise.

Management Support

It is doubtful that any action in the company can be successful without management support, or that is what we are told. Any new venture requires this support, the introduction of technology must have it, and change in any form has less of a chance of success when support is lacking. This appears to be good management logic. However, remember that unsupported end user computing has worked because motivated people will not let the system get in the way of accomplishment. But isn't it defeating your purpose to set up roadblocks for motivated people when the alternative is greater productivity through support?

Support from management ranges from approving of an individual's sitting at a terminal or personal computer to do his or her work to approving new equipment without justifying it to death to leading the way by using the new systems and equipment and letting others know you, the manager, are using it. One of the most effective ways to introduce change is to give it to the boss first and let others see him or her use the new capability. If the use is just for show and nothing comes out of it, the truth will eventually be revealed.

But if middle and upper management actually utilize the new capability and expect others to do the same, support will be evident.

The use of new systems, capabilities, and equipment by management does not have to be hour after hour of hands-on use. Much can be achieved by having an intermediary or assistant push the keys and give the result to the manager. However, consider for a moment the advantage of the manager's learning to use such capabilities as databases that can be queried for unusual data by short, simple commands. A report raises questions, and the manager can turn to his or her terminal and direct queries to the source of data and review the result. This may raise further questions that can be answered by further query. The result is fast answers, little staff translation, the best use of the resource, and management use and support of the capability.

Another aspect of management support is the way that approval of new capabilities and equipment is received. It seems to be a management and data services position that users always want new toys and that it is the responsibility of the reviewer to protect the company from the insatiable wants of the users, regardless of the impact of the equipment or system. On the other hand, users do seem always to be optimistic about the value and benefit of another video display terminal, personal computer, or application and not sensitive to the cost. Somewhere there must be a meeting of these two diverse views, a place where review is to support productivity, creativity, and the best use of resources and where the users will know they will be supported for valid requests. This is the environment of management support. Realizing that the users are closest to the problem and most likely have a valid response to it, management can provide a supportive review, not a halting one. Such support involves positive responses to requests, the requirement of a reasonable amount of justification, and an expectation of a reasonable response time for review and acquisition.

Data Services Support

The discussion so far would indicate that data services is less than positive in its attitude and response to the requests of the users. This organization seems to present a well-thought-out series of roadblocks that users must first recognize and then pass in order to get an application development under way or to acquire new equipment. Data services seems to be supporting the firm by judiciously holding costs in check through its administrative and developmental techniques. This organization does have a responsibility to be productive in the use of computer technology, and it receives many requests for service. What we want to address, though, is that the firm's objectives may best be met by serving the objectives of the individuals and departments.

One view of support to users would be the allocation of some resources specially designed to assist users. This may mean a readily available person to answer questions, search for data, seek out lost reports, and assist in acquiring equipment. Many data services organizations do not yet have this resource, but the numbers that do are growing. Data services may be a ''business within a business,'' but it does not yet realize the need to market itself to its customers. Most competitive firms that fail in marketing and customer services find staying competitive difficult, if not impossible. Data services has so far avoided the dangers of a lack of marketing orientation because of the high demand for its services. Due to this high demand, data services has tended to become a closed system, looking inward for efficiency.

Two specific events have caused data services to address support of end user computing and customer service in an apparently positive manner. The first was the increasing expenditures for outside timeshare services. Data services saw significant amounts of money going out that could be better spent within data services. Thus data services management took a position that outside timeshare must be reduced and gave it a high priority.

The second event that has changed the view of data services toward the users has been the advent of the personal computer. Users purchased computer power without the approval or assistance of data services and were able to gain productivity outside of the formal computer resource of the firm. Data services realized that the users had an alternative to its services since anyone could have a computer for less than $5,000. The control of the purchase and proliferation of personal computers also became a primary objective of data services, and a way had to be found to give the users a data services alternative. Since the users knew that access to computer power was possible via personal computers and outside timeshare services, it was not possible simply to stop the access to these resources without providing suitable substitutes.

Data Services Alternatives

An obvious alternative to acquiescing to outside timeshare and personal computers is for data services to take on a customer-oriented perspective and be more attuned to the users' needs, even if these needs cannot be met immediately by present resources. The advantages of choosing this tack are, first, that it does not run counter to the user's present path and, second, that it does not try to stop the users' successful actions. Thus some data services organizations initiated customer service groups, help desks, telephone hotlines, and other ways to interact with users. Marketing has not been a forte of most data services organizations, so the initiation of newsletters, seminars, and noontime presentations is quite new to most people, users as well as programmers.

The second step by which data services regains control is to provide users with an in-house alternative. This means that data services must determine what the user wants and somehow provide the service. First an alternative must exist; then the use of the resource can be pressed. Data services reviews its mainframe resources to see how it can satisfy the requirement for scheduled production processing, maintenance and change programming, new development, and the needs of the users, specifically, how much computer processing time there is, the amount of disk storage, languages and capabilities, and security measures.

If processing power and disk space are adequate, it is likely that the complement of languages is not sufficient or appropriate for use by the end users. How can you ask a user to give up a personal computer and familiar spreadsheet and use COBOL for financial analysis? Thus data services must acquire capabilities that supplant those offered by the personal computer and outside timeshare. But remember, data services does have one resource that PCs and outside services do not have: mainframe-resident organizational data.

Thus they have the one thing that the users cannot get elsewhere (other than by manual means) and have it in a form that can be readily accessed by them. With data, computing power, storage, and mainframe languages that offer the query, analysis, and reporting capability that is superior to PCs, data services has a strong possibility of actually winning the users back.

It should not be assumed that data services will be totally directed to mainframe usage and ignore the personal computer as a resource. It is possible that even with the power of the mainframe computer and resident data, the users will still prefer the autonomy and friendliness of the PC. Given this attitude on the part of users, data services would be fighting a losing battle to try to replace this resource entirely. So the next best thing to do is organize the PC world and support it. Thus data services initiates PC support in its customer support group. It determines which machines are the most prevalent or the most likely to survive and begins to provide a positive support program for these devices and the most popular software. It probably finds that a variety of PCs exists and quietly takes a stand that there will be an official, approved hardware complement, with nonofficial versions being left to fend for themselves. Classes in house or at the vendor's facility are organized, and a few programmers are designated to begin hardware and software review and evaluation. The immediate thrust is to be viewed as supportive; the long-term goal is to support and control.

A Support Environment for the End User

Whether the support environment developed by data services has a goal of control and the reestablishment of power or is a new way of invoking its charter, data services must provide a new atmosphere of user support. The environment can be mainframe, personal computer, or a mix, but it must be user-oriented. The users must begin to change their view of data services, and that organization must begin to realize the need for customer support and service. To do otherwise will continue a history that ignores present pressures and capabilities and stifles potential user productivity.

The form of the support is people and computer resources. Supported end user computing must include data services personnel who interact on a one-on-one basis in a personal manner. The attitude must communicate that no user question is stupid and that all requests are sincere. However, this does not mean that users roll over the customer support group and get anything they desire. A compromise must be established: an environment in which the user's needs are seen as valid and security of the system and data are not violated. As for computer resources, the thrust must be user-oriented capabilities that provide solutions, not more languages that require significant training and a sequential thought process.

FROM THE USER VIEWPOINT

We have indicated that support must be provided to the motivated individual who wishes to be involved in end user computing. What would that support be like from the vantage point of the user?

Whether users are college-trained in personal computers and mainframe languages or not, they will always require training when new equipment and capabilities are furnished. Thus as an end user begins or continues to use computer-based capabilities, some form of hardware and software training must be provided. This can be PC-based tutorials, classroom instruction, videotapes, computer-aided instruction, one-on-one assistance, or courses at the vendor's site. In reality, this training consideration is not new. Training is inherent in all business activities, and the use of a computer is certainly no exception. While many tasks can be learned via on-the-job training, education and training for new computer capabilities are often significantly more effective and efficient when first given in a formal environment and reinforced on the job.

Even when training is available at a high level, the user often needs to discuss a thought process or problem with someone well versed in the capability being considered. This means the need for (1) a consulting group to which the user can turn for assistance and (2) highly skilled departmental specialists. The former are data services personnel who support all aspects of end user computing. This can range from equipment ordering and setup to syntax resolution and general trouble-shooting support. The departmental specialists are more informal but more available since they are in the area and are end users themselves. The advantage of the in-area support is that assistance is quite close and the end user does not feel intimidated. Both kinds of support and counsel are necessary as neither fulfills the total need.

Another support function provided by the consultants is aid in finding and accessing mainframe-resident data. This means helping the user determine the existence of the data and its location, determining the owner and gaining permission to use the data, accessing directly or making an extract copy, and, finally, addressing the data and using it as required. A few firms have a data management or librarian function that centralizes the information on data, but this valuable service is not widespread. Often the user will have to search for quite a while to get the data being sought.

Two other areas of support that must be addressed to make the end user effective is the availability of usable tools and system access. For personal computers, this can mean gaining access to an existing device or ordering a new one. For PC software, it can mean borrowing a copy where permissible or ordering additional copies. In the area of mainframe access, quite often this entails much effort and equipment. Terminals must be available, accounts must be established, and the user must be trained in system control syntax.

CONCLUSION

> *End user computing is an idea whose time has come.*

The application development backlog has caused stagnation of computer use expansion. Users are willing to take an active part in rectifying this situation. The price of personal computers allows easy entry into the process, and many users have the background and motivation to take on the task. Whether they are convincing management that the cost of outside timeshare is affordable or that the only solution is purchase of personal computers, users are willing to address the problem by themselves. Fortunately, there is an alternative. This option avoids many management, cost, support, and security problems and provides the users with a legitimate, recognized, and formal environment in which to be productive. This supported environment for end user computing is called the *information center*.

SUMMARY

- Users are diverse, varying as to background, capability, and attitude. The users of concern are those that use the computer on an as-needed basis to solve a problem in a functional area of the company, such as accounting, personnel, or inventory management.
- Experts in the field of MIS recognize support of end users as desirable. End user computing is viewed as inevitable and will bring with it the need to change the data processing organization because it "offers just too many benefits" to ignore.
- End users perform eight basic tasks and require a relatively small, select group of capabilities to support these tasks. The capabilities provided should not require the user to be highly computer-literate, just willing to learn problem-solving processes rather than computer syntax.
- Users require management support, data services support, and computer support. All are vital to achieve the highest level of productivity.
- The way in which data services are provided is changing. The data services organization is under significant pressure to change.
- A number of firms are demonstrating a variety of ways to enhance productivity through supported end user computing. The concept has been operationalized successfully in excellent firms. There is no reason that most other firms cannot follow suit and achieve a similar level of productivity through such a support concept.

Key Terms

End user	End user computing
Consulting	Support
Rows and columns	Spreadsheet
Written communications	Word processing
Records management	Database management system
Data search	Data query
Data analysis	Statistics
Pictorial display	Graphics
Computer instructions	Computer programming
Computer communications	Telecommunications
Solution model	Solution adequacy
Solution correctness	

DISCUSSION QUESTIONS

1. Discuss considerations for each of the six categories of end users. How are they different, and how must they be treated differently?

2. Develop three advertisements for the bulletin board to promote the new EUC support group. Each one will be addressed to one of the three groups (waves) of users. How will you make the ads different to appeal to rather than alarm each of the diverse groups?

3. Define an organizational setting, and name six things done there that could be done with end user computing. Then indicate which of the basic eight tasks each is.

4. Can you think of basic tasks that users do that are not covered in the eight basic tasks?

5. Which of the eight basic tasks appeal to you?

6. How do MIS and DSS differ? Could we have knowledge-enhanced MIS?

7. What is missing from the map of problem resolution?

8. What is different in the view of management and data services in regard to (a) data, (b) information, and (c) end user computing?

9. What is wrong with use of outside timeshare?

10. What does proliferation of personal computers mean? Is it good or bad? Why?

CASE STUDIES

The following cases introduce the concept of end user development and its support environment in major Texas firms. To some extent, the case illustrates features and problems before the concepts have been fully developed. Presenting cases provides practical examples of the concepts as well as a model by which the concepts can be investigated.

GENERAL DYNAMICS CORPORATION

The General Dynamics Corporation is the result of mergers of aircraft corporations, electronics companies, and a material services firm. The process began in the 1920s and resulted in a corporation with four aerospace manufacturing divisions, coal-mining operations, ready-mix concrete sales, and atomic submarine manufacturing. The Fort Worth Division, with sales in excess of $1 billion, is the subject of this interview. The facility in west Forth Worth, Texas, was built in 1942 to assemble B-24 bombers and now manufactures military fighter aircraft, such as the F-111 and F-16 models, and electronic systems for the United States Air Force. The division employs 16,000 people, over one-half of whom are engineering and other professional staff.

The division is supported for computer resources by the Central Center of the corporation's Data Services Division. This center has some 1,000 DP employees, who provide full data processing services to the business and engineering organizations of the Fort Worth Division. Besides the usual computer operations, technical support, and programming functions, the center also responds to portions of the primary contracts to support airborne computer software.

The use of computers for business purposes began in the late 1950s, using some of the earliest IBM machines. In the early 1960s, an engineering computing laboratory was developed to support the research and engineering tasks of aircraft design. In the early 1970s, the two computer facilities were merged to form the present Central Center. *Engineering end user computing* has been an organized but minimally supported function since the mid-1960s. Engineers would learn FORTRAN on their own and be certified as co-op programmers through a center-administered test. At that point, an engineer could use the computer as long as he or she had a direct budget to support the project.

Informal end user computing began in the business community in the mid-1970s. In 1975, the Foresight language was purchased for use by the corporate office in St. Louis, Missouri, which receives DP support from the Central Center. It was used by corporate financial analysts and Central Center personnel for modeling and analysis. In 1976, the pricing organization bought a generalized system from Rockwell International. This was a user-controlled table-driven DBMS that operated in the IMS environment. This capability allowed the pricing department to create an on-line proposal status system in three worker-months of effort that was thought to be impossible with less than two worker-years of IMS effort via formal methods. The generalized system capability was believed by the center to be too resource-intensive, so in 1978 a DBMS was sought to replace it and provide a capability of more generalized use than IMS. The result of the search was the selection of RAMIS II.

In 1978, the technical services section of the Central Center purchased SAS for internal use. It was discovered by select users in late 1979. The users trained themselves and began using SAS in a batch mode. As the demand for SAS grew, training was purchased from SAS Institute.

In 1979, the corporate office requested a project that would create a database of historical contract cost information by which the pricers could manipulate and analyze pricing data and produce independent estimates. This resulted in the center's purchasing from Boeing Computer Services the Executive Information Services (EIS) software. Not only was EIS the vehicle for the creation of the database, but it also contained a high-level language in which pricers and financial analysts could model and perform analysis.

The Information Center of the Fort Worth Division

By the end of 1979, the Central Center had users actively employing SAS, EIS, Foresight, and RAMIS with minimal support. The center personnel assigned to support EIS and RAMIS were part of data administration and were also the project team for the pricing database. It soon became apparent that the informal, unsupported, and uncontrolled end user computing was growing rapidly, and the decision was made to separate the EIS/RAMIS support personnel to an individual group for the support of end use computing. This, and the beginning of EIS and RAMIS training, began in February 1980.

This was around the same time that IBM announced the information center concept, and the decision was made to call the support of end user computing by an alternative name, Information Network Systems. IBM soon announced a service by this name, so the name was changed to Infonet Services. (For consistency, we will use the term *information center* here instead.) All capabilities supporting end user computing, in-

cluding TSO and CMS timeshare, were placed under this group. With the formal announcement of the information center, the training backlog quickly went to two years and has remained there ever since, though the training effort has doubled each year for the past two years.

The staff of the IC began with four members from the Data Administration Group and has grown to 22 members. The user population has grown to 1,300. Additional languages and services have been added, including APL, SCRIPT, GDDM, Tel-a-Graf, and ADRS.

The support of end user computing began in an all-mainframe environment. While EIS and RAMIS began in a purely VM environment on a dedicated IBM Model 168, end user and production support is provided by a system of six large IBM 30XX Series mainframes. The Model 168 replacement, a Model 3083, is utilized 98 percent for user support, though it is not yet technically considered a dedicated processor. Of the total computing power, 35 percent is used by the end user community.

There is no physical information center at the Fort Worth Division or in the Central Center. The users access the capabilities via some 2,000 Model 3270 terminals, five Tandem minicomputer installations, five IBM Series One computers, and several IBM Model 8100 installations. (Each of the other two Data Services Division centers supports ICs on the East and West coasts. Communications among the three centers are supported by a satellite network, and communications are provided to Europe for support of the multinational F-16 contracts.)

Personal computers and office automation were initially introduced to the corporation by its CEO through non–Data Services channels. These capabilities have grown rapidly in the past three years and were recently placed under the auspice of Data Services. The initial offerings of PCs were the Apple models II and III, but the new standard is now the IBM PC and the DEC Rainbow to be more compatible with the mainframe and office automation environments. The initial quantity of 275 PCs grew to 1,000 within 2 years. With placement of the PCs under the IC, training is being provided on a scheduled basis, in addition to the tutorial capabilities on the machines. Communications from the PC to the host mainframe are just now being provided.

For several reasons, one being the conduct of primarily defense contracts, security considerations are of great concern. The reduction of outside timeshare use and cost was a prime consideration in the development of the IC. Access to outside timeshare remains today only for special nonduplicated applications. Dial-in communications supported the multidivision use of EIS initially, but this computer access has been replaced to a large extent with hard-wired communications. Some departments have insisted on dial-in access for off-site computer support, and this is provided via registered modem terminals. All data is secured by either ACF2 in the MVS environment or VM Secure for the VM environment. A formal data administration organization, including database administration, data management, and quality control, has existed for several years.

Due to the military contract nature of the business, all use of the computer has chargeback and accountability for services. This includes logon ID, password, and account number(s) for costing. The IC training is charged to overhead except for specially arranged departmental classes. Until 1982, all computer costing data was provided via paper report. In late 1982, at user request, some data for certain departments was also placed in TSO files for user access and analysis. Soon thereafter, computer charge data for all accounts was placed in a database that the account owners can access and use for analysis and forecasting. All computer users must budget DP expenditures on an annual basis.

The primary objective and benefit of the IC are the increase of productivity of the professional staff of the Fort Worth Division. This is achieved through timely access to data, automation of manual activities, and the elimination of waiting for the output of other people and groups. To support this positive trend, future plans include proactive marketing of the services, integration of products, PCs, and the mainframe, and the creation of a PC communications network. New ventures include branching into support of engineering end user computing as a special category, change of chargeback to more directly pay for IC services, and more direct support of decision support systems.

OTIS ENGINEERING CORPORATION

Otis Engineering Corporation, a Halliburton company, is a worldwide manufacturer and supplier of oilfield products and services for the oil and gas industry. Headquartered in Carrollton, Texas, Otis became one of the four Halliburton Oil Field Service and Product Division companies in 1959. In spite of the downturn in the oil industry, Otis continues to devote its resources to research and development and engineering to maintain its position in a highly competitive marketplace. Otis has over 135 sales and service locations with approximately 4,000 employees around the world. Though Otis revenues are not reported separately, the Oil Field Services and Products Division as a whole contributed just over half of the Halliburton Company's $5.5 billion total revenue.

Otis began using computers for engineering support in 1959. The company originally processed in conjunction with a sister division, Brown and Root in Houston, Texas, but separated DP operations in 1980. In April 1984, Halliburton began operating a data center in Arlington, Texas. This is a cooperative effort for several Halliburton companies and divisions. The data center has IBM Models 4341 and 3081 that are used by Otis, plus a Model 3083.

Otis Engineering's Information Center

In early 1982, the Model 4341 computer was in heavy use for numeric control and also had numerous end users working on it in the VM environment. The users were accessing resources in an uncontrolled and unaccountable manner, i.e., informal end user computing. To gain control of this environment, the director of DP/MIS formed the information center in March 1982, promoting a member of the applications programming staff to the position of IC manager. The object was to determine and control the end user community, absorb some of the functions of the operations analyst of the 4341, and initiate better control of DP training. This has been accomplished using the IC manager and two staff members. The user population has grown from 80 users on VM/ROSCOE only to 80 to 100 on VM where ADRS and the production data resides and 60 to 70 on MVS using Easytrieve, SAS, and IFPS. The primary segment of the user population is first-line supervisors. Finance and engineering are the largest users of IC services and use it primarily for intradepartmental applications.

The auditing department originally purchased Pansophic's Easytrieve for use of the PANAUDIT program. Easytrieve is now the mainstay of the IC, with ADRS the second most used application. The IC has three main rules: (1) We don't do user programming, (2) no daily production jobs or systems development, and (3) no interdepartmental work. To assist with the significant backlog of jobs that fail the IC rules, there are three levels of steering committees that set the priorities for DP development tasks. Thus it is not DP that determines order of priority.

There was no use of personal computers at Otis at the time of the interview. The IC operates in a mainframe-based environment. Most departments use the facilities, especially accounting and engineering, although engineering continues to do a large amount of work via outside timeshare. (The

advent of the IC has not changed this use of timeshare since it is for specialized engineering applications.) The IC runs under a special class initiator within the mainframe to avoid conflict. Training is provided via videotapes. To instill a more determined interest in the IC products, the end user is required to purchase manuals ($60) prior to gaining a logon ID from the IC. The IC staff also provides IDs for DP users. The computer literacy of the users ranges from zero to DP professionals.

One problem with the present facility is that the production IMS databases are on one mainframe and the most used IC languages are on another. Communications between the two computers are minimal and do not support the sharing of data between the two environments. Otis's plans include improved mainframe-to-mainframe communications, which should be of great assistance to the users.

Very little of the data (around 10 percent) is sensitive or software-secured. That which is protected has control via ACF2 rules. A file of data availability and definitions is accessible by users from an on-line library. Use of the UCC-10 data dictionary is just beginning. The Otis IC staff, who control data access, allows direct read-only access to production databases as an alternative to extract files. This practice is necessary due to the small staff size and appears to work well because of the low-sensitivity nature of the data.

Otis did not directly charge any user for DP or IC services in the early 1980's. All costs are allocated to a DP budget that is considered overhead. Thus the company had limited visibility as to IC usage. To change this, the DP department first began giving out dummy bills to the departments to show computer use and then began direct charging in 1985. The total cost of computer usage, either IC or DP, is a serious consideration due to the slow recovery of the industry in which Otis works. This economic condition has also constrained the growth of the IC staff and any IC marketing and promotion efforts.

The IC manager believes that the use of PCs at Otis is inevitable and will bring security and data proliferation problems. The IC manager plans to intensify training if the staff can be increased.

The primary objective, and benefit, of the IC at Otis is to help the users do their own computing and thus address the DP backlog of requests, both visible and hidden.

The IC has improved the timeliness of reports to management and relations between DP and the users by making the users more aware of MIS problems and procedures. The IC is well received and has a good future.

Future plans include support of PCs, acquisition of additional fourth-generation languages, moving to a dedicated mainframe, extraction of production data to more accessible files, and determination of career paths for IC personnel.

REFERENCES

3-1. Rockart, John F., and Lauren S. Flannery, ''The Management of End User Computing—A Research Perspective.'' *CISR WP #100 MIT Sloan School of Management*, February 1983.

3-2. Rosenberger, Robert B., ''The Information Center.'' *IBM Application Development Marketing Center*, Rockville, MD (1982), pp. 1–20.

3-3. '''Programming' by End Users.'' *EDP Analyzer*, May 1981, pp. 1–12.

3-4. ''The Security of Managers' Information.'' *EDP Analyzer*, July 79, pp. 1–13.

3-5. Rosenberger, Robert B., ''The Productivity Impact of an Information Center on Application Development.'' *Proceedings of Guide 53* Dallas (1981), pp. 918–32.

3-6. Hammond, L. W., ''Management Considerations for an Information Center.'' *IBM Systems Journal* 21:2 (1982), pp. 131–61.

3-7. Benson, David H., ''A Field Study of End User Computing—Findings and Issues.'' *Fourth International Conference on Information Systems in Supplemental Proceedings* December 1983, pp. 1–25.

3-8. ''The CRWTH Information Center Survey.'' *CRWTHNews for Better Training* 2, 1 (1984), pp. 3–8.

3-9. Edelman, Franz., ''The Management of Information Resources—A Challenge for American Business.'' *MIS Quarterly* March 1981, pp. 17–27.

3-10. Ryan, Hugh, ''End User Game Plan.'' *Datamation* December 1983, pp. 241–44.

4

The Information Center
Concept: Staff
and Premises

BEGINNING OF THE IDEA

The information center (IC) is a coordinated, formalized way of supporting end user computing. It was originated and tried by IBM-Canada in 1974 as a means of gaining relief from the building backlog of data services requests. With internal success, IBM presented the concept to its customers as an alternative to the stagnation being experienced in application creation.

The information center concept has a structure, a definition, and an outcome. The concept consists of certain kinds and amounts of support to the end user, options available to data services, and management issues, which result in benefits to the user and the firm. Many authors believe that these premises, options, issues, and benefits are obvious and certain. Others raise warnings and additional issues.

L. W. Hammond of IBM in his landmark article on the information center [4-1], gives the following description and prescription:

> An Information Center (I/C) is a portion of the Information Systems (I/S) development resource organized and dedicated to support the users of I/S services in activities such as report generation and modification, data manipulation and analysis, spontaneous inquiries, etc. The fundamental premise underlying an I/C is that if provided proper education, technical support, usable tools, data availability, and convenient access to the system, users may directly and rapidly . . . and willingly . . . satisfy a part of their business area requirements that depend on an I/S environment.
>
> The objective of an I/C is to provide users access to data on their own terms so that they can solve their own business problems.

Both sides must provide people who bring with them an appropriate set of skills to apply to the task. The I/C staff provides the technical support and consulting services; the users provide the application knowledge, task requirements, and people to do the work.

The type of work the I/C is intended to support is the short job, the one-time query, the simple report, the minor change, etc., and not the work that requires the discipline of formal project development procedures. It is not a replacement for or a way around the longer schedules usually required to develop a system. The typical characteristics of this kind of request are that: the time frame to respond is short (hours or days); the request is not unreasonable; the data does exist to satisfy the request; but no single existing report contains all the data.

Figures 4-1 and 4-2 display the IBM-Hammond concept of the information center. This is an evolution of the EUC support group presented in Chapter 3 and delineates specific characteristics of support.

Another perspective of the information center is by Robert H. Torgler [4-2], manager of the IBM Business Professional Center in Bethesda, Maryland:

The Information Center is neither a process nor a product, but a strategy a dp manager can use to support and manage a company's burgeoning information needs. Business professionals (the users of info centers) need more than mere computer access. They need guidance, education, and ongoing support. It is the dp manager's responsibility to decide how to deliver these

A. Basic premise
    1. When provided
        a. Proper education
        b. Technical support
        c. Usable tools
        d. Data availability
        e. Convenient access to the systems
    2. Users may directly and rapidly satisfy a part of their business area requirements that depend on an IS environment.
B. Definition
    1. Portion of information services
    2. Dedicated to support the end users
    3. It is a product, a place, a concept, a process
C. Charter
    1. Support end users
    2. Help users do their own work
    3. Provide training, consulting, hardware and software support
    4. Give users access to data on their own terms so that they can solve their own problems
D. Type of work supported
    1. Short job
    2. One-time query
    3. Simple report
    4. Minor change
    5. Not work that requires the discipline of formal development

Figure 4-1 The information center concept

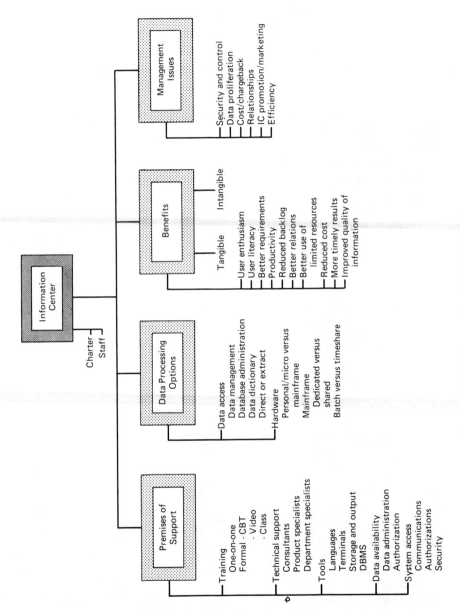

Figure 4-2 IBM-Hammond model of the information center

90

services—applications on the company's mainframe, distributed systems, personal computers, and/or other approaches. He must also ensure that access to sensitive information is controlled, computer resources are managed effectively, and the integrity of the databases is maintained.

Many other authorities have defined the information center in various ways. One calls it "a formal organizational entity which has a manager and a staff devoted to supporting 'do-it-yourself' computing" [4-3]. Another says, "Fundamentally, the Information Center is a department chartered to promote and support end user computing" [4-15] and "The premise and promise of the Information Center is simply stated: users can solve many of their own problems when provided with proper tools and techniques" [4-16]. A more pragmatic analyst [4-4] observed:

> Though "Information Center" may mean different things to different people, one common denominator does tend to emerge: widen the use of computers throughout an organization to take the strain off the data processing department. If Information Centers have a payoff, it is relieving the load on data processing's shoulders and increasing the productivity of more workers.

Torgler [4-2], explained:

> According to one Information Center manager, the Information Center was the direct result of a major shift in strategy resulting from the recognition that all the information requirements of a widely varying user community could not be satisfied adequately by a central group of DP professionals.

Thus several authors indicate that what IBM-Canada originated was an idea that they put into practice using people, hardware, and data resources. The idea may well be more important than the equipment resources because the idea supports the value of the users in solving their own problems. As will be noted later, there are a variety of ways in which the information center concept can be installed. Regardless of the mode of installation, many companies are providing this formal support environment for end user computing.

More than 400 companies opened ICs between 1981 and 1983, with 1400 installed as of late 1983 and 2100 by the end of 1984, just 5 years after IBM began introducing the concept to its customers. Estimates at that time indicated that between 42 and 53 percent of large IBM customers had ICs installed by the end of 1983, and one source projected that 90 percent of all larger IBM installations would have ICs by the end of 1984. The Data Processing Management Association during this time reported that 41 percent of its members responding to a random survey said that their organization had an IC by the end of 1983, with 19 percent indicating that they would be implementing one sometime in 1984 [4-5, 4-6, 4-7]. Another survey found that two-thirds of the respondents expected to support two or more information centers by 1985 [4-6]. As for non-US companies, one organization indicated that 80 percent of larger companies in the United Kingdom had ICs by the end of 1984 [4-6]. While this appears to be historical information, it shows the rapid acceptance of the concept in the early to mid 1980's. As for its future, James Martin, a noted author and lecturer in the information systems field, predicts that more than 6 million users will be serviced by centers by 1990 [4-5].

One reason given for the success of the information center is its support by IBM. One consulting firm [4-9] came to this conclusion and notes:

> IBM has done an effective job of promoting this very important concept, which has legitimized end user personal computing in the DP world. We can safely say that IBM's original commitment to the IC is the basis for the concept's success.

As to the benefit of this marketing thrust, these consultants add:

> The Information Center stands as the most viable concept for providing knowledge workers with the skills essential to the firm's long-term success. The benefits from the Information Center are therefore not the reduction of backlogs, but the providing of new revolutionary tools to the knowledge workers for continued professional development.

Finally:

> Four things . . . have contributed to the development of the Information Center in organizations: the emergence of the personal computer, the proliferation of "user-friendly" software, the integrated systems business plan objectives, and the growing data processing backlog. [4-10]

Among the options noted in Chapter 3 that are available to end users we listed outside timeshare and personal computers. With reference to these, Peter Bittner [4-11] notes:

> The Information Center has a number of advantages. Computer resources remain under one organization within a company, thus allowing better utilization of equipment and personnel. Duplicate data do not have to be maintained on several computers. Future integration of data from data applications into a data management system can be easier. A pool of experienced Information Center specialists, centrally located, can support a large number of users in different user departments. The demand on the rest of the dp staff is minimal.

Another writer [4-12] observes:

> Getting control of these mushrooming micros is a big issue with MIS directors. More and more companies are setting up Information Centers (ICs) as a way to aid end users and bring back centralized control to the selection, purchase, installation, and maintenance of systems, software, and services.

Not all authors give complete support to the information center concept. One reminds us:

> There is no free lunch; the Information Center is no exception. Some of the problems to look for include: (1) technical orientation instead of business orientation in the information resource center, (2) duplication of effort, (3) poor dissemination of information, (4) excessive computer

usage, (5) unauthorized updating of information in data bases, (6) security in the form of unauthorized access to sensitive information, and (7) executives spending too much time on writing queries. [4-13]

Thus we have an indication of the source and consensus of thought on the information center concept. Now let us address the parts of the concept.

Do-It-Yourself Computer Solutions

The information center concept, along with user-oriented software, lets this city's employees solve programming problems on their own.

The municipality of Anchorage, AK, has made dramatic improvements in data processing (DP) efficiency as the direct result of a new organizational concept spreading among large DP users—the information center. "It used to take up to a year and a half to get a data processing solution to a specific problem," says Michael Thompson, the municipality's information center supervisor. "Now we can get answers within hours."

The information center concept, built around user-friendly software that lets even DP novices write their own programs, springs from the need to find quick solutions to everyday DP problems by giving more people access to computers. Information centers are staffed by a minimal number of DP professionals who familiarize first-time users with software and aid them in program development.

Thompson notes that in the past a DP committee determined priorities, and simple problems would often get pushed off in favor of more important ones, leading to user frustration.

Also, demands on Anchorage's IBM 3031 and 4341 were greater than average. Due to its remote location, the city owns and operates most of the utilities, and its legal department must monitor all parcels of land within the 1,950-square-mile area the municipality covers. As a result, 42 percent of the system's time is devoted to utilities, 17.5 percent to schools, and 40.5 percent to general government.

The development of an information center as a way to give users with minor application needs access to the computer system began in 1979, says William Lewis, manager of data processing. At that time, the municipality acquired IBM's Virtual Storage Personal Computing (VSPC) software and made it available to 11 users including the departments of Transportation, Law, and Public Works. Users were given an IBM 3278 terminal and computer workspace to use in solving their own problems.

"The package works well for us," Lewis says. "It lets a user develop simple programs by extracting specific information from large data bases. With it, laypersons can attack a problem and develop a solution in two to three days. Within the VSPC network, the various departments can use the capability at their own discretion with limited human support." And limited human support means savings to the municipality. Center Supervisor Thompson says it only takes one person to run the information center. "It basically functions as a consulting service, and the cost to the user is minimal."

Thompson says that anyone who thinks [he or she] can use the center to solve a problem can come to him with a brief description of the situation. "If it sounds good, I can move on it right away." He also says the VSPC is so user oriented that it takes only "about an hour's training on the data base," and within several days, DP novices can be writing their own programs.

VSPC-developed programs have helped the municipality's legal department inventory a land area almost as large as Delaware. The Transportation Department was able to determine the average length of stay and therefore turnover rate in the city's parking garage using the VSPC program. The person monitoring the permits has developed a simple program to keep track of insurance policies, accidents, and other information pertaining to licenses. Yet another user-developed program will minimize fuel consumption in autos by optimizing traffic signal timing. With autos running more efficiently, less carbon monoxide will be emitted, and city air pollution will be reduced.

With the information center introducing more people to the computer, Thompson says, "it's like a light bulb going on. Once people see how the system can solve their problems, they are coming up with more uses for computers." [4-13a]

> *The fundamental premise underlying an IC is that if provided proper education, technical support, usable tools, data availability, and convenient access to the system, users may directly and rapidly satisfy a part of their business area requirements that depend on an information systems environment.*

ORGANIZATION AND ISSUES

Figure 4-2 shows a model of the information center concept as presented by Hammond and IBM [4-1]. The indicated areas of interest are (1) the staff, (2) premises of support, (3) options open to data services, (4) issues to be addressed by management, and (5) benefits to be realized. This is the order of discussion we will follow. We will investigate the details of the concept and then examine how these parts provide significant benefits.

The Staff and Its Charter

Part of the strength of the IC is in the staff supporting the end user. Hammond [4-1] describes this organization as

a formal organization within I/S that has a manager, staff, a mission statement and charter directing its efforts, and, usually, a set of objectives covering tangible measures (such as return on investment, revenue-to-expense ratios, budget headcount or budget dollars) and/or intangible measures (such as user satisfaction, quality of service, morale).

The first resource encountered in an information center is a staff to aid and assist the end user. The staff, per se, often begins with only a single person, sometimes two, designated to plan for and initiate the information center concept for the firm within the data services environment. The leader is usually referred to as the *information center manager* and has the responsibility of laying out the IC facilities, preparing plans, acquiring and training additional staff members, and informing the users that the new capability exists.

Research findings indicate that the IC manager is the most important single resource of a new information center. It is generally the attitude, motivation, and activity of this individual that gets the idea off the ground and implanted in the firm. Comments by 20 IC managers indicate that one of the most important ingredients of a successful information center is the presence of a champion in the form of the IC manager. To be the most effective at creating an information center, the IC manager should have no duties other than the information center.

The characteristics of the IC manager are similar to those of other staff members in that he or she must be personable, possess the ability to work with data services management and company management at all levels, and be very creative and persistent. The manager should have a reasonable technical background that is tempered with business knowledge and an ability to sell ideas. This person must persevere against opposition and win the support of upper management. While over half of present IC managers come from a DP background, they all recognize the need for an understanding of the business world and a people orientation. IC managers usually report to the head of data services or the manager of application programs.

The IC manager's orientation is short-term and day to day. The time horizon of IC planning is operational rather than strategic, with an average planning period of six months or less. Though long-term considerations are important to the survival of the IC, most of the manager's efforts will be in the short term.

Staff members in addition to the manager are usually of a homogeneous type. That is, until the center has become stabilized in its services and the users have matured in their use, the staff members all perform a variety of duties. Later, specialization will take place as members tend to concentrate on the area they do best. The duties being addressed have to do with the premises of support: consultation, training, data access, and general user support. Each of these duties will be described in turn.

> *The duties of the IC staff deal with consultation, training, data access, and general user support.*

From the nature of duties for IC staff members, it would seem natural for these personnel to come from within data services and have extensive DP backgrounds. Many, if not most, ICs draw the initial staff from application programming but attract many candidate staff members later from the user groups inside the firm and from non-DP sources outside the firm, such as teachers, business students, and nonexperienced computer science graduates. Although the title of the duties would indicate a need for quantitative or computer-related backgrounds, the nature of the duties calls for interpersonal skills and a user orientation, qualities not generally found in DP-trained people. Thus it is important to recognize the ability to look outside data services for IC staff members. This is even more vital when you realize that programmers and analysts are already in short supply within data services and on the open market and transferring them to the IC may only make the formal development situation worse.

A successful IC staff member has:

1. A people orientation
2. Good communication and interpersonal skills
3. A technical knowledge but a generalist attitude
4. A business background (ideally)

These are not the attributes of most programmers, analysts, and computer science students. This is not to imply that DP personnel are less than personable; it is simply to observe that the profession is often self-selecting, drawing into the field technically oriented, left-brain (math-oriented) people who tend to have less developed interpersonal skills and graces. Thus the IC manager has the task of selecting not the best programmers and analysts from application development but trainable, people-oriented, computer-literate individuals who can aid the users while working with all of data services.

It may be no surprise that study findings indicate that over half of present IC staff members are women and that nearly half are under 30 years of age. These two traits, sex and age, account for the shift toward motivated, friendly, and user-oriented IC employees. Whereas the original staffs came from application development, many of the new staffs are coming direct from college or from non-DP backgrounds.

Hammond and other writers suggest a support level of one staff member for each 20 users. In reality, this is both optimistic and nonspecific. When an IC first begins operations and must support a large, untrained user community, the demands on the staff will be significant. Therefore, it will be very desirable to provide a large staff in order to have good one-on-one contact with the users. Unfortunately, this is the point in time when most ICs take a wait-and-see attitude and constrain the number of staff members. As the IC and its services stabilize, especially in a technically oriented user community, the user-to-staff ratio can be high without sacrificing service. That is to say, as the users become more mature and competent in use of the applications, there is less need for support, and each staff member can service a larger number of users. Where a user-to-staff ratio of between 15 to 1 and 20 to 1 is desirable in the beginning, a ratio of 30 to 1, 50 to 1, or even 100 to 1 is quite acceptable with a stable, trained, technically oriented user community. Table 4-1 indicates how the number of IC staff members vary over different types of user communities and different phases of IC maturity. The number and type of permanent IC staff are dependent on the number of departmental specialists (users who help users) as well as the characteristics of the users. The duties of the job titles listed in Table 4-1 are explained on pages 103–4.

One of the benefits of the existence of an information center is improved relations between users and data services. IC managers indicated that users had a very high opinion of the IC staff, and this view carried over to the rest of data services. Thus the existence of one user-oriented support group significantly affected the nature of relationships for the entire organization. The view of the IC staff was the result of its support of the users and

TABLE 4-1 NUMBER OF IC STAFF MEMBERS REQUIRED

User community (user type)	Phase of IC	Number of staff per 100 users		
		Consultants	Product specialists	Departmental specialists
1. Technical	Just starting	3	1	2
	Moderate mature	1	2	3
	Stable use of IC	$\frac{1}{2}$	$1\frac{1}{2}$	3
2. Nontechnical	Just starting	6	0	1
	Moderate mature	5	$\frac{1}{4}$	1
	Stable use of IC	4	$\frac{1}{2}$	1
3. Management	Just starting	6	0	0
	Moderate mature	6	$\frac{1}{2}$	0
	Stable use of IC	5	1	0
4. Highly varied (heterogeneous)	Just starting	6	0	1
	Moderate mature	5	$\frac{1}{2}$	2
	Stable use of IC	4	1	2

the users' view that these people were not only pleasant and helpful but also highly competent. With this improvement in relations and user acceptance, one would expect that the IC staff would be well accepted by data services itself. Although there appeared to be no animosity between the IC staff and, specifically, application development members, the IC staff has no special job description and no career path beyond the IC. For the most part, the future for the IC staff members is ''back to programming.'' This is a problem for the IC manager in recruiting new staff and for the staff in planning a career. The one bright spot was the indication that transfer to the user departments was an increasing opportunity, but this would deplete the total data services staff.

As with most new ideas, people who create them and others who write about them believe that formal guidelines and objectives should be instituted and followed. Thus we would expect to find a *charter* or *mission statement* indicating the nature of the IC and the duties of the staff. In reality, the services of the staff are at such a high level of demand in such a short time that many ICs never get around to creating or formalizing an IC mission statement. Even those that do write down the idea of the center and what will go on there often do not present the document officially to their customers. Thus one has a staff that is in great demand but must determine for itself the exact nature of its duties. Naturally, this is a prime duty of the IC manager. The content of a charter will be addressed in a later chapter.

As noted earlier, Figures 4-1 and 4-2 present a model of the information center concept. As originally described in the IBM-Hammond model, the IC is presented with four views: (1) premises of support, (2) options open to data services in establishing the IC, (3) issues that must be addressed by management, and (4) benefits to be derived from the information center creation. These four views are presented in order, with the intent of specifying the makeup and capabilities of an IC.

THE INFORMATION CENTER AS A CAREER CHOICE

—Wanted—

Bright, imaginative, dynamic individual!

Must desire challenging work environment and enjoy
    working with people.

Strong college background in computer-based
    information systems and/or MIS *required*;
    some in management preferred.
Must be patient, attentive listener.

Must be willing to learn and even more willing TO TEACH!
    Must be willing to leap tall buildings in a single bound at the drop of a hat—
    should the need arise!

No experience necessary.

Could you answer an ad like this? If you meet the qualifications of this want ad, you probably are the type of individual who could find career success in a company's information center. But, would you *want* to drop your résumé in the mail and respond to such an ad?

A firm's information center is a unique work environment, unlike any other you will encounter if you choose a more traditional career path. To be successful, an information center must be equipped with a pool of diverse talents. Thus, its manager and its staff must possess an unorthodox variety of skills, as suggested by the ad. It could be that answering the want ad is a whole lot easier than answering the interviewer's potential question—"Would you like the job?"

The Information Center Environment

Members of a firm's information center (IC) typically operate in a relatively unstructured environment. First, it is unstructured in the organizational sense. Since it is an outgrowth of the Information Services (IS) department, members of the information center (usually small in number) will reside within the IS department. Often times, viewed as a stepchild of IS, the IC staff operate without formal organization and, sometimes, without a manager.

Second, the IC is unstructured in the physical sense. End users who visit the IC arrive seeking solutions to computer-related problems. Thus, it is necessary to provide them with a practical workplace which offers computer access and space to work. So if plush, private offices with mahogany furniture are the backdrop of your dream career, the IC may not be for you. As an IC professional, however, you will at least have opportunities to glimpse the finery of modern office interior design. IC staff spend a fair amount of time visiting end users at all levels of the organization. Freedom of movement is a big plus in this line of work and being "chained to your desk" is unlikely for the productive IC person.

Finally, the task environment of the IC lacks structure. The type of work that the IC is created to support involves short jobs, one-time queries, minor changes, and generally, requests which require immediate and varied responses. Because of its dynamic nature, the IC task environment presents a never-ending challenge for creative thinking and problem solving. Additionally, the tasks may originate at any location within the organization, requiring the IC staff to maintain an awareness of a wide variety of ever-changing user perspectives.

The information center is a newly created work environment in most organizations. The necessity of its existence is still questionable as far as some top managers (and users) are concerned; others simply are unsure of how to organize it and where to place it in the organizational hierarchy. These uncertainties place a certain amount of stress on IC members. As if the task objectives of the IC were not difficult enough to achieve, its personnel must continuously justify their usefulness in the interest of the long-run survival of the center. On a brighter note, stepping into a department during its emergence could open countless doors for an innovative, hard-working new member.

The Information Center People

Working in an IC obviously involves association with a few people possessing a diverse set of talents, namely, the IC staff and the IC manager. Successful IC professionals are technically knowledgeable and exhibit certain mental capabilities and personality traits. They are the liaison for end users and the resources needed by these end users to solve their computing problems. These "resources" may exist in many forms—computer hardware, computer software, data, instruction, advice or even development groups. IC members must be able to help assess these needs, arrange for the tapping of the required resources, and provide a means for delivery of a resource solution. Accordingly, they must have certain technological skills, people skills, problem-solving skills, teaching skills and general business sense.

A career in the IC would certainly involve establishing a goal for the position of IC manager. The manager of the IC must have skills similar to [those of] his or her staff. Because of the disparity between small staff size and increasing request loads, it is usually necessary for the manager to roll up his sleeves. Additionally, the manager must be a shrewd salesman—justifying the IC existence to management and users, alike. To do this, he must continually act as a watchdog for opportunities to quietly carve the IC niche firmly in the organization, knowing when to brag and when to remain quietly productive.

So, Would You Like the Job?

As usual, the disadvantages seem readily apparent:

1. The unstructured organizational environment of the IC may pose a threat to job security. It may also hinder upward mobility within the firm due to lack of formal promotion procedures and erratic visibility.
2. The unstructured task environment is extremely demanding. This situation is not helped much by many firms' desire to keep IC staff at a minimal level.
3. Being a successful IC professional requires that you not only keep pace with the newest technology, but that you aggressively seek new ideas for users. Your survival depends on your ability to keep them coming back for more.

The advantages of an IC career are not always as easy to pinpoint, but they exist in large numbers for those who are ready to reach beyond the mundane and explore a career path in a newly discovered "territory":

1. The dynamic environment of the IC offers a never-ending challenge to creative people who loathe routine and excel in tackling impromptu, unstructured tasks.
2. Stress associated with a given task never remains for a prolonged period of time. New problems arise daily and are usually solvable within a short time span. This

task environment has the psychological advantage of producing a continued feeling of completion and accomplishment.

3. The diverse tasks supported by the IC offer you a variety of experience such as working with the very latest technology, learning to work with people, making decisions, and viewing a company from a wide range of perspectives.

4. If your ego needs massaging, another psychological benefit is that you will always be in demand by others and you may even gain the image of being an expert.

There are probably countless advantages and disadvantages associated with the IC as a career. The ultimate decision is, of course, based on what you as an individual might want out of your career and the compatibility of the IC with your personal goals. This overview hopefully will give you some ideas about the match between you, your career needs and desires, and a career in a company's information center. [4-14]

PREMISES

The IBM-Hammond model indicates premises concerning support provided by the information center. These have to do with (1) training, (2) technical support, (3) tools, (4) data availability, and (5) system access. That is, under the premise that these items are supplied to the right people, at the correct time, and in an adequate amount, the benefits of the IC will be realized. Thus these five items form an underpinning for the information center concept, like legs to a table. Even with five legs, a table becomes unstable if one breaks or is shortened.

Training

Training involves instructing users how to use the IC software and hardware and consumes a very large amount of the staff's time. Training is the most important IC staff activity, other than direct consultation with users, and provides users with the skills and information that are necessary for productive operation of the software and hardware provided. Whether the training is to groups or individuals, in mainframe or PC use, it is the activity that makes the staff and users most productive.

The primary method of training is to lecture a group in a *classroom* setting, followed by hands-on laboratory practice with the hardware and software. One firm visited had a PC classroom that accommodated 40 students on 20 microcomputers. The instructor had a PC that displayed on a 48-inch TV screen. Two students were situated at each computer and took turns at the keyboard. The student stations also had room for documentation and note taking. The training was designed to make the student, whether clerk or company president, literate, if not competent, in the software or hardware in question.

The next most popular method of training, especially involving personal computers, is *self-study* or *tutorial*. The most primitive level of this technique is the use of only a reference or training manual. The manual is studied with the hope of remembering enough to use the software or equipment later. The next higher level is programmed instruction, where questions are asked at intervals to reinforce the written material to that point. Of greater value is the tutorial software that many PC software packages include. These tutorial disks allow the student to follow the instruction on the computer with dynamic action and real displays on the screen. Often the computer asks for input from the student and indicates whether the response was correct as a primary form of testing.

The most advanced form of the tutorial method is *computer-aided instruction (CAI)*, or *computer-based training (CBT)*, which is intended for a significant amount of involvement and interaction between student and software. On the PC, it may be difficult to determine the difference between a tutorial and CAI/CBT. However, on a mainframe, CAI and CBT can be quite intensive and the only alternative to the manuals. In such an environment, the student is taught and tested on a continuous basis. The program can differentiate between different students using the same program and give final results at the end. Though admitting that these programs have great potential, many IC managers questioned their quality and indicated a lack of time for their staffs to develop such programs.

A method of training that has existed for many years is the use of *videotapes* to train users of hardware and software. The visual recording and playback of a classroom or studio session can be more dynamic and interesting than just the reading of manuals. The advantage is that users can check out cassettes at their convenience and learn or review subjects on their own time schedule and at their own pace. Students can review specific sections several times if needed. This can be a primary form of training as well as support for the classroom. Though videotape training generally does not involve hands-on use of the equipment or software, this can be arranged with IC staff personnel.

Another type of training, one that can be of significant value to new ICs with low staffing levels, is the use of the hardware and software *vendor's facilities*. The firm that developed the equipment or capability will usually train personnel in its use for a fee and will have an extensive schedule of classes. This offers the advantage of not requiring time and services of a limited IC staff organization but has the apparent disadvantage of incurring an out-of-pocket cost that adds to the expense of the IC. This training cost may be minor in relation to the productivity it provides in a timely fashion, however. Vendor training expenditure will be a trade-off of IC staff capabilities, users' needs, and funds available.

A final form is the most intensive on the part of the IC and students but can pay handsome dividends for training management users. It is the use of an IC consultant for *one-on-one training*, preferably at the users' work area. This means that the consultant will spend an amount of time with just one student. Although this is generally not the best use of the consultant's time, it can be just right in exceptional cases.

Whether the training method is classroom, videotape, or CBT, the number of classes offered and their duration will be a function of the capabilities present in the IC. Classes tend to average 8 to 12 hours in duration and are often offered in half-day increments to reduce interference with other work. A company with four or five software packages employed by the users will tend to offer four to eight classes. The best place for the training is out of the users' work area, preferably in the IC area. The classes should be scheduled and well advertised with provisions to accommodate special requests for departmental groups. It should go without saying that training is part of the users' job and is offered and accomplished during normal work hours.

Besides the specific training of users, there is a need for additional materials, such as *supplemental manuals* and *reference guides*. This expense is logically a part of the IC responsibility and can be a method of feedback as to the needs and learning rate of the user community. Here again, the departmental specialists will tend to be the intermediaries between new users and the IC staff and will themselves require more documentation than the general user population.

A question that is raised with the training issue is the requirement for the completion of training prior to the access and use of IC capabilities and services. It would seem natural and logical to require such instruction and training before using the computer; however, 70 percent of the firms interviewed had no such requirements. Thus it appears that most firms realize that training is a key factor to the productivity of the users but believe that the IC is safely usable without extensive prior training.

A final consideration of training is the *retention* of the training and *use of skills learned*. This is the concern for linking the formal training received with the real tasks to be achieved. Consider the following two scenarios as examples of the problem. Be aware that the problem evidences itself in two ways: linking the training to the tasks and determining appropriate tasks.

Mike has been told by his manager that he will be receiving a PC soon and that he should immediately sign up for classes. Because Mike has no prior experience or training with PCs, he goes to the IC to see what training is available. From the schedule, he signs up for Intro to PCs, which starts the next week, and Use of Spreadsheets, which convenes three weeks hence. He feels that this will prepare him for the arrival of the new equipment and use of the software. Though he does not know what tasks are appropriate for computer-based support, he has been told by friends that a spreadsheet is the most used PC product, especially an integrated one that includes database and graphics.

Mary has just received her PC and has not even had time to open the boxes. She feels there is no hurry since she does not know how to set up or operate one. Her boss sees the boxes in the corner and tells her to get it set up and start using it because it looks bad to have the resource idle. Mary goes to the IC and signs up for the same courses as Mike.

Mike and Mary return from training. Mary sets out to set up her PC, with help from the IC. Then she begins to think about what tasks she can put into the spreadsheet. She tries her phone directory, with little success. (The spreadsheet does not have a database capability.) Then she thinks about putting in her budget, with some success. However, the budget just doesn't seem as good an example as they did in class. This is frustrating, especially since she missed two weeks of work and has many jobs awaiting her attention. She sets the PC aside for "just a few days" and gets to the business at hand.

Mike returns to his work, still waiting for the arrival of his PC. It is delivered three weeks later. His boss expects him to get to it immediately. Mike assembles the system and thinks about which tasks to put in a spreadsheet. It has been three weeks since class, and he has forgotten exactly how they did their assignments. Reviewing the notebook is a little help, but still it is not clear which is the best task to work on. "Maybe tomorrow," Mike thinks, and returns to his usual work.

Several problems occur in these scenarios. (1) Mike's equipment arrived three weeks after training, and he has forgotten what he studied. Instead of coming back to an operational system, Mike had a significant delay, which broke the link between training and at-hand tasks. (2) Mary had her machine, but the link between the training exercises and her office tasks was not obvious. It was not clear what were the most appropriate tasks to use for the PC and just how any task was like her new training. (3) In both cases, neither person stopped to consider which tasks they had that might be supported by the new PCs (or even mainframe capabilities). Had this been done, different training might have been in order. Because of several conditions in the environment, neither Mike nor Mary could make the link between the training and the tasks at hand. This was intensified for Mike because of the delay in the arrival of equipment.

Problems such as these can be alleviated by taking two actions. (1) Schedule the training to coincide with the availability of equipment, and (2) provide training in class that addresses the types of tasks the users have and includes specific work for each user on a problem at hand. Mike did not receive his equipment for three weeks, which caused a loss of skills and knowledge learned in training. Even with no delay, moving from the classroom textbook problems to the user's real problems is a shock. When the user does not have an idea of where to start in transferring tasks to the computer-based environment, the result can be frustration and delay. By having the user bring one or more real problems to the classroom, the instructor can guide the user in making the transition. Often the problem brought to a spreadsheet class will be more appropriate for a database tool. The IC staff member will be able to recognize this and demonstrate to the user where the mismatch lies. The user can then bring another problem, in order to get the desired training and linkage, and determine if a class in database is in order.

The purpose of the training is to teach skills, give the user the knowledge to use the skills, and then begin the transition from manual to computer-based modes. Skills alone are necessary but not sufficient. The other part of the equation, education (knowledge), is vital to a successful transition.

> *"If you think the cost of education (training) is high, you should see the cost of ignorance."*

Technical Support

Technical support involves the type of job and support provided by the IC staff to the users. Of interest here is the level of specific support, such as one-on-one consultation and troubleshooting, the level of expertise in specific capabilities, and the softer support of administration.

The primary job of the IC staff member is day-to-day support of the end user. This tends to take many forms, ranging from assistance with hardware to training, but the user's primary attitude is that the person is available for *consultation* on a matter at hand. For example, a user needs to know what is wrong with his or her statistical analysis program.

The program runs and provides part of the output desired but stops short of completion. The IC staff member takes the time to work personally with the user, review the program, make recommendations, discuss other tasks, and send the user away feeling that he or she has been heard and helped. The consulting offered is time-consuming on the part of the staff but very productive for the users. It is this person-to-person advice and assistance that makes the IC so useful and accepted and significantly instrumental in improving the relations between the users and data services.

The next area of technical support is *product specialization*. One or more staff members have the time, talent, and charter to become experts in a specific IC application and to offer a very high level of assistance and consultation on that application. Assume that a user employing the Statistical Analysis System by SAS, Inc., is trying to get the general linear model (GLM) procedure to perform linear regression. The IC consultant may have directed the use of the GLM procedure, but he or she may have to defer to the product specialist for detailed instructions. The product specialist would be aware of whether this procedure is appropriate for the task at hand, review its use, and recommend other procedures within SAS that would address the same problem. Such a person can review sophisticated syntax and catch nonobvious problems. To perform this service, the product specialist must have a high degree of training and experience in the capability in question. Without this background, it is best to advertise the person as a general consultant, not a product specialist.

Generally, the product specialist works with the more advanced users, allowing the general IC consultants to assist the recently trained. Where there may be one consultant for 20 users, there may be only one product specialist for every 100 to 200 users. In general, this person addresses a more narrow range of problems, but at a much more technical level. Also, it would not be unusual for all but the larger ICs to have product specialists trained in several languages or capabilities.

There may be a fine line between consulting and product specialist positions, as most ICs have individuals performing both duties. The two jobs would therefore be on a continuum, with the staff member being a general consultant to aid most users but assuming product specialist capability when warranted.

General . . . . *Level of understanding* . . . . Detailed

|———|

Consultant   *IC staff position*   *Product specialist*

Though not technical, the IBM-Hammond model indicates that ICs should provide *administrative support*. This is a job assumed by the IC, as with training and consulting, but in reality is seldom provided. Internally, administrative support takes care of the IC paperwork, schedules, reception of visitors in a physical information center, telephone answering, and other duties required for a smooth-running organization or facility. As the IC becomes a focal point for the users addressing computer-related needs, administrative support can also assist in completing requests for service on the larger projects and other data services–required documentation.

Since the information center may not have significant centralized resources, administrative support may not be in place. If the form of consultation is most often a telephone hotline for hardware resources in the user's areas, there will not be a concentration of IC staff members. Thus there will be minimum administrative support. If the IC manager is actually a manager in data services, his or her secretary may provide administrative support to the IC and its staff while supporting the manager. The need for this service will be contingent on the physical form of the IC and the services provided.

A method of support for the end user and a way to amplify or extend the services of the IC staff are the use of *departmental specialists*. These are individuals in the user departments who are the more advanced IC customers and are able and willing to aid others. As end user computing takes hold in an organization and the number of direct computer users increases, some individuals stand out because they learn quickly, possess insights into the IC capabilities and ways of attacking problems, and are natural candidates to assist others. These department members take the added informal duty of being available as the first point of assistance for other users. When the task is too long or complex for the departmental specialists, the user is passed on to the IC staff consultant or product specialist. The use of departmental specialists takes part of the support load from the IC staff and apparently reduces the direct costs of the IC. It is also a way to significantly expand the influence of the IC staff without increasing the staff size.

Tools

For a carpenter, the tools of the trade are the hammer, saw, and other devices. For the end user, the tools are (1) computer languages and applications. (2) hardware, (3) data storage, (4) output from the computer, and (5) higher-level data storage and access via database management systems (DBMS). It is one thing to have tools available; it is quite another to have them supported and made usable.

The *languages* that are popular in data services will be the obvious ones to support in the IC but of the least value. Procedural, nonfriendly languages like COBOL, FORTRAN, and PL/1 are difficult to teach, are hard to use, and require very strict adherence to rules of structure. The end user requires other languages because the use of the computer is a means to an end, not a primary job assignment. Thus the fundamental software tools of the IC should be, to the extent possible, nonprocedural, user-friendly, high level, English-like syntax fourth-generation languages. These often quoted qualifiers are not used lightly, for it is these characteristics that make the IC and end user computing so powerful. To reinforce this attitude, we must define these qualifiers and see how this software compares with that provided to data services.

It is the fourth generation of languages that embodies the other attributes noted. One extreme of generation notation is the lowest level of language, the first generation, machine language of 1's and 0's. To preclude the programmer's or user's having to do all the work, languages were developed that moved closer to English and require less specific direction of the central processing unit. We appear to be at the fourth generation presently, which provides languages that allow more freedom on the part of the user and allow the language translator to provide the specific instructions.

User-friendliness refers to the feeling the user has during or after using a specific language or capability. Thus COBOL may be user-friendly to a seasoned programmer but highly unfriendly to the end user. Friendliness refers to the work that the user must accomplish to gain a given outcome, the forgiveness of the computer to actions of the user, and the ability included in the language or capability to protect the user from taking undesirable actions from which he or she cannot recover. When an application is created for the user with languages other than the one with which the end user is familiar, such as COBOL, it is very possible to include features of friendliness, capability, alternatives, and protection in the application per se, with enough time and talent. This is because the creator can design a system to do a specific task and takes into account the nature of the task and the user. When an end user language is created, it must take into consideration many users and uses. Thus a general language or capability may not be as user-friendly as a specific application of that language. Presently, languages that profess to be user-friendly continue to require a certain level of training and experience on the part of the user. With evolution, ease of use will increase, and training requirements will decrease. Table 4-2 lists the four areas that must be addressed for a user-software interface to be considered friendly. This indicates that the subject is nontrivial or easy to achieve.

Low-level languages require that the user direct the computer, step by step, how to perform a task, whereas a high-level language requires instructions without significant details. In FORTRAN, the summing of a column of figures in a two-dimensional array requires the zeroing out of a summing variable, a loop to include all of the elements in question, and a summing statement. In SAS, you simply use the syntax PROC SUM to sum all columns in the array and inspect the one in question for the answer. Thus SAS in this example is a significantly higher-level language than FORTRAN, even though the latter is considered a high-order or high-level language.

A nonprocedural language is not sensitive to the order of the commands. Contrary to statements made in the journals, most languages are very sensitive to the command ordering. Thus the user must pay attention to what he or she is writing and in what order. For example, printing before sorting will not give the same results as printing after sorting a file.

Whether a specific language uses English-like commands would be up to interpretation. SAS's PROC MEANS would be far from English-like for an executive but very friendly for someone accustomed to the structure and syntax of FORTRAN. COBOL was intended to be English-like but is very verbose and structured. Thus the descriptives *English-*

TABLE 4-2 INTERFACE FACTORS

Learning	Behavior	Adaptability	Error Control
Accessibility	Humanization	Control	Forgiveness
Comprehension	Regularity	Flexibility	Recovery
Segmentation	Predictability	Variety	Security
Guidance	Responsiveness	Leverage	Reliability
Informativeness	Information overload	Simplicity	

TABLE 4-3 EXAMPLES OF SYNTAX IN FOUR LANGUAGES

Command syntax	Language	Characteristic
ADD 1 TO COUNT.	COBOL	English-like.
PROC SORT; BY NAME; PROC PRINT;	SAS	Several powerful commands in a small amount of syntax.
COLUMNS 1985 THRU 1990 SALES = FIRST SALES, PREVIOUS * 1.06 } FIRST SALES = 10000	IFPS	Order of sequence arbitrary. Years 1986 and on created by IFPS based on 1985.
LIST SALES BY DEPARTMENT; ACROSS MONTHS;	RAMIS	Reasonably English-like. Small amount of syntax.

like and *user-friendly* are subject to interpretation. Until computer languages are evolved to resemble or understand the user's native language, very few will allow users to express themselves freely.

Table 4-3 gives examples of syntax in several languages. Note that each offers a characteristic of user-friendliness, but still any given user may not consider the base language friendly.

> A user-friendly computer language should allow the user to instruct *what* to do, *not how* to do it.

There are two views of *hardware support* in the IC. One indicates the provision of a physical information center facility in which the IC staff members have offices, training facilities, and publicly available terminals, printers, work spaces, and documentation. This is the IBM-Hammond model of an IC and assumes that users do not have their own resources but choose to come to a centralized facility. Hardware support in this case is the provision of equipment in a publicly accessible facility.

The other view of hardware support relates to a decentralized aspect of end user computing. In this case, the users have terminals or personal computers in their work areas and access IC systems and data primarily via timeshare for mainframe processing, telephone hotlines for aid and assistance, and public conference rooms for training. In this situation, there are no public IC facilities for general use.

In the decentralized hardware situation, the IC staff assists the users in acquiring their own equipment and supports its use thereafter, from afar. This means that the IC staff is knowledgeable about available and authorized hardware (and software), appropriate acquisition procedures, and necessary resources affecting the purchase or lease. Upon arrival of the acquired hardware, the IC staff assists in installation and trains in use.

The foregoing reference to hardware was primarily mainframe-oriented. With the use of personal computers, the physical entity is usually a single group of components, but the considerations are the same. Help is needed in choosing and purchasing a PC for the user, and often PCs are made available for public use in the IC facility.

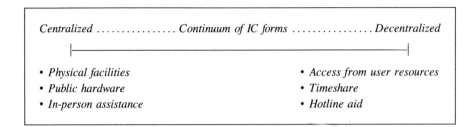

Centralized .... *Continuum of IC forms* .... *Decentralized*

|———|

• *Physical facilities*
• *Public hardware*
• *In-person assistance*

• *Access from user resources*
• *Timeshare*
• *Hotline aid*

After the user has access to computer hardware and software, *data storage* will be required to hold his or her unique application and data. For the PC, this means floppy disks, purchased at a very low cost. However, for the mainframe environment, the IC staff will often be called on to ensure that adequate centralized, secure program and data storage space is available. Adequate means that there is enough to hold permanent copies plus space to use for temporary storage. Security means three things: (1) Unauthorized access is prevented so that the data is not changed, damaged, or accessed by the wrong persons; (2) the files are not routinely deleted by data services to provide disk space for use elsewhere; and (3) backup copies of the files are made on a scheduled basis so that recovery is possible in case of inadvertent deletion or destruction of the data.

Even when mainframe security is provided, users must be trained in file maintenance capabilities such as directory or catalog commands, compression of files, and archiving to tape to conserve space. File storage generally results in an expense to the user. Thus users must be made aware of this expense and learn how to effect a balance between cost and benefit of stored data and programs.

Secondary storage for personal computer data and programs is generally done on internal hard disks or inexpensive external flexible disks. For the hard disks, the users must learn about and create backup copies themselves. When using flexible disks, they must learn that this medium is not secure and can be easily damaged. Thus data storage for the users is a nontrivial matter in that it requires the users' attention and easily incurs significant costs.

It can be said that the purpose of computer use is the output. If you cannot see the result of the application, preferably in a printed or plotted (hard-copy) form, the expenditure and time were wasted. Thus the *output from the computer* is of significant value to the user. For a PC owner and user, the output is generally restricted to the capability of the attached printer or plotter. With the mainframe, where larger quantities of printed output are the norm, the ability to print large volumes of reports, of a good quality, within a reasonable time frame is important and practical. Thus the IC may have printers within the facility to provide these services. In the absence of this, the IC staff will be called upon to assist the users in obtaining reliable, high-quality, fast-response printing and plotting services. This can mean feedback to the central facility or assisting the larger user department in acquiring its own line printers where volume warrants.

Under the subject of languages, we discussed capabilities that appeared to concentrate on analysis and reporting. Of equal value is the ability to query data. Thus the access to and use of *database management systems* (*DBMS*) will be a capability to be considered by the IC staff. DBMS and databases can be considered files that are surrounded by added intelligence. It is this added intelligence and the availability of query capabilities that make DBMS of such value to the user. This means that a user can ask questions of the data repository and receive just the data he or she needs with a minimum of syntax, structure, and training, as opposed to use of a file system. The use of database technology requires greater initial cost, consideration, and concern but can provide the firm with a significant increase in data use and productivity of the computer and data resources. Data redundancy is reduced, data sharing and use are increased, and formal as well as ad hoc applications can be created faster and at lower cost. While the tendency for an IC is to support the DBMS that is the standard of data services, this will be successful only if this capability is friendly to end users. For example, 70 percent of the firms interviewed used IBM's IMS database environment, which requires knowledge and use of DL/1 and, generally, COBOL. Neither of these languages is friendly or user-oriented. This would invite the IC's purchase of another DBMS, such as FOCUS by Information Builders, Inc., RAMIS by Mathematica, Inc., or SAS by SAS Institute, to support the user community. These DBMS feature fourth-generation languages, have good database capabilities, and are easy for the user to learn and use. One firm interviewed routinely copies the transaction databases into a FOCUS database for user access. This means that user access is simpler and does not interface with production databases.

With the availability of tools, end users can satisfy independently a significant portion of their business-related needs that require computer support. With training and support, the time and cost to do this can be low and the productivity of both users and data services can be increased. The net result is the use of all resources in the best manner.

Data Availability

Data availability means finding where the data is located and getting to it. It would seem obvious as to what data existed, where it was, and how to gain access, but it is not. In file-oriented organizations, several groups, unbeknown to one another, may be creating duplicate files. The data in the various files may not agree, and groups may be unaware of the existence of certain files and go wanting for the data. Few organizations, even those that use database technology, have a data library in which all stored data is cataloged. With such a service for both files and databases, a user wanting access to specific data can request information on existence, owner, and nature and gain permission to access it. Since this service seldom exists, the IC staff may be called on to help the user ferret out needed data and support the techniques of access. This often means knowledge of the human and computer-based security systems and how to request, access, and acquire the data. Thus the IC staff must be knowledgeable in languages, hardware, storage, security methods, and data sources.

Knowledge of the existence of data is only part of the search. As indicated, most data is considered of value and is secured by its owner. This *security* usually takes the form of a system or file password, or a rule in computer-based security systems like IBM's RACF, ACF-2, and TOP SECRET. In any case, once the data is found and its owner determined, either the user or the IC staff must approach the owner for permission to access the data and acquire the needed password or have an access rule written. For the user, this path of permission may be lengthy and complex, but for the IC staff member who has traveled it before, data access can be just a phone call away.

Data availability and sharing should be a concern of the IC staff. Regardless of the view of the creator-owner, data is a corporate resource and should be protected and shared as such. The creation and maintenance of data incur an expense, and that expense can be apportioned among users to reduce the per-use cost. The IC staff should be sensitive to data deposits and become part of the movement to database technology. With such an objective, the IC can enhance total productivity and reduce total data cost.

System Access

Where data availability involved finding and accessing data, system access is getting to the computer. For a personal computer user, it means simply turning the machine on. This assumes that the user has access to a PC when needed. If this is not the case, the IC staff can assist the user by having PCs in the IC or helping to purchase systems for the user. Once a PC is available, the other IC services of training, software, and hardware support will be important.

In the mainframe environment, access means much more. The first concern is the availability of a terminal for the user, either in the IC or in the user's area. Next are the account for collecting charges incurred, training in use of the terminal, logon sequence authorization, timeshare and job control languages, and data access. It is the complexity of mainframe access that has made the PC so popular. However, the mainframe has several advantages not found on the PC that make it continue to be a primary choice of many users. These are (1) sources of data, (2) processing power, (3) capabilities not found on the PC, and (4) faster, larger quantities of hard-copy output. This makes the trouble of system access on the mainframe worth the effort.

It is the presence of routinely captured (transaction) *data* that makes the mainframe of great interest to the end user. Accounting and financial analysts need accounting data to perform their analysis and reporting. The PC alternative is manually to reinput the data from reports or to gain access to the mainframe from the PC via communications and download the data. This mixed (cooperative processing) environment of mainframe data to PC for analysis causes other problems of data redundancy and integrity, which require further controls. However, use of mainframe data on the mainframe provides the users with a valuable resource in an easily controlled environment. This, added to processing power and output, provides a highly useful and valuable total environment.

Although PCs provide ready access and reasonable *processing* power (superb processing power when compared with mainframe of just a decade ago), they are still slow in comparison with large mainframes. When the task requires a significant amount of number crunching, manipulating of data, or other computer processing, the PC may take longer than the time available, and the mainframe is the only practical alternative. The point is not the difficulty of processing but the amount. Searching through a database of a million records, sorting such a file, and adding four fields throughout the records can require hours on a PC but only a minute on a mainframe. Executives will wait minutes but not hours or days.

The question of the value of *capabilities* on the mainframe versus those on PCs is a current important issue. One of the great values of the PC is the availability of powerful and friendly applications, such as spreadsheets, databases, and word processing. These are generally not universally available on the mainframe. This has added to the attractiveness of the PC and moves groups of users to it. However, the mainframe remains the primary environment for many applications, such as specialized and highly powerful languages, modeling capabilities, and other capabilities requiring a significant amount of processing power. Even when the PC capability is sufficient, the data must be manually entered or downloaded from the mainframe to be used. With the mainframe capability, the processing is faster, the data is available, and output services are of greater capability. However, this must be compared with the ability of the user and the training required.

End-user computing addresses small tasks that require a small quantity of *hard-copy output*. Such is often not the case as users become more competent and tasks become more complex. While a single-page summary report and a few graphs may satisfy the executive, users often want to see the details that produce the summary page, and this requires printing or plotting dozens or hundreds of pages of output. Even when the output per alternative is kept low, the ability of the decision-making user to consider many alternatives creates a large quantity of output.

Printing from PCs is usually slow. With a variety of mainframe devices that are shared among many tasks, low-cost, high-quality, high-volume output is possible on a quick-turnaround basis. Thus the end user will find the mainframe of value even with access to a PC and its friendly software.

CONCLUSION

The story of the information center is spread over Chapters 4, 5, and 6. This chapter addressed the history of the concept and the IBM-Hammond model and discussed the first parts of the model, staffing and premises. The thrust has been to present the information center as an organized concept for the formal support of end user computing. To quote Hammond again [4-1]:

> The fundamental premise underlying an I/C is that if provided proper education, technical support, usable tools, data availability, and convenient access to the system, users may directly and rapidly satisfy a part of their business area requirements that depend on an I/S environment.

In the next two chapters, we will discuss various options available to data services in organizing an information center, some issues that must be addressed by management, and the benefits that can be expected from the expenditure for an IC. Even before that discussion, the IC can be seen as a viable concept when only the considerations of staffing and premises are addressed.

SUMMARY

- IBM originated the information center concept in 1974 to solve internal problems associated with formal development. The idea was to provide formal support to the most valuable resource in the organization, the users.
- An information center can be a physical place or just an idea. It can be initiated in a mainframe, PC, or mixed environment.
- The most important resource of an information center is the champion who organizes it and directs its staff. This individual generally becomes the IC manager.
- The IC staff must be oriented to the users and have interpersonal skills as well as a reasonable technical background. These skills and a willingness to help users have been instrumental in improving the relations between data services and organizations in general.
- The premise of an information center is that it will provide training, technical support, tools, data availability, and system access. Given these capabilities, the IC has proved to be a valuable resource.
- Capabilities appropriate for an IC are not necessarily those found useful by programmers. Therefore, it may be necessary to acquire capabilities in addition to those appropriate to data services uses.
- Part of the job of the IC staff will be to seek out data and gain access to it and the system for the user. This aid makes the mainframe a useful tool.

Key Terms

IBM-Hammond model	FORTRAN
Premises	COBOL
Computer literacy	BASIC
Computer education	Fourth-generation language
Data	User-friendliness
Information	Nonprocedural
IC charter or mission statement	English-like
Training	Database management system (DBMS)
Education	Primary storage
Information center	Secondary storage
Do-it-yourself computing	Password protection
Consultant	Data access
Product specialist	System access
Departmental specialist	Centralized facilities
Interpersonal skills	Decentralized services
Computer-aided education	Computer-based training

DISCUSSION QUESTIONS

1. Discuss what is meant by centralization and decentralization of resources. Show the difference when referring to computer resources and other resources.
2. What is the difference between education and training?

3. Would you hire a 45-year-old third-grade teacher to be an IC staff consultant?

4. What is the difference between a charter and a mission statement?

5. What would it take for you to be an IC manager?

6. Does your college have an information center? What is the user-to-staff ratio? Is that an appropriate figure?

7. What services would you expect from the vendor of a major software language? Should the vendor charge for these services?

8. Which job appeals to you more, consultant or product specialist?

9. How would you go about cultivating a cadre of departmental specialists?

10. What is wrong with using COBOL or FORTRAN in an IC? After all, these are the primary languages taught in college.

11. How is it possible for a language to be nonprocedural? What does it take for a computer to accept English-like syntax?

12. Do you really agree that there are still reasons that users will be attracted to the mainframe after they have access to personal computers?

CASE STUDIES

MOSTEK–Thomson Components

MOSTEK was started in 1974 by three former Texas Instruments engineers. The primary product was semiconductor devices. This had been a very successful venture until the Japanese entered the market. This foreign competition caused MOSTEK significant hardships, including a drastic decline in profit, reduced employment, and a change of products leading to only 50 percent reliance on semiconductor production. The new ventures include government contracts for electronic devices.

At the time of its economic depression, MOSTEK was purchased by United Technologies Companies (UTC) and later by Thomson Components. UTC was instrumental in the MOSTEK recovery. Total MOSTEK employment is presently 5,000, which remains lower than peak figures.

The firm has been computer-intensive since its beginning, having much the same corporate style as Texas Instruments. An example of this corporate style is the placement of mainframe terminals on or near the desk of most of the salaried personnel who might use them in their jobs.

MOSTEK's Information Center

The present IC manager was hired by the director of DP to provide a customer service function. He began by teaching the use of the Easytrieve language. At that point, there was no informal end user computing, so there was no user base from which to draw. Since then, SAS and IFPS have been added, and PANVALET has been used extensively for data storage. The staff has grown from the lone instructor to eight members, and the user base has reached over 750 people.

The objective of the support of end user computing was to give relief to the ap-

plications backlog and teach users to be more self-sufficient. The physical IC, installed in January 1984, has dedicated facilities for training, consultants, PCs, and administrative support. This installation has followed the IBM model in facilities and has received excellent management visibility and user support.

The largest group of users is first-line supervision, followed by middle management. While finance and accounting are the lead departments in IC use, all departments participate. Reports and analysis are the most intense use, with modeling and system prototyping following closely. The clerical staff uses word processing extensively but is growing impatient with the limited IC word processing capability. Unlike most ICs interviewed, the use of the MOSTEK IC was reported to peak in the early morning and in midafternoon.

MOSTEK is one of six companies interviewed to use computer-based training (CBT). It is using the IIS facility on the firm's Amdahl computer as well as self-study training on the PCs. The IC offers 12 courses during the first shift, attended by employees from all three shifts. This means that some people must acquire training outside of their normal work hours. The IC charges for training, $50 to $150 per course. For the most part this is done so that the users will not sign up for training and then fail to attend classes.

The support of end user computing was mainframe-based until UTC purchased the company. At that time, the executives were trained in Hartford, Connecticut, and each received an IBM personal computer. Thus top management was formally introduced to PC technology and has been highly supportive of the PC and IC concepts. The PC training and support continue, but the purchase of PCs is now entirely up to the user departments.

The IC is active in the acquisition process for PCs. The acquisition effort is large enough to pass the actual buying effort to the purchasing department, but installation and support are performed by the IC staff. The policy is that any truly IBM-compatible device is acceptable. This is carried out to the extent that different manufacturers are recommended for different users, secretaries, executives, and professionals. There are presently 250 PCs installed, and the rate of request continues to increase. Of note is the overt lack of PC connections to and communications with the mainframe. This is due to potential problems with security—the lack of an audit trail. This will be well thought out before PC-to-host communications are instituted.

MOSTEK uses two computer environments, TSO and CICS. TSO has limitations as to the number of users logged on but is required for use of ISPF with PANVALET. Although many users use just CICS for FOCUS and SAS, support of two environments imposes additional training requirements.

MOSTEK and its parent company are very sensitive about corporate data. The concern is not as much for the financial records of the business as for the computer-aided design (CAD) data on device design and competitive pricing information. ACF2 is the security capability employed, and all files except user-owned files and common PANVALET areas are protected. Access to data is via formal authorization from the owner.

The IC manager believed that a successful IC could best be achieved from a combination of management support and user support. Either alone was insufficient. The management of an IC must be outgoing and actively market the IC rather than sit around and wait for users to find it. This is contrary to other firms' belief in marketing cautiously so as not to be overrun with user acceptance. The IC manager believed that the users have latent needs that are not understood. These users require support in uncovering the needs and effecting solutions.

The primary objective, since the IC is in place and has been advertised to meet data and information needs, is to venture out of the physical IC to help users define and address their needs. The IC manager believes marketing is much broader than just advertising and promotion. It is active assistance to the user. To provide this, the IC will answer or determine the answer to almost any question raised by users. "We are a service organization," noted the IC manager.

A primary benefit of the IC has been in its role as the public relations branch of DP and the resultant improvement of DP's image. The application development area is usually viewed as ineffective, and the IC has helped change this image. The second benefit has resulted from training the users and motivating them to meet their own needs. The result has been users who are more interested in their jobs.

The plans for the IC involve active marketing and more active consulting, seeking out areas in which to help. In addition, the IC staff plans to review user-developed programs to improve efficiency and determine ways to support the PC expansion process even more effectively.

EasTexas Industries, Inc.

EasTexas's principal business is providing wireline and well evaluation services for companies engaged in the drilling, completion, and workover of oil and gas wells. The performance of these services involves the lowering of an armored cable, equipped with sophisticated instruments and sensing devices, into the well to measure specific parameters at various points in a well's life.

Annual Report

This oilfield support and services company was founded in 1959 and presently has headquarters in Forth Worth, Texas. EasTexas has used computers most of its corporate life for engineering and business applications. It has reached a level of sales of $316 million during this time and employs 4,700 people.

EasTexas's Information Center

In the early 1980s, some of the DP programming staff at EasTexas wanted a higher-level programming language than COBOL and pressed for the acquisition of Easytrieve by Pansophic, Inc. This language was chosen for its IMS access methods. Once acquired, several application programmers started using Easytrieve. This use came to the attention of a cost accounting manager, who wanted Easytrieve access for his own use. Some DP personnel feared end user access to the language and data, but the manager insisted and eventually gained access to Easytrieve. Other people saw his success and purchased training from the vendor. Manufacturing was the next department to use it and acquired training tapes. At this point, end user computing was not supported, although it was specifically allowed. It is questionable as to whether this is informal end user computing, but was sufficient to cause management to recognize the need for support. Thus when the IC officially started in June 1982, there were eight end users. The opening of the IC coincided with the hiring of the IC manager, who was the only staff member at the time. The staff has since grown to three, and the end user population has expanded to 70.

The objective of the IC was to isolate the programmers from the users, support the users in doing their own work, and provide a central point for user training. Part of the IC initiation decision process was supported by attending IBM Guide user group sessions. Once the decision was made to install an IC, an extensive search was conducted to find a special person as the IC manager. The person chosen for this position came from a non-DP environment.

The prime users are salaried staff personnel, who use it mainly for reports and analysis. Most applications are for personal use, with departmental applications in second place. Accounting continues to be the biggest user, whereas engineering and data processing do not use the capabilities to any extent. Though Easytrieve is the primary language, SAS and SAS/GRAPH are well utilized.

Computer-based training (CBT, from Deltak) has been tried but is still in evaluation. Meanwhile, videotapes and classroom sessions are the primary training methods. There is still some outside training by vendors. Of note is that Deltak CBT training has no up-front charge but has a variable charge for each training session. This seems an advantage not necessarily offered by other vendors.

The IC shares the company's IBM Model 3081 computer. Acquisition of terminals for IC use is not a problem as there are some 400 Model 3278 and 3178 terminals in the user areas for application access. Personal computers are just beginning to be supported by the IC. There are presently a small number of IBM PCs in house, and the IC has dedicated about 1.5 of the IC staff members to support the PC acquisition and use. Only about 20 percent of the PCs can access the mainframe, uploading of data is not permitted, and downloading of data seems to pose no problems.

EasTexas does use chargeback for services, but there is no forecasting of budgets, nor are the departments held accountable for use. Chargeback is mainly for information. This practice started in February 1984, and DP plans to require budgeting and forecasting in order to gain greater control.

The reduction of timeshare was not a specific issue addressed at the time of the IC installation. The external timeshare was mainly for the budgeting group and was of a nature that could not be replaced by internal EasTexas capabilities.

Data security is provided by the TOP SECRET (TS) software. To gain access to data, the user sends a form to the TS administrator. The TS file is changed, and access is controlled at logon. One feature that is to be changed is that the level of security is fairly high at the file level. This creates a problem in that a person with file authorization can access a lower level such as a field, if known, when the field should be restricted. The data that is accessed is mainly image copies of the IMS databases that are created routinely via production jobs. Users with special needs can request the IC manager to make an ad hoc run against the IMS databases. In rare cases, users can access IMS databases via batch once the database is in a down state.

The two main risks that the IC manager believed the information center created were potential unauthorized access to data because it was now easier to get to and the use of a file copy to create a report that appeared to be based on the source file. These were characterized as potential problems, not experienced ones.

The primary objective of the EasTexas IC is to provide first-class training and services to any end user desiring access to data stored on the computer. The primary benefit is that the IC allows end users to get the information on a more timely basis than would be possible through traditional DP methods. End users ask for services that they would not ask from traditional DP organizations, are becoming more DP-literate, and now are better able to explain their requirements.

Plans for the future include the promotion and marketing of the IC, expansion of the training effort, and increased management visibility and involvement in the information center.

REFERENCES

4-1. Hammond, L. W., ''Management Considerations for an Information Center.'' *IBM Systems Journal* 21: 2 (1982), pp. 131–61.

4-2. Torgler, Robert. H., ''The Information Center—A Review of the Concept.'' *Proceedings of the Eighth Annual SAS Users Group International Conference* January 1983, pp. 427–33.

4-3. ''The Security of Managers' Information.'' *EDP Analyzer* July 79, pp. 1–13.

4-4. Smith, Amy E., ''A Concept Comes of Age.'' *Business Computer Systems* November 1983, pp. 173–84.

4-5. Rifkin, Glenn, ''The Information Center: Oasis or Mirage?'' *Computerworld* 15 June 1983, pp. OA/13–16.

4-6. ''The CRWTH Information Center Survey.'' *CRWTHNews for Better Training* 2, 1 (1984), pp. 3–8.

4-7. Clarke, William, ''It's A Jungle Out There.'' *Computerworld* 23 February 1983, pp. 31–33.

4-8. ''DPMA Members Feel the Sudden Impact of Info Centers.'' *Data Management* February 1984, p. 22.

4-9. Research Memorandum #2371—*The Information Center in Large Organizations. Massachusetts: International Data Corporation*, February 1983.

4-10. Seidman, Marsha, ''Coming of Age—The Information Center Grows Up.'' *Data Training* January 1984.

4-11. Bittner, Peter B., ''The Information Center.'' *Datamation* In Reader's Forum October 1982, pp. 207–9.

4-12. Friedman, Selma, ''The Information Center: Taking Control.'' *Micro Manager Supplement to MIS Week*, May 1984, pp. 22–25.

4-13.   O'Connel, Daniel J., "The Information Resource Center: Why So Popular?" *Computerworld* 29 September 1982, pp. OA/35–37.

4-13a. "Do-it-yourself Computer Solutions," reprinted from *Infosystems*, (Hickcock Publishing Co), May 1983, p. 70.

4-14.   Jackson, Pamela Z., "The Information Center as a Career Choice," unpublished paper, University of Georgia, November 1986.

4-15.   Rhoades, Wayne L., Jr., "The Information Center Lends a Helping Hand," *Infosystems*, January 1983, pp. 26–30.

4-16.   Hargar, George, "Information Center: The User's Report," *Computerworld*, 26 December 1983–2 January 1984, pp. 70–74.

5

The Information Center Concept: Options and Issues

DATA SERVICES OPTIONS

In instituting anything new, whether it is a change in organizational structure, introduction of electronic mail in the office, or a new machine in the factory, management generally has a number of options it can exercise. The same is true in the use of computers: Data services can initiate the change by choosing from various alternatives. With the formal support of end user computing via the information center, the options that must be addressed have to do primarily with data access and hardware. Since we have already discussed the support provided in training and the IC staff, indicating alternatives there, the options at this point tend to be more in the line of ways of doing data services' business and how this organization keeps control. These same thoughts will be continued in the section on management issues, but the problems to be discussed there tend to be more organizational, whereas the options here tend to be more technical.

Data Access

Data access addresses the way that users learn about and get to data. We shall take a closer look at four aspects of data as it pertains to end users: (1) data management, (2) database administration, (3) data dictionaries, and (4) methods of accessing production data.

   Data management and administration comprises the consideration of storage, quality, security, and use of data. It can involve the use of databases or files, data dictionaries, librarians, and technicians, but the primary consideration is the storage and protection of the data resource of the firm. It can be compared to the function of the head librarian at a library. The librarian considers books, whereas data management addresses individual files of data, but both must be acquired, stored adequately and efficiently, protected and secured, and made usable.

The question of data management for the information center has to do with how the users gain knowledge of and access to data. For example, the use of centralized *data dictionaries* to describe the location, ownership, and characteristics of all company data provides a single point of access for users in their search for needed data. Although many firms employ data dictionaries, they are usually not available to end users or are not in a form of great value for them. Thus the users must rely on the IC staff or seek out the data on their own. The establishment of a data management function and a data dictionary are options to be exercised by data services management. The decisions concerning these functions will have far-reaching effects and thus will not be made at the convenience of the end users. However, the establishment of an information center may be the emphasis to realize the value of the data resource and to begin its management in a formal, centralized manner.

Figures 5-1 and 5-2 show examples of two of the entries in a data dictionary. Figure 5-1 describes a specific data element, and Figure 5-2 shows the contents of a file. There would also be a cross-reference showing where data elements are stored, data flows, and primary sources of data. The purpose of a manual or computer-based data dictionary is to be a single source for "data on data," an authority where a user can find the existence, owner, and characteristics of any data element, data source, or data storage site.

The use of database technology requires the discipline of *database administration*, a subset of data administration and management. The individual database administrator (DBA) is responsible for the technical aspects of the database—creation, reorganization, backup, security, and access. This is normally a concern for large formal systems, but the

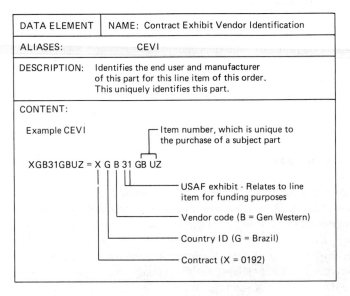

Figure 5-1   Data element page/screen of data dictionary

FILE	NAME: Invoice File	
ALIASES:		
DESCRIPTION:	Selected data from the VOCOL database. Data is stored pending merging with STATUS AND PRICE file data.	
COMPOSITION OR CONTENT:	(CEVI + PO + Item + POR Code + POR Quantity + Buyer + Vendor + GDPN	Vendor-Unit-Print)
VOLUME/SIZE:	43,000 records	
WHERE LOCATED:	Tape FW5C.FW5CG.JB3(0)	
SEQUENCE OF RECORDS:	CEVI	
IMMEDIATE ACCESS REQUIREMENTS:	None	
COMMENTS: This is a tape produced from the VOCOL database. It is produced by a programmer in the Material Department on request, with some delay. See Tom Smith for details.		
Date: 14 February 1988 Originator: H.H. Carr		

Figure 5-2 File page/screen of data dictionary

addition of end users wanting access to the production data will have an impact on the DBA. With the increased traffic that comes with end user computing and the information center, the databases will be exercised more and will require more attention to structure, organization, security, and frequency of access. The options to be exercised have to do with how access authorization is established and the effect of end user computing on the databases. The use of database technology will be of significant value for the end users because of the concentration of the needed data and the formality of the database care.

Production databases are actively used for the operational activities of the firm and contain the basic data upon which the company operates. Disruption of these databases will have serious consequences; data services, in general, and the DBA, in particular, are therefore very sensitive about who accesses the system and in what manner. To avoid disruption of service or damage to data, some firms periodically make *extract copies* of production data and allow end users to access only these file copies. The copying can be done at night, and the data is considered current within the time frame of the users' problems. This method reduces the activity to the databases and potential competition for access and insures against damage to the production databases by end users. The penalties are in the form of extraction time and copy storage space, but both are often small in comparison with the benefit.

The second alternative for the data access option is to allow *read-only access* to production databases. This insures the most current data and avoids extract expense and storage space for copies. However, these advantages are gained at the expense of greater activity on the databases and the potential of end users interfering with other users of the system. If this happens, the use of extract copies is an easy alternative. Half the firms interviewed found read-only access to be acceptable, nondisruptive, and effective.

The last alternative is to allow *direct read-write access* to the databases. Although few companies allow this freedom, it is possible that this will be necessary when the results of the end users' query and analysis of data necessitate the changing of data on the original database. Obviously, only experienced users should have this access, and the need for recovery techniques is greatly increased. A variation of this is to allow read-only access and effect rewrite of data via the data entry group in data services.

Hardware Options

Hardware options involve the choice of using personal computers or mainframes and the methods of service on the mainframe computers. This may not be a specific option in many firms where information centers are initiated for the purpose of controlling PC acquisition. In other companies, the PC may not yet be an alternative, so the primary consideration may be how the mainframe is used. Figure 5-3 shows the results of a study on the distribution between mainframe and PC use in ICs. Of the 311 ICs responding, about half used both forms of equipment, and the remainder were split 2 to 1 in favor of PCs.

The choice to use *microcomputers* or *mainframe computers* or a combination of both has to do with present resources, available funds, staff availability to support each, and the nature of the end user community. If departments are already acquiring PCs, often without the authorization or knowledge of data services, the support of the PC by the information center will be a welcome service but a significant task for data services. Where the thrust is to control these PCs, something more than absolute control will be required. In either case, the IC is an excellent support opportunity for the new PC and should be well received by the users.

Support for PCs tends to be somewhat different from that for the mainframe. Mainframe environments support centralized processing and output even though the terminals are located in the users' areas. The use of personal computers is a decentralized concept (unless they are in the centralized IC facility). These systems tend to be the property of the users. This means a widely distributed processing environment, one that may have a variety of hardware and software types. Thus support for the PC environment may include setting standards for equipment and publishing a list of authorized and supported software. This may run counter to the wishes of the users but may be the only way to contain a runaway environment

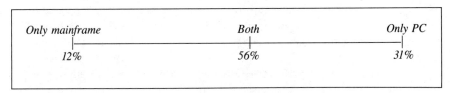

Figure 5-3   Use of mainframes and PCs in ICs [5-1]

because the IC staff can practically support only limited types and numbers of equipment and software.

Another feature of the PC environment is that the production data is resident on the mainframe and must be accessed and downloaded to the microcomputers. This requires communications equipment and software, additional training, and the creation of duplicate files. The hardware and software costs are a one-time expense, but the duplicated files may have a long-term effect. The IC managers interviewed believed the primary problems associated with PCs to be this proliferation of data files and the use of the copied file, often changed, as an authority. Though these managers believed this situation was manageable, it was a persistent and obvious problem.

The one consideration, which may be a surprise in the present use of mainframe technology, is the use of batch processing as opposed to on-line, interactive services. While more than 90 percent of IBM sites have timeshare software for terminal use, the cost of interactive computing is greater than for batch processing. Thus a decision needs to be made as to the encouragement, or requirement, of the service used by the end users. It has been noted that users who are accustomed to receiving two-week turnaround on computer requests can now receive four-hour service in the batch mode, and thus two-minute response for the higher-cost interactive service is unwarranted. Where the output is a report that does not tend to create another question that requires attention, the batch mode is the better and cheaper mode because it requires less in the way of computer resources. The file of commands can be created at the terminal in an on-line mode, but the actual processing is done in the batch mode. However, when an answer tends to prompt another question, as in ad hoc query and analysis, the use of on-line, interactive capabilities is not only worth the added cost but is vital to timely decision making. It would be penny wise and pound foolish to save a few dollars in batch mode to lose a contract due to the absence of decision support information.

It may be that the best of both worlds can be achieved by training the users in the use of interactive and batch processing for each application, cautioning them about the benefit of each. Creating a file interactively and processing it in batch mode tends to be the more effective and efficient method for complex tasks, as time is needed to review the syntax and structure of the problem. Quick tasks may best be handled interactively in that the task is completed in a short time, freeing the system for others.

```
 Quick . . . . . . . . . . . . . . . . . . . . . . . . . . . Response . . . . . . . . . . . . . . . . . . . . . . . . . . Slow
 Higher -----------------------------Resource usage/cost-----------------------------Lower
 |                                                                                      |
 On-line                              Processing mode                             Batch
```

The last consideration of the mainframe environment is whether to have the end users share the computer with production tasks or to obtain a *dedicated processor* for end user computing. With the recognition of end user computing and its subsequent acceptance, the amount and percentage of processing by end users has been steadily increasing. It has been predicted that end user computing will require in excess of half of the total computer

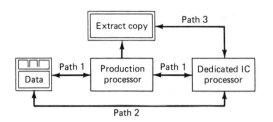

Figure 5-4 Paths to data from separate IC processor

resource by the mid-1990s. With this demand, and the possibility of interference with the normal production tasks, the dedication of a computer to end user computing has great merit. With such a separate machine, production databases and processing are protected, and an environment can be created to protect the users from themselves. However, a firm with limited resources may not have the freedom to dedicate a processor for end user computing and must share existing capabilities. This is quite acceptable if processing power and data storage facilities are adequate.

The use of a shared processor does have one advantage over separate computers. Where users are sharing the computer with production work, the production data is readily available, from a technical standpoint. Given permission and access, there are no technical problems concerned with getting to the needed data since it resides on data storage addressable by the user's machine. However, in a separate-machine environment, special care must be taken to be sure that both processors can access the data. Where direct communication to the data is not provided for the end user machine (path 2 in Figure 5-4), a pass-through capability (path 1 in Figure 5-4) must exist, or extract copies must be available for the IC processor (path 3 in Figure 5-4).

The options for data access and hardware alternatives open to data services are basically technical issues. Each alternative has a different support requirement and different effects on the end user. Any given alternative can be made to work; however, data services must create an environment that supports end users while not being disruptive to production processes. Production systems support the day-to-day business of the firm, whereas end user computing supports a longer-term decision process. Both uses of the computer are important, and options must be considered in light of each.

MANAGEMENT ISSUES

In introducing and discussing the information center, Hammond and other authors urge caution regarding certain aspects of end user computing and its formal support environment. The areas of concern involve issues that management must address and resolve. Managers of successful information centers indicate that these management issues can be resolved but that they must be considered overtly to avoid problems. The issues of concern are (1) security and control, (2) data proliferation, (3) data integrity, (4) cost accounting and chargeback, (5) user–data services relationships, (6) the promotion and marketing of the IC, (7) computer efficiency, and (8) benefits.

Security and Control

Security and control are two aspects of determining who does what on the computer. *Control* in the area of end user computing addresses the issue of centralization of power and the faith that data services and management have in the end users. Various authors show concern with allowing hordes of non-computer-trained employees to have access to computer resources and company data. The denial of access to processing and data is a form of power; information is power, computer access is power, and denial is power. End user computing is a direct frontal assault on the data services power base, at the issue of centralization of computer resources, and the power that it brings. Since there is more formal work than can be accomplished by application programming, data services is obviously important. The greater the backlog, the greater will be the cry from the departments for more computer and programmer resources to relieve the backlog. This supports a large data services budget and organization. With end user computing comes an alternative to formal development and an acknowledgment that data services has not addressed the entire workload. Machine resources can be purchased at a low cost as a trade-off for programmers in short supply. Letting the users do their own computer-based work is cost-effective and provides an alternative to data services' human services.

Data processing and data services organizations are only four decades old. They have evolved during a time when management theory and practices were evolving and changing. End user computing was introduced at a time when the personal side of the firm was being addressed anew. The introduction of a new method of providing data services (EUC) was introduced coincidentally with an acute shortage of programmers and a different method of personnel management. At the same time, the view that information is a resource like capital and labor began to be accepted as it was realized at what cost the data resource was being created and maintained. All of these forces converge in the subject of control. The outcome is that data services and management must face this issue and realize that a change is in order.

The change in question is a new method of providing data services. This redefines who does what. In the simple view, programmers are isolated from the users except as necessary to coordinate and interact on formal development. A few members of application programming are designated as the IC staff with a charter to be the prime interface point with all users of computer services. The users, with the support and training provided by the IC staff, perform a majority of their own computer-based tasks. Management supports the acquisition of PCs, terminals, printers, other computer hardware, and software. Data services management redefines its charter from one of absolute control of the computing and data resource to one of custodianship, development of formal applications, and support of all users.

It would appear that a revolution is in the making. Revolutions are often the result of building pressures. The result is that a discontinuity occurs and the organization follows a different path. The pressure of official and invisible backlogs have fueled the revolution for end user computing. One view is the disruption of the conduct of data services business. The other view is that a change is overdue. The point is that users have shown an ability and willingness to be part of the solution, and end user computing supported by the information center appears to be the best alternative. Thus it would seem that data services has only two options to exercise: to accept a new way of offering services that has user support or to try to enforce an older and apparently outdated standard.

It is not my intent to lecture on the pros and cons of organizational power and whether any particular part of the firm should be in a special position of authority. Nor is it my intent to throw stones at the data services organization. Data services is experiencing significant pressure, as noted several times. Many organizations are responding to this pressure as well as actively evolving their management and conduct. The issue of control will likely evolve, also, to one of caring custodian of a valuable corporate resource.

The management of *security* is concerned with the protection of data and computer resources. The initial view of allowing users who are not trained in computer practices to have access was that it would degrade the security of the computer and the resident data. Since computer use in general, and data access in particular, had been the domain of data services personnel or terminal-only users trained by them, opening up the use of languages, capabilities, and data called forth the specter of violated systems and damaged data.

Security originally meant the protection of expensive hardware, hence the locked machine room, into which all computer equipment was placed and into which only data services personnel were allowed. While show windows were included to display the new equipment, access was restricted in the belief that harm would come to the machinery or it would be stolen. Later the threat of sabotage became a concern as outside organizations or disgruntled employees sought to disrupt businesses by interrupting their computer processing. In response to this new threat, computers were placed behind stronger walls without windows, and access was restricted further. In some cases, the existence of the machine room was kept secret. However, as time passed, it was realized that the data was of equal, if not greater, importance, and access to the data was made easier by remote timeshare terminals. This meant that (possibly new) security measures were needed to ensure that data was not accessed by unauthorized personnel and that it was not changed, damaged, or stolen.

Hardware security is generally achieved by locking the equipment in a room or to a table or requiring it to pass through an inspection point if moved out of the firm. This, of course, is in addition to the informal watchdog function provided by the departmental users. Software security is more difficult, since data, programs, or even complete software systems can be copied without anyone knowing that anything has happened. The advent of the movie *War Games* and headlines about hackers have made people more aware of this subject, but this has not changed the need for security; in fact, with an increasing number of people having computer and data access with production terminal–oriented timeshare as well as end user computing, the potential for overt and accidental damage has increased.

The most prevalent method of comprehensive mainframe data security is through computer-resident software. Applications such as ACF2, RACF, and TOP SECRET contain rules that allow only specific access. For a user to gain access to a file, a rule must be created by the data services security personnel. Then the system will allow that specified user to access that specified file or application. If the firm does not have such software, the next method is to have password protection. Many applications provide for this access control, and this method can be included in new applications. Either way, security can be added and is quite effective in protecting the data.

The advent of dial-up services from remote locations to the computer makes the system more prone to intrusion and potentially less secure. It is possible, in systems that have a low level of security, for a person to dial into the system and keep trying until discovering an authorized logon code and password. This same technique can be used for accessing data. For companies that are security-conscious, four-attempt automatic lockout systems can be effective. Other hardware and software systems such as computer callback can provide added security. This capability requires that a human or machine call the potential user back at a specified number before further connections are made. Thus, while the advent of end user computing does add more users, many of whom are casual users untrained in many aspects of data processing and security, measures and methods exist to protect the equipment and data to the extent that costs are reasonable and safety is adequate.

This concern for security started with the overt attempts to access, change, or destroy data. Surprising to many is that outside attempts are considered low on the list of threats to data. Just above the outside threat is the internal threat of the disgruntled employee who wishes to do harm. This also is viewed as a problem, but not a significant one, and it can be addressed with proper measures. Of greater concern is the accidental incorrect input, change, or destruction of data by competent employees. An example is where read-write access is authorized for normal production use and data is inadvertently changed or damaged in day-to-day operations. While this is of great concern for production access, the problem can be avoided in the end user environment by using read-only databases or extract copies. Thus security can be maintained.

Our discussion of security trends has focused mainly on the mainframe environment. Personal computers present a different set of problems. PCs store their data on removable flexible disks and on internal hard disks. The former can be subject to various methods of damage, ranging from spilled coffee, dust, and smoke to spiked golf shoes. The modes of storing disks include desktops, desk drawers, file cabinets, briefcases, and safes. If users are not conscious of the potential for copying these disks, the data on them can be easily stolen. Hard disks are difficult to secure, and cases exist of individuals coming by during the night and erasing all data on them with such simple commands as ERASE *.* or FORMAT. Also, material produced from PCs tends to be less formal than mainframe or typed data and is therefore treated more casually.

This bleak picture of PC security is specific to end user computing. However, a response is available. Most of the IC managers interviewed believed that the basic form of all security is the attitude and practices of the users. With training, users learn about backup copies, locking up disks, locking machines, and securing written material. While the potential for copying and transporting disks seems ominous, the view exists that it is no easier to copy a disk than to take a paper copy to the duplicating machine, and the latter method requires less effort and training. Thus PC security is less software- and machine-oriented than believed, and practical protection is possible.

An issue adjacent to security is *privacy*, the protection of data on individuals to the extent that only people with a ''need to know'' may review the data. This is a management matter not affected by end user computing because it involves the basic issue of who can see what and should be in effect for all data. This concerns the owner of the data and the authorization for access. Privacy for end user computing is not a new concern and presents no new issues.

> When asked what problems were raised by the existence of end user computing and the information center, 35 percent of the IC managers interviewed mentioned security, whereas over half expressed the belief that this new environment posed no new or increased problems. Later comments by these same individuals indicated that security could be maintained in an end user computing environment and that the new environment did not cause any problems that could not be handled.

Data Proliferation

Data proliferation is the creation of duplicate (and uncontrolled) files. Generally, it describes the duplication of data when a PC user downloads all or part of a mainframe file for manipulation and analysis. Once copied, the file is in two locations; when changed, it is in two forms; and when kept without update, it is in two states. The problems that arise from proliferation involve data security and data form.

Data security was covered in the preceding section. With downloading, the data is out of the mainframe environment, with its software and password security, and is in the less controlled PC environment. Thus persons who could not access the mainframe file can now copy the PC file. In fact, the issue of downloading seems to concern moving data from the overt protection of the mainframe to the noncontrolled PC environment. Though this is true, much data is not sensitive, the data movement is one-way, and training should be in place to ensure that persons with downloading authority are versed in PC security practices. Again, this problem is solved by management practices, and the IC managers interviewed expressed the belief that the problems of security were controllable.

The problem of *data form* is a more serious one, in two instances. The first is the use of changed data for presentation as if it came from the original, authoritative file. Reports from data that was downloaded from the mainframe to a PC and changed can be quite misleading and conflicting. This is recognized as a problem in existing information centers, and the managers involved indicated that the solution is to insist that reports can come only from the original file. Thus the technical problem has a management solution.

The second aspect of the data form problem of data proliferation is that files are downloaded and left on the PC long enough that the data becomes out-of-date and does not match the original file. Old data, regardless of source, is a general problem that is only emphasized by the use of PCs, end user computing, and downloading. With the ability to download and manipulate data, the decision process is enhanced. With the management practice of only using the original file for reports and presentations, the problem of outdated files, like that of changed files, is minimized.

Data Integrity

Data integrity concerns the reliability of data, addresses the protection of data from inadvertent change, and ensures that data is initially correct and retains this quality. Integrity is concerned with write access to data. With more users having read-only access, integrity is affected only to the extent that the copied or downloaded data is changed and used, a practice addressed under proliferation. When a user is given write access, the integrity of the data is in the hands of the user. If write access is in the form of uploading data from the PC environment, a greater potential for disaster exists; however, only 15 percent of the IC managers interviewed allowed upload, and then only when the data passed through a review authority.

To emphasize the problem of integrity, or rather the lack of a problem, only 7 of the 20 IC managers interviewed cited integrity as a potential problem with the practice of downloading data to PCs. Each of these 7 managers went on to say that the problem was containable with such practices as prohibiting uploading of data. Thus what appears to be a serious problem with end user computing and downloading of data is controllable in the final analysis.

Cost Accounting and Chargeback

This concerns the data services practice of charging for mainframe computer usage. Though most of the expense of using a computer is a fixed cost because the firm will tend to neither add nor subtract hardware, software, or people based on high or low usage in the near term, many firms allocate the usage to the departments involved. Though a fixed cost, accounting practices spread the expenditures to those incurring them to give visibility and indicate who is responsible for them. Charging is generally a process of measuring the seconds of computer processing, time logged on to a terminal, lines of output printed, and space used for data storage. The units measured are then converted to dollars, and the user is charged for these services. The intent is usually to allocate all costs but not to make a profit. (Some companies use data services as a profit center, especially if the organization sells services to organizations outside the firm.)

The IBM-Hammond model indicated that end user computing should not be presented or viewed as a free good because that would tend to degrade its use and lower its value. Hammond also recommended offering special low prices or even providing free services to new users or on pilot projects to show the value of end user computing early on and gain support, after which the charge would revert to the normal price. Obviously, this is for a mainframe environment, as PCs are generally considered a true fixed cost, even a sunk expenditure, with no method to allocate their cost.

It would appear that charging for end user computing on the mainframe in the same manner as for production processing is appropriate. It might be acceptable to not charge if the environment were one of a dedicated processor, but then again, charging points up who is using which service and provides information for planning. However, the results of existing practices give a different view. Of the 20 firms studied, 15 used charging, with generally the same procedures used for information center and production processing. However, of these firms only 8 held the users accountable for expenditures. Thus only 40 percent of the firms believed it was necessary or desirable to require forecasting, allocation, and accountability for computer use. This is an important point, that a significant number of companies view the use of the computer as vital and do not wish to impede its use by accounting practices.

Though Hammond strongly supports the practice of charging and accountability for computer use, other authors have indicated that these practices are a significant impedance to effective use of this technology. The practice is viewed so poorly by these latter authors that they consider chargeback the greatest impedance to effective computer use. When the issue is further reviewed, data services is not consistent. All firms interviewed charged the fixed and personnel costs of the information center to data processing overhead as opposed to allocating costs based on usage. This views the IC as cost-comparable with other significant assets, such as buildings, and recognizes that allocation is artificial. This gives a precedent for providing access to the computer on a nonchargeback basis. Seven of the firms interviewed already have this no-charge practice, and one firm charged $3,000 per year per terminal as a fixed charge. Both practices would encourage use, and good local management would ensure proper use.

The view of the value of computer services is important. Its value is embodied in the accounting practices of the firm. These practices are the responsibility of the upper levels of management. It is important for executive and data services management to view the computer and computer-resident data as a corporate resource, not a company liability. It would be considered foolish to charge for use of desktop calculators or telephones (though the cost of long-distance calls seems to receive undue attention and control). If computer services were viewed in the light of their importance and not in accordance with their cost, accounting practices would likely change. I contend that this is one purpose of executive management, to determine value first and practice second. As in the field of architecture, "form ever follows function."

Relations between End Users and Data Services

This is an area in which Hammond predicated the information center would have a significant positive influence on the way end users and data services personnel relate to each other. Historically, the departments have viewed data services as an organization peopled with individuals who were interested in the computer, not in the business of the firm, who spoke in strange tongues, and who were difficult to communicate and work with. When the time came to create a new capability for users, the programmers and systems analysts wanted users to know all about the system, put it in writing, accept whatever was delivered, and, above all, not make any changes.

Meanwhile, programmers and analysts had a problem dealing with the using departments. The users seemed to be illiterate about technology in general and computers in particular. When asked about the systems they wanted developed, the users were unable to explain or describe them in any detail. Data services perceived a total lack of computer knowledge. These "bean counters" did not understand the object of programming, systems analysis, and other technical aspects of data services and believed that the computer was there for the user's pleasure without regard or respect for efficient processing or storage. Furthermore, the users were seen as constantly changing their requirements and never being satisfied with the end result. Clearly, the users and data services did not see eye to eye.

Hammond recognized the information center as a way for users and data services to bridge the gap of understanding, since each brought something to problem resolution. The users would bring problem knowledge and people to work the problem, while the IC staff would bring support and the needed technical base. With the people skills of the IC staff, there would be less animosity and "speaking in tongues" and more communication. Since the users had someone to listen to their needs, the IC staff would be perceived as associates and counselors.

It was quickly seen in the early ICs that a rapport developed between the IC staff and the users that had far-reaching effects. As the IC staff was seen as people to provide assistance and help, either on the phone or in person, the users came to realize they were no longer alone. The IC staff not only provided training in class but would consult and aid on a one-on-one basis and would take the time to understand the users' business. The IC staff was seen as competent and willing to provide help. A positive relationship quickly developed between the users and the IC staff and even spilled over into all of data services. Not only was the staff of the IC viewed as helpful and a part of the solution, but the user departments' image of all of data services improved, and so did relations. Whether this change was the result of programmers' seeing what the IC staff could achieve with inter-personal skills or whether it was only a perception on the part of the users, it is possible that the improving of relations between data services and the users may be one of the greatest benefits of the creation of the information center. Because of the effect on subsequent efforts in the area of new developments as well as maintenance and change of existing systems, the bettering of relations will be of significant benefit.

Promotion and Marketing of the IC

Promotion and marketing involve the advertising of the information center in order to make its presence known, create a customer base, and attract users. It is envisioned to be similar to promotions by a new fast-food establishment, in a somewhat milder manner. The proposed methods are bulletin boards, user groups, lunchtime presentations, memos, and newsletters. The object is to advertise the facility and its capabilities to a great extent.

Opinons are divided on IC promotion. It is recommended in the literature but was discouraged by most of the IC managers interviewed. The managers indicated that generally, the IC staffs are kept small by management and are not able to handle large audiences. Thus in many cases, the opening of the IC was accompanied by no announcement at all, and the only form of advertisement at a later date was a newsletter. Only one-fourth of the ICs had any form of active marketing; an additional 30 percent had a low level. The stated reason was that the IC would not be able to deliver the advertised features in the manner expected, and the user community would be greatly disappointed. Most of the few dis-couraging user comments about the IC or relations related to a small staff not being able to provide service at the level desired.

The issue of promotion is one of management support. When an IC is adequately staffed by data services, it can be proactive in its activities and seek out opportunities. However, most of the time, the size of the staff is kept to a level that can just meet the minimum needs, and then it must actively refrain from attracting attention or too much enthusiasm. This is quite contrary to the potential of the center. ICs have demonstrated the ability to allow users to be highly productive and act as a kind of an amplifier but are not allowed the human resources to effect this service.

Although the management issue of IC marketing and promotion was originally one of ensuring that it took place so as to make full and proper use of the facility, the real issue is one of management addressing the need for staff and the ability of that staff to support the users. With the use of personnel from outside of data services, staff members will be more readily available and will reach a staff size that is able to better serve the user community. Only at that time can active marketing efforts be justified and the results supported.

Computer Efficiency

Efficiency has been a subject of discussion since the introduction of the mainframe computer. The concern originally was that computer resources were costly and scarce, so only cost-saving applications were supported by the machine. In addition, these applications must run in a manner that used the computer fully and well. With such high cost, it was important to keep the machine working in a way that returned the most for the processing cycle. Thus the intent was to keep the processing level at 100 percent to the extent possible and to have it operate in an efficient manner. To do this, jobs were scheduled to keep the input queue filled, and programmers were rewarded for writing code that ran efficiently.

There are now considerations that make efficient use of the computer questionable. The first is that machine and other hardware costs have been reduced drastically, to such an extent that the hardware is much less costly than the software and the human resources needed to run it. Whereas the cost of hardware used to be 80 percent of the total cost, the machinery now accounts for only 20 percent of the cost. Thus, when needed, new hardware resources can be acquired at low cost.

The reason for running at a lower level of computer efficiency (or utilization) is due to the change in use. Originally, processing was in the batch mode, and there was no interaction between the processing and the users. The machine crunched numbers and provided printed output that was used by the personnel of accounting and finance. The saturation of the processing power did not affect the users' job and was not important to them. The only thing that was important to the users was getting the job into their hands. Thus data services scheduled the computer to the maximum extent possible and only acquired new hardware when the work exceeded possible processing time. However, with the introduction of timeshare capabilities, users actively work on the computer and interact with the programs. A computer that is working at 90 to 95 percent of its capability will always have a backlog of tasks and will take a significant amount of time to respond to a user's request. The request can be as simple as the entry of a single character of data or as lengthy as a database query, but the result is that it always seems to take an undue amount of time for the computer to complete the action. (This phenomenon has to do with random events, such as timeshare tasks and queuing theory. As the utilization of the machine goes above 60 percent, the probability that it is busy at the receipt of a task is high, and thus the task must wait. It has been recommended that computers supporting interactive timeshare should be operated at below 50 percent busy.)

The reason that the response time for interactive users is important is that the users are now more costly to the company than the computer processing time. Thus the trade-off is human costs versus machine costs. Now the efficiency of machine processing is influencing the effectiveness and efficiency of human processing. By obtaining additional processing power and running the computer at 40 to 50 percent utilization, users receive significantly quicker responses and are better able to do their tasks. Lower machine saturation (efficiency) has a direct positive impact on user productivity. The view that the machine had better be kept busy must be replaced with the attitude that it is vital for the computer to be responsive to users.

The second issue in ensuring computer efficiency is the use of extremely efficient code. Originally, programmers wrote computer instructions in machine language both out of necessity and to make the processing as efficient as possible. Though this seems logical, machine code is difficult and time-consuming to create and maintain. With the advent of compilers, the programmers could create code more quickly in a more English-like syntax. This source language was then translated into code that the computer could understand. However, it was believed that the process was less efficient than possible, and a concentrated effort was applied to make the programmer's code as "tight" and efficient as possible through creative programming. The problem with unique and creative programming is that it is difficult to trouble-shoot and maintain. When someone other than the author worked with the program, it took a significant effort to determine what the code was doing. This was, again, a trade-off between computer efficiency and human (programmer) efficiency. With a large number of programs to maintain and a shortage of programmers, it is appropriate, if not vital, to take the time, use less creative code that is understandable by most programmers, and save human time later. Since computers are now less expensive and more powerful, less efficiency in the code can easily be made up by the machine.

The reason that computer efficiency is a subject in end user computing relates to the age-old view of the need for machine efficiency and that end users will be wasteful. Imagine dozens, even hundreds, of ill-trained users, using inefficient fourth-generation languages, for questionable tasks. Now consider these same users being able to employ user-friendly languages in a responsive environment to satisfy time-critical decision needs. The trade-off, again, is machine use and efficiency for human effectiveness and productivity. With the use of lower-cost, powerful mainframes and fixed-cost, inexpensive personal computers, the question of computer efficiency should die, but the death continues to be a slow one. We have seen the application of technology always to involve high cost, so we continue to view the situation as cost-oriented rather than benefit-related. Even if fourth-generation languages are less efficient than procedural languages (and that is highly questionable), and if users are less efficient than programmers, in the absence of an adequate supply of programmers, especially those who understand the user's problem, the user-plus-computer option is the most effective, efficient, and productive combination available.

Benefits

The concern for benefits of end user computing is indeed a subject at issue. A full discussion of this topic will be provided in Chapter 6. However, a look at the issue is appropriate here.

Whenever a new technology is introduced, its authors are quick to note its benefits, or else the technology will not be accepted. The imperative of "technology for its own sake" does not usually sit well with boards of directors and review committees. A medium-sized hospital may be tempted to introduce open-heart surgery facilities to appear up-to-date, but it is unlikely that this level of funding can be expended in most such organizations without a reasonable return on investment. Thus it should be in all cases of technology.

The benefits that are quickly presented are those that are at the heart of the problem. Thus the proponents of ICs to support end user computing indicated early that the IC would reduce the backlog of requests and generally support the users in ways in which they were not being assisted in the past. This was a way to sell the information center concept and achieve the real intent of data services management, to control PCs and reduce outside timeshare costs. However, with time, it became obvious that ICs did not reduce backlogs, and in some cases the instance of an IC increased the number of requests from the departments. If reduction of the backlog is not the prime benefit, what is? This will be discussed in Chapter 6.

SUMMARY

- Data services has several options available for providing an end user computing environment, and management must address a number of issues.
- The information center can be instrumental in providing effective and efficient access to data for end users.
- The use of user-oriented data management and administration can significantly support use of the information resource.
- Information center support can be provided for mainframe, microcomputer, or mixed environments. Each has different considerations, but all can be effective for the user and the firm.
- Security of equipment and data can be provided in an end user environment, usually with training plus the same capabilities used in the production area.
- Data privacy is an issue with all forms of data and is not a special consideration for end user computing.
- End user computing is a new way of providing data services. It will change how jobs are done and who does them. Data services organizations are evolving to provide a different set of services.
- The primary concerns in end user computing are security and data proliferation. Security can be adequately addressed with training and software capabilities. Data proliferation results in problems that can be contained with proper management practices.
- Accounting for computer services appears to be widespread; however, holding the user accountable for costs is not. It is important to view the computer and its resident data as a corporate resource and not a company liability.

- The information center has been responsible for improving the relationship between users and data services.
- Information centers must be cautious in their marketing efforts so as not to attract more business than they can adequately support. This tends to be an issue of management allocating adequate resources prior to extensive marketing of the IC.
- Computer efficiency is no longer an important issue; user productivity is. It is vital to realize the value of low machine use in relation to appropriate response for user actions.
- It is more important for a computer program to be maintainable than for it to run efficiently. The cost of change and maintenance can be significantly higher than the cost of processing.

Key Terms

Data access	Relations between users and data services
Data dictionary	Computer cost versus user cost
Database	Maintainable programs
Database administration	Tight code
Database administrator (DBA)	Computer efficiency
Read-only access	Chargeback
Read-write access	IC promotion
Shared processor	Data integrity
Dedicated processor	Data proliferation
Control	Privacy
Data management and administration	Security

DISCUSSION QUESTIONS

1. Discuss the difference between file-oriented applications and database technology. How does the use of each affect the end user?

2. Assume that you are a data manager and are in charge of administration of all data for the firm. What would the organization look like? What resources would you have?

3. You want to use accounting data that is available from extract copy files. You determine that the file is updated (extracted) only once a month. Should this be a matter of concern?

4. Under what conditions do you believe that read-write access is necessary?

5. If you had to choose just mainframe or just PC resources for EUC, which would you choose, and why?

6. Do you really think you could make a case for a dedicated IC mainframe?

7. Why is there such a concern for security of data?

8. Is data privacy really so important?

9. If data is downloaded to a PC from a mainframe file or database and it is analyzed there, how would it be possible to use the original mainframe data rather than the downloaded data?

10. Should charges for the IC be allocated back to the user, or should it be a fixed-cost service?

11. How would the use of special interest groups help the IC? For example, if you had a large number of SAS users and you had an SAS users group to meet and discuss problems and opportunities, how would it help the IC, or is it just of value to the members?

CASE STUDIES

MIDDLE-TEXAS & COMPANY, INC.

The company, with headquarters in Dallas, Texas, mines, processes, and makes construction materials that are sold in five states. The primary revenue-producing components are ready-mixed concrete, aggregate and concrete products, concrete additives, portland cement, and metal building systems. The firm employees 3,600 people and has sales of $390 million. One unusual item is the purchase by Middle-Texas of fly ash from coal-burning power plants and its use in the company's concrete or for resale. This pollutant continues to be a very profitable product for the company.

Middle-Texas (MT) began using computers for business purposes in the early 1960s. The initial venture was via outside service bureau timeshare services. The company soon purchased an IBM system and brought the applications in-house. They moved to a Honeywell computer in 1967 and now use a Burroughs Model 7850 mainframe.

This was the only company during this study that was not using IBM mainframe equipment. This is believed to be true for two reasons: (1) The information center concept is considered an IBM environment concept, and (2) it appears that there was not a significant amount of user-oriented software on non-IBM mainframes.

Data services created a report generation program (R-GEN) in 1977 for the accounting department. This batch-mode capability could access and manipulate data and format the desired report under user control. This was the first end user product at MT. It was supported by the application development programmers for about six months, and then training and support dropped to a minimum. R-GEN was rewritten in 1979 and remains a useful capability today. Meanwhile, some users outside of accounting were using FORTRAN in an informal end user computing mode, without support.

Middle-Texas's Information Center

In early 1981, the user departments were applying pressure for computer-based assistance in preparation of the annual budget reports. Data services reviewed the request and purchased IFPS to let the users create their own financial models and reports. This was the beginning of the formal support to end user computing and the information center at MT. The support was intense at the beginning, with two people providing training and consulting service. After about six months, the support dropped to the present one person, one-fourth time.

Since the beginning of the IC, the user community has grown to about 40 people. The users tend to be self-sufficient and usually require assistance from the support person only for unusual problems. Training of new personnel is provided by the IFPS vendor, EXECUCOM, either at the vendor's facility in Austin, Texas, for individuals or at MT for group training. In either case, the users pay the vendor's charges.

The motivation for supplying IFPS was to give the users a tool to perform their own work outside of MIS. It was believed that this methodology would be less costly than formal MIS development. When nontrivial projects are required by users, the tasks are described, justified, and submitted to the MIS committee. In review, the project may be accepted for formal development or may be referred back to the user for development using the IC capabilities. In this case, the IC staff does not act as a clearinghouse, but the MIS committee acts to forward minor tasks back to the users and the information center.

In early 1984, additional capabilities were needed. Due to the lack of products for the Burroughs environment, data services opted to purchase microcomputers for the users and support spreadsheet, word processing, and charting packages. Data services purchased 15 IBM PCs and is providing an equivalent of $1\frac{1}{2}$-person support. This brought the total staff of the IC to about two people who were supervised by the manager of systems programming. With this low level of support, marketing is kept to word of mouth.

On-line mainframe computer access is routine at MT, with the user community having 125 video display terminals. They process on-line about half the time and access needed data through data extract copies. In some cases, direct read-only access to the DBMS is provided. A total of 95 percent of the production data is secured by either the timeshare environment or the provisions of the DBMS.

MT has no computer chargeback system of accounting. Information center and DP users alike are provided with computer services free of charge. The acquisition of a logon ID and password is the primary control. Data services does monitor use, but the departments do not forecast or respond to costs. This issue has been discussed annually for many years, without change.

PC connection to the computer mainframe is provided and seems to pose no problem. Though it is believed that some security and integrity problems could occur, none have surfaced. The concern of integrity relates to the use and presentation of copied and manipulated data via a faulty model without noting this.

SOUTHLAND ROYALTY COMPANY

Southland Royalty Company observed its 60th anniversary during 1984. Since its formation in 1924, Southland has grown to be one of the nation's largest independent producers of

oil and gas. The Company explores for, develops and produces oil and natural gas in most major geological provinces in the United States.

This unusual corporation was founded in 1924 for the purpose of controlling holdings in oil-producing properties. Southland had only five employees, and its primary function was the collection and distribution of oil-interest royalty payments. The company's operations changed to petroleum exploration and production in the southwestern United States in the 1960s as the result of an employee benefits trust from Continental Oil Company. This action was taken by the founder of Continental at the time of change of ownership of that firm. Southland has developed into an oil production firm with annual sales in excess of $300 million through the services of only 500 employees, over 400 of whom have joined Southland since 1978.

As a company employing so few people, Southland did not start using the computer until about 1978. The entry into this venture was via outside timeshare. Southland's DP department wrote specific programs to meet specific needs in engineering and accounting applications. Between 1978 and 1984 Southland acquired an IBM 370 Model 125 and then moved to the present IBM model 4341-2 processor. With in-house computing power, outside applications were internalized as it was practical and economically feasible. Bringing an application from outside timeshare for the sake of cost reduction was not a prime motive. Outside timeshare remains a valuable resource, costing in excess of $100,000 per year, with the primary use in accessing specialized applications and databases.

Southland Royalty's Information Center

The installation of the formal support of end user computing by the information center was the result of user pressure and frustration with the existing environment. Until 1983, the processing was batch-oriented, which provided no support to users. Since the company was organized into decentralized districts, six IBM Model 5110 computers were located in the field to support local processing. The intent was to program centrally, process locally, and combine centrally. Unfortunately, the centrally created programs were changed locally, and the result was disappointing. Meanwhile, the accounting department personnel were doing a large number of spreadsheets manually and requested assistance. Engineers were using outside timeshare services in an unsupported fashion and were requesting a better environment. In addition, a petroleum engineer had written a graphic plot program that had received wide publicity and was receiving many requests to run it for financial reports.

Thus informal, unsupported end user computing had developed and exerted major pressure for the development of a formal information center. Another way of expressing this is that the IC was created by default due to circumstances.

In June 1983, timeshare facilities were installed on the in-house mainframe, and OmniCalc was obtained to support the users. This was the beginning of the IC, with one programmer from the Management Science and Special Programming Group appointed to support the users on a part-time basis. Since that time, six IBM Personal Computers have been acquired and receive support from the same individual. As the IC manager stated, "When the advantage of having PCs became greater than not having them, we bought PCs."

Due to the small support staff and informality of the environment, training is up to the users. It is via self-study and hands-on tutorial and use, with the IC staff available for question resolution. Two eight-hour courses are available. Even with this method of training, 30 users have become proficient in the mainframe and PC usage.

Accounting and engineering are the biggest users of the IC capabilities, with departmental applications accounting for 80 percent of use. Data acquisition, manipulation, and analysis are major uses, supported primarily by mainframe OmniCalc and PC Lotus 1-2-3.

While not done as part of the IC, the introduction of the ADABAS DBMS and NATURAL language have caused the two major parts of the company, exploration and production, to tend to merge data storage, access, and applications. The use of the DBMS and language is primarily a DP function but is seen as becoming more attractive to the users with time.

The introduction of the IC has made more users aware of the data that is available. People are communicating more on the use of data and applications. Thus the IC has increased data use and has improved data integrity via increased communication and awareness.

The overt marketing and promotion of the IC has not been a consideration. However, MIS is now using the IC as a central focal point to make the company aware of what exists in the way of services and data. The application programming group has found that various groups do not know what exists and will be developing or using outside timeshare programs that are in existence internally. The IC acts as a central point for questions about capabilities and refers the individual to the application programmer with the specialty. This has avoided any IC-IS staff conflict, by design, and has improved intracompany coordination.

Computer access, chargeback, and security are handled in a very unusual but effective manner. Most data is not secured. Existing data security is by application program control. The specific method is that when the transaction to access the data is requested, a security screen appears on which the user may indicate his initials and password. If he does, he will be given access to the sensitive fields to which he has been authorized access. If he does not enter anything, he still gains access, with only certain fields available. That is, he can browse and receive most of the data he requires, just not the fields that are secured. In addition, there is no logon procedure and no chargeback for use of the computer for the IC or other applications. Cost is a consideration only when cash flow is a consideration, upon purchase of new equipment.

Meanwhile, acquisition of PCs and their connection to the mainframe may present security, data proliferation, and data integrity problems. As Southland moves to the use of PCs, DP is attempting to provide an environment that will avoid these problems.

Southland has a formal data administration function that will extract data for users. Users can upload data to the mainframe for their own use but not to the production sources.

The objective of the IC is to provide the best tools to people to help them do their job and to support them in their tasks. The primary benefit received has been better information. The IC staff is small and still has other IS duties. Even with dual duties, the IC staff acts as a contact point and go-between for the users and the many application programming areas. This had avoided conflict and has made the use of internal applications and data more effective.

QUICK-TEX CORPORATION

The Quick-Tex Corporation is the parent company of a large number of convenience stores located across the United States. It has approximately 50,000 employees in the stores division and operates manufacturing facilities that supply the stores. The nature of the computer-based information system is on-line data input and batch output to support the high volume of retail sales, which exceeds $10 billion.

The computer has been used by Quick-Tex Corporation since the early 1960s, and applications are accounting- and finance-oriented. The company is highly decentralized and uses some 2,000 IBM 3270-type video display terminals to enter activity data on a daily basis over leased communication lines. To support the data services activities, Quick-Tex has some 300 to 350 data processing personnel and uses an IBM Model 3081K environment.

Quick-Tex's Information Center

End user computing began about 1979, and the information center has evolved gradually from this concept. Users were frustrated with the application development backlog and began requesting support. The staff has grown to four members, while the user community had grown from 2 to 75 members of the corporate office staff. Only the corporate staff was initially supported by the IC. Future plans call for expanding outward to the 450 offices, but with great care.

The initial language supported was SAS, and now the offering includes IFPS, RAMIS, and STRATA. The personal computer exists in the corporate office but is not yet supported by the IC. Once PC-to-host communications are installed, the PC proliferation will begin. The IC will support PCs, but training will come from a training section elsewhere. At present, the IC provides no formal training, neither mainframe fourth-generation language nor PC. Users arrange for, go off-site to, and pay for training from the vendor.

Users are located in most departments, with high use in accounting, human resources, and data processing. There has been no effect on the two- to three-year backlog of development requests, and the IC manager expects the IC to have none. The primary use of the IC is data query and ad hoc reporting, for departmental and companywide applications, by senior clerical staff and middle management.

It was uncertain who wanted the responsibility of IC direction when the IC was formalized because the IC staff was considered so small. The IC has no designated manager and is currently under the direction of the manager of application systems and programming. (For consistency, the term IC manager will be used.) The senior IC staff member is from the field of office automation, whereas the IC manager has only limited experience in that area. If the activity in office automation reaches a high level, to whom the IC would report might be called into question. Presently, it is firmly an MIS function.

The IC manager believes that TV and magazine advertisements were a major factor in influencing end users in the quest for personal computers. Though the IC manager saw the personal computer as a force coming his way, he felt it would go the way of the video game. With use, the end user would be dissatisfied with the PC as soon as he could gain the same application on the mainframe, where the data resides.

The present users work directly with the IC languages. It is believed that expansion of the IC concept beyond the corporate office will require menus for interface due to the less sophisticated nature of the users. The use of menus will be quite a change, one that will require significant thought and work.

Of note is the level of 90 percent batch processing by the IC users. Due to the high prevalence of timeshare in most DP environments, it is often assumed that processing will take place in the interactive mode. The IC manager sees no reason for providing such a responsive environment to a person who is accustomed to waiting two days to two weeks for a report. He believes that this reduces costs and helps lower contention for communication lines.

With significant support of data file extracts, DP uses extensive disk storage. The IC manager believes that this was a reasonable trade-off for the apparent increase in productivity for end users.

The IC manager believes that data services had adequate security procedures in place and that the IC was just another environment in this respect. Data owners gave permission for use of data through an official signoff form, and access to the files was through logon security files. There were no data dictionaries in use, and on occasion the end user would have to go to the director of MIS to determine who owned the required data. The IC manager believes the greatest contribution of the IC was the access to data and that no security problems have resulted from this.

Charging for mainframe usage in the information center is in transition. Presently, the use of the computer is budgeted and allocated to the general and administrative (G&A) expense. This means that there is no visibility to end user computing levels or the activity of the IC. The IC manager indicates that this would change in the future and believes that a dedicated IC mainframe would make the usage more visible and the end user more accountable. At present, the end user is directly charged only for equipment and communications.

The IC manager believes it is important to support the user in two areas: (1) provide access to the data the user requires and (2) show the user the cost of his request and let him determine its value. This practice is DP-wide; the IC is not an exception. Purchase of PCs or mainframe terminals is at the user's expense.

A specific issue the IC manager sees with PC proliferation is that highly paid personnel such as managers might spend a significant amount of time as programmers. This activity seems very counterproductive. The IC manager's belief seems to be firm that the correct path for the corporation is database orientation and fourth-generation mainframe languages that could directly access already available data. This would avoid the PC-programmer problem mentioned.

The primary objective, and benefit, of the IC is to assist the end user in accessing the data he or she requires. The IC staff makes extract copies of data and ensures production files against disruption and loss of integrity by protection from access and upload from copied files. The only concern that the IC manager has about extract copies is their use for reports without noting that the report is from other than the official data source.

The users of the Quick-Tex information center are highly pleased. Benefits are not measured, and there has been no need for justification of the IC or IC projects. Relations between the IC and IS staff are good, "because they are part of MIS." All in all, the IC is viewed as an asset that needs to be expanded to the total corporation.

Future plans include a more structured IC, increased user involvement, enhanced languages, and expanding the IC to the entire corporation. The spread of PCs has begun, and a PC-to-mainframe link is planned.

REFERENCES

5-1.   Magal, Simha R., Houston H. Carr, and Hugh J. Watson, "Critical Success Factors for Information Center Managers" Working Paper Series, *University of Georgia End User Computing Research Center Working Paper #21.*

6

The Information Center Concept: Benefits

EXPECTED IC BENEFITS

The subject of information center benefits was introduced in the discussion of management issues because there are differences of opinion as to what to expect. Here we will take the predictions of the literature and temper them with data from interviews with managers of ICs. Out of this should come realistic expectations. A total of ten benefits are referenced in writings to one degree or another:

- Reduced backlog
- More timely results
- Better relations
- Increased productivity
- User literacy

- Reduced cost
- Better requirements
- Improved quality of information
- Better use of limited resources
- User enthusiasm

Reduction of the Backlog

The belief is that an information center will work off and thus reduce the formal queue of requests. Users will be able to respond to some of their own requests and therefore assist application development in completing these actions. However, none of the IC managers indicated that the IC achieved reduction of the formal backlog.

Remember that the real backlog of user needs is made up of both the formal approved backlog and the unofficial, invisible, unknown list of needs and requirements. This latter list is never presented for attention because the users believe that the tasks are too small, not important enough to data services, and of restricted timeliness. However, it is the invisible queue that is specifically addressed by the IC capability. The IC is designed for jobs for which the user is best suited: short duration of development, short useful lifetime, simply query, analysis and report, and limited user-population access.

Whereas the items in the formal backlog are important to the continuance of the firm, the items in the informal queue, which can be five times as large, are important in a near-term sense. Formal applications, such as payroll, inventory management, and cash management, tend to involve data gathering and information reporting. IC applications tend to be decision-oriented, for the near term, and affect the competitive posture of the firm in the long term. Transaction applications are important and require formal development, but not at the expense of the small tasks that support week-to-week decisions. By addressing the items in the informal queue, the information center does reduce the backlog; it is just not the backlog the authors had in mind.

The reverse of the reduction of the formal development backlog may take place with the support of end user computing by a competent IC staff. As users become more computer-literate and see the computer and computer-based systems as productivity items, they may well request additional large, formal systems. As they understand what is needed and how to express these needs, the users will convey these ideas as added requests. Thus both backlogs may lengthen.

> As Service Merchandise's Mr. Denton explained, "One of the key aspects in IBM's original proposal was that the center would reduce backlog. Well, ours has increased. As computer awareness rises and users become more literate, they have more requests."
> [5-1]

Reduced Cost of Application Creation and More Timely Results

These are both goals of data services organizations and management. As the complexity of applications has grown and the need for maintenance and change has been recognized, formal development has increased in both time required and cost. Since the intent of the formal SDLC methodology is to record the entire need and create a solution in a manner that can be tested and maintained by other than the original programmers, the SDLC is, by necessity, laborious and time-consuming. This means high cost and long development time. In addition, part of the time, and thus the cost, is the result of the need for communications between the users and the programmer.

When the user develops the application via end user computing, either with IC staff assistance, programmer support, or in isolation, the need to communicate is greatly reduced. The user just has to be able to understand all of the parts of the problem and devise a solution that addresses the entire problem. Although this may potentially mean less analysis and an incomplete solution, it does provide for a solution that the user wants, in a time frame of his or her choosing, at a cost determined by the user. Thus end user computing with IC support does provide a way to shorten the development time and reduce the cost of specific applications. However, again, these are not from the backlog of formal applications; they are generally from the invisible queue.

> *The question arises: Are information centers answering their call? To the extent that they improve productivity by spreading computer usage, the answer is yes. Mr. Lockard conducted a companywide study at Corning Glass a few years after the information center was introduced. "The user departments were able to document $1 million worth of hard savings," he said. "And they also identified another $1 million in soft savings. They were saving time, and they know that additional savings were there." [5-1]*

Better Requirements

Users learn through experience and begin to present applications that are better defined, more stable, and better communicated. This is the result of end users using the IC and creating their own applications. Not only do these small tasks receive computer-based attention not available before and involve less cost and time to develop than would normally be expected with formal development, but the experience also trains the users to be a part of the formal development process and to present better requirements for formal development. Through this experience, the users have a greater knowledge of computer-based solutions and can communicate more effectively with the programmers. In addition, the users' expectations are more realistic as they have exposure to computer-based resources. Though the programmer still requires education and training in the users' business, communications increase simply by evolving users experienced in use of the information center.

Better Relations

The information center has been very successful in improving interactions and communications between users and data services. Programmers and other members of application development have not generally given much time or effort to the marketing and customer service side of their business. The only times that these people interact with the users is when new applications are being developed or when problems develop. With the size of the formal backlog, programmers have little time for small talk and user handholding. Thus the programmers are seen as less than personable. Partly due to this, users have little tendency to seek out the programmers except when desperately needed. The users and programmers seem to live in different worlds and have divergent views of the goals of their organizations.

With the advent of the information center has come the IC staff whose primary job is user interface and customer service. At last, the user has someone to ask about any aspect of computer-based solutions and applications, someone who takes the time to listen and help. What a change! Not only will the IC staff counsel on problems, large and small, but they will also answer questions over the phone, assist on PCs, schedule training, work on a one-on-one basis, and show a genuine interest in the user's problem and business. This is their business. The intent here is not to harass programmers but to realize that the very existence of the IC staff is to do what application development has not done in the past.

The creation of the Information Center, a group chartered to interface with users, has caused a change in the way that these users view data services. The IC managers stated that the score indicating the level of relations between the users and the IC staff was 50% higher than that for the users and data services. Further, the managers said that the user–IC staff relation was responsible for an improvement in the user-data services relation and that relations in both areas were continuing to improve. In one sense, the IC is the outward and visible sign that data services is trying to understand users and their needs. One IC was initiated for just that purpose, and many others were taking on the charter of being the primary contact point for all data services–user interactions.

Increased Productivity

Emphasis on productivity is a popular trend in organizations as management attempts to get more output for a given input, be it human or machine, labor or cost. Productivity is like efficiency—the higher the better. This has been the thrust of computer use for four decades. However, with a shortage of programmers and a lengthy backlog of requests, the potential for increased productivity has reached a plateau. Specifically, the backlog is caused not by a scarcity of hardware but by a scarcity of people to design, program, and implement software. With the advent of end user computing and its support via the information center has come the ability to bypass this roadblock. Utilization of end users for ad hoc reports and small application development supplements the programmers. Allowing the users to develop applications that the programmers cannot get to adds more resources to the solution area and supports the users where needed. As with the addition of equipment in the factory, the addition of the computer in the office provides increased capability and greater productivity. Specifically, with computer and data resources, the users can have faster data query, better analysis, the review of more alternatives, and faster output—all of which lead to increased productivity.

Critics and some IC managers have made negative comments about productivity. They have seen users spend too much time programming tasks that would be done more efficiently by others. Finance managers have been seen creating spreadsheets or BASIC programs instead of attending to management issues. There is no question that a few users find the means of the solution very interesting and spend an inordinate amount of time with the problem. However, this will pass as users learn to deal with the application and as the excitement of programming evolves into the excitement of solution.

> *The idea of productivity is to reduce the cost relative to the benefit.*

Improved Quality of Information

This tends to come with the ability to access the required data. As the data resource is made available and accessible, users will have more suitable data for the problem at hand, and the exercise will result in the use of better and higher-quality information in the solution. By the use of data librarians, data dictionaries, database management systems, query languages, and the IC staff for support, users can access the proper data, draw it into mainframe files or download it to the PC, and use manipulation and analysis techniques to support the decision process. As the data is readily available, the process improves. Manual searches are avoided with the use of production files, and old data is deleted as the ease of access to current data increases. The result is that users who have ready access to appropriate, current data will make good use of that resource and produce decision information of a high quality.

Better Use of Limited Resources

This addresses the involvement of the users in the creation of computer-based solutions. Data services programmers and analysts are considered a human resource to effect the development of computer applications. With a shortage of programmers and an excess of formal and invisible requests, there is a need to apply other resources to the solution. Users are one such additional resource. Meanwhile, the limited resource of programmers can be applied to tasks for which they are uniquely qualified, formal development of large applications.

Another way of stating this benefit is that by using the IC staff to support the users and having departmental personnel perform their own ad hoc tasks, the programmers are free to attend to other tasks. With isolation, programmers can keep their attention on the formal, complex tasks of development and are not interrupted by user questions. Just as use of the IC increases the productivity of the users, the insulation afforded the programmers provides for increased productivity for them.

Meanwhile, the added resource of the user is applied to the problem in a very productive manner. These users are the most knowledgeable about the problem and are best able to effect a solution. When they are directly involved with the solution, it is not necessary to communicate to others for development. The users may not be as technically proficient with the computers as data services programmers, but they are far more knowledgeable and experienced in the actual problem area. Thus to apply the user to the problem is to apply the best resource available.

User Literacy

When achieved, knowledge of the computer allows individuals and departments to understand better the uses of the computer and to communicate more effectively with data services. In the 1970s, colleges began to offer computer classes at business schools and have thus contributed to the computer training and literacy of many graduates. However, a large portion of the user departments remain neither literate about mainframe and PCs nor comfortable with technology. Potential computer users, ranging from clerks to corporate presidents, need familiarity with computer resources and training to become literate in their use and usefulness. The information center can and does support this function.

The author has seen highly qualified and competent secretaries freeze at the keyboard of a computer, heard department managers complain about typing on a terminal, and witnessed professionals continue to use manual methods due to a lack of knowledge of computers. As users receive training from the IC staff and use the equipment and software, they gain knowledge of the machines, their capabilities, and ways in which this technology can improve their job and their productivity. The IC staff expects a variety of users, ranging from the technically competent to the professionally qualified but machine-fearful. Part of the skill required in the IC staff member addresses the problems of lack of literacy and fear of the machine. The IC provides the training, counseling, consulting, and time to support all types of users. With literacy comes use and productivity.

> *Computer literacy expands one's view of the possible.*

User Enthusiasm

Enthusiasm is another facet of training and familiarity with computers. Where fear reigned before the IC, enthusiasm now abounds. Secretaries and executives alike openly express delight in mastering a capability and being able to use that capability to solve a problem personally. The IC supports making the user comfortable and competent with technology, which gives the person a different view of that technology. In this, the IC staff is counselor and confidante, friend and helper, teacher and supporter, champion and cheerleader. The interpersonal skills required for the IC staff involve not just being a pleasant teacher; they are essential for overcoming user fears and inhibitions and aiding the metamorphosis from standoffish opponent to enthusiastic user.

> *The IC staff is counselor and confidante, friend and helper, teacher and supporter, champion and cheerleader.*

CONCLUSION

All ten benefits can result from the creation of an information center. Interviews with managers of active and successful information centers reinforce this belief and support the ideas of end user computing and the environment provided by the information center.

The IC and its customer support role represent a change in the charter of data services, a new way of providing computer-based services to the firm. The need for professional systems analysts and programmers remains, but there is now also a need for personnel to support users in achieving their own computer-based solutions. These support people tend to have different traits and capabilities from programmers in application development. The differences are complementary, and the firm is the winner as users are added to the solution arena. The benefits of the installation of an information center are significant, the most predominant one being increased productivity for all concerned. These benefits are not presented in isolation but in relation to the options available to data services and issues that must be addressed by that organization's and the firm's management. The outcome may well be a different way of doing business. It certainly will affect the way many individuals perform their job as well as the job they perform.

SUMMARY

- The information center does not cause a reduction in the formal backlog of requests. On occasion, it will cause an increase in this queue. However, it does address the invisible backlog of needs that have never surfaced as requests for service.
- Use of the IC can reduce the cost and time to complete applications that the users can address.
- With the experience gained in end user computing, users increase their computer literacy and are able to specify service requirements better and more clearly. This has a direct effect on formal systems development.
- The IC is responsible for bettering the relationships between the users and data services. As users receive attention and assistance from the IC staff, they relate better to computer resources and all of the personnel of data services.
- Supported end user computing increases the productivity of both the users and the programming staff of data services. This is the result of applying more resources to the problem solution (the users) and insulating the programmers from day-to-day interruptions by users.
- As users have access to corporate data, the quality of the information used in decisions improves. The information center concept directly supports access to the corporate data resource.
- Support of users via the information center creates users who are more enthusiastic about their jobs and the use of computer resources.

Key Terms

Benefits of the IC	Queue
Backlog of requests	Productivity
Formal backlog	Quality of information
Informal backlog	Resources
Relations with data services	Computer literacy

DISCUSSION QUESTIONS

1. How do you determine that an apparent benefit is worth the cost?
2. Differentiate between the formal backlog of requests and the informal (invisible) backlog.
3. What are the costs of developing a computer-based application? Why does one take such a long time?
4. How can a user create "better requirements?"
5. Why are relations strained between users of computer services and the programmers in data services? What is it about the IC that changes this?
6. How does productivity differ from efficiency or effectiveness?
7. What affects the quality of information?
8. What is computer literacy, and how can it be improved?
9. Why should we be concerned with users' being enthusiastic about their jobs? Aren't they paid to do those jobs?
10. Do you think the IC is of great benefit, or is this all propaganda?

REFERENCES

6-1. "Information Centers: Diverging from IBM's Original Concept," *PC Week*, February 24, 1987, pp. 42–43.

CASE STUDIES

FMC CORPORATION

This Chicago-based company has evolved greatly during its history. Today it specializes in heavy machinery, chemicals, and other industrial products and had sales of $3 billion, and current employment of 40,000. The company began using computers in the early 1960s for accounting functions. Late in that decade the computer was adopted in the factory environment. The computer is now used extensively in areas of production control and engineering, including the techniques of CAD-CAM.

The Information Center at FMC

By 1981, specialized users were informally employing Foresight, APL, and SAS. Informal end user computing was viewed by DP as not particularly effective. Meanwhile, the backlog of requests for application development was lengthy, and DP was viewed as unproductive by the user community. The DP opinion of the backlog was that simply adding people in DP would not produce the desired results. What was required was an environment that allowed use of capabilities that supported the user and products that were non-DP-oriented. The intent was to be responsive to the needs of the users, resolve a large number of the application requests in a nontraditional MIS way, and improve general productivity. The result was the first of seven information centers to be installed at FMC operating units. This first was set up after ten months of planning; five months passed before the IC decision was made, and five months transpired between the decision and the opening of the first center in January 1983. The seventh FMC IC was announced in May 1984.

The FMC computer center in Dallas supports a staff that counsels and advises the operating-unit ICs. This group is composed of a manager of information centers support and four staff members. The other ICs have staffs ranging from 3 to 11 members, including the local IC managers, constituting a total staff of 40. The end user population has grown from 4 to over 3,000 (2,800 logon IDs). The details that follow are representative of the seven centers, according to the corporate manager of information centers support.

The primary departments using the IC are finance and manufacturing. Reports, queries, and analysis lead the list of uses, in personal, department, and corporate applications, in that order. Electronic mail and office automation are planned for the near future and will have a close association with the IC.

Training is provided through varying methodologies at the different IC locations. Both instruction by IC staff and purchased outside training are available. For the most part, training is scheduled and provided during working hours. Although neither training nor certification is required for IC access, the IC manager views certification as a desirable process, including the certification of department managers prior to their being allowed to select PCs.

Computer support to the various operating locations of the corporation is provided from a centralized location in the Dallas area. The FMC processors include one dual 3084, one quad 3084, two 3081s, one 3033, and one 4341. The ICs operate in shared environments, using VM and MVS operating systems. The most used language is RAMIS, followed by Foresight (prior to 1985), IFPS, and SAS. A dozen other applications are used to varying degrees. The mainframe processing is 85 percent on-line, with access provided via several thousand Model 3278 terminals.

Microcomputer support is provided via 210 IBM PCs and 100 Apple, Radio Shack, Wang, and DEC microcomputers.

DEC, Wang, and IBM PCs are acceptable for end user DP needs, while DEC and Wang are the ones acceptable for office automation uses. There is presently no corporate standard for a basic configuration other than these acceptable choices. The specific needs of the user are considered in recommending a machine. There presently is no PC-to-host communication.

The use of timeshare has not been widespread at FMC and was not a consideration in the installation of the ICs. The only use has been for specialized outside databases.

FMC has a data administration function but no central data control for the users. Users have to seek out the data they need. All data is secure, but often only a phone call to the ACF2 security officer is required to have a rule written for access to a copy. FMC is very sensitive about production data but is less concerned about the end user data. Since data is extracted on a routine basis, the difference between production and user data may be hard to detect. In any event, the use of data has increased due to its availability through the ICs.

An issue was raised by the IBM model about the advisability of the IC staff performing actual coding for the users. Within the FMC information centers, about half of the staff members spend most of their time coding projects, and the others concentrate on user consulting. The IC manager viewed this level of program coding as high and undesirable and has plans to reduce or eliminate it.

FMC charges for all mainframe access, either IC or production. However, the users do not see chargeback as a problem. Some of the ICs provide no-cost accounts for new customers. At least one IC has used varying charge rates as a method of resource control, such as an increased tape-use charge to move people to DASD and charging more for MVS to get users to move to VM. The reduced rate for VM services is also cited as an example of costing as a marketing ploy.

One indicator of the success of the FMC ICs has been a reduction in adverse comments in user surveys. Another is a documented cost savings resulting from the rewrite of a production system in EXPRESS. The project cost of six months' effort plus the expense of running it for the first year was less than the cost of maintaining the old system for one year. In addition to these success stories, the IC manager cited as major benefits received from the IC the positive effect on the users' view of MIS, increased FMC productivity, and the ability to manage information to stay competitive.

One of the manager of information center support's objectives is removing the ICs from the development of systems, that is, stopping program coding. A second major objective is for the end user community to be self-sufficient in the area of computer support. To achieve this, the FMC information centers plan to provide (1) migration paths from PC products to mainframe products, (2) data dictionary for the end users, (3) computer-based training, and (4) easier, stronger products to enable end users to perform more sophisticated tasks.

ELECTRO-TEX CORPORATION

Harry Smith began a company in 1966 that has experienced widespread success. He saw a need for outside management of corporate DP resources and established Electro-Tex Corporation. ETC has established a wide reputation and significant corporate income, with sales now in excess of $500 million annually. ETC has 13,000 employees worldwide. Since the business is computer-oriented, the number of DP personnel was quoted at 5,000.

A feature of the extensive computer environment at ETC is a satellite-based communications network that connects the various data processing centers and provides CPU access from the many ETC and customer terminals. Another feature of the ETC computer environment is the lack of database orientation. Due to the nature and volume of data processed, the company believes it can achieve greater productivity through access methods other than DBMS. Such methods have been developed within ETC. The information center uses APL/DI as a relational database, and the company supports IMS and IDMS for its customers, but the production files are presently not using DBMS technology.

ETC Information Center

The present information center resulted from a project to solve a specific problem. A time span of 30 days was required to produce financial reports from the corporate MIS system after month-end closing of accounts. The vice-president of finance found this of significant concern and requested that the person who is now the IC manager create reports within a shorter time frame. The result of that project was that the time span from month-end closing of records to reports decreased from 30 days to less than two days. This project demonstrated the ability to both bypass the delays associated with MIS application development and to gain access to existing data. Based on this success, the IC was formally started in July 1982, just four months after the original request for the financial report previously mentioned. Part of the ability for such a short time span was that IBM worked closely with ETC in defining and establishing the IC concept. IBM brought a team to ETC to assist in planning, and the IC manager went to IBM facilities to see the results of other firms' efforts.

The staff of the IC grew from three to the present seven members in 3 years, while the user base expanded from 8 to 225. The staff is composed of six men and one woman who are expected (1) to maintain the IC and customer interface, (2) to provide training, (3) to refrain from programming for the users, and (4) to assist the end users in their computer needs for timely, accurate report-

ing. The IC manager believes that the best way to assist the user is to provide personal interface, usually in the user area. "It is not unusual to find the IC area empty," he notes. Another way the user is supported is by providing additional, individualized training for users who relate well to the IC capabilities and show a tendency to be departmental specialists.

The primary use of the IC is for queries, analysis, and timely reports. It is used at all levels of the corporation and by many departments. Two specific applications are the creation of a database for the legal department and an applicant-tracking system. The primary languages are ADRS, APL/DI, and GDDM, all IBM products. Also used are STAIRS and PROFS, as well as the ISPF and DMS productivity tools.

Being a computer-based services company, a spare IBM Model 4341 was located and dedicated to IC support at the time of the IC initiation. This CPU was recently augmented by IBM's latest addition to the 4300 Series machines, the Model 4361. The primary access device is the IBM Model 3279 color terminal with color printer support. Personal computers are just beginning to be used for access, and most of them are connected as dumb terminals. However, some PCs access the mainframe to download data in order to perform statistical analysis.

The computers that support the information center also support a programmer productivity center. Both are considered information centers by the IC manager but have very different charters.

Users do not have access to the production data, however, the IC periodically extracts files and makes them available to IC users in read-only form. The users can easily gain access to the extracted data but are prevented from uploading data to any level. Accessible files are password-protected, and access is controlled in the logon ID of the user. IC user logon IDs and passwords are provided by the IC. Unlike many firms, the time at which automatic terminal logoff occurs is after several hours of inactivity. This time span was established after problems were encountered with short logoff time spans of 10 to 30 minutes.

The IC manager believes that PC proliferation will bring problems of security, such as the ability to take data out of the facility. Another concern is that the IC provides a concentration of data and resources. In spite of these considerations, the IC manager is a strong supporter of the IC concept for providing data access and computer resources.

There is no chargeback for use of the information center. The IC manager believes that cost will be a deterrent and that the resource should be utilized to the best advantage. Problems are not expected until the present CPUs saturate and additional monies are required for additional CPU power. Complementing the no-cost structure is the ability to provide rapid response on the IC mainframe.

Promotion of the IC has slowed recently. The primary method for marketing the IC concept is now user communication and user group meetings.

The primary objective and benefit of the ETC IC is to meet the computer and data needs of end users. This extends to all levels within the company and has high visibility with the board of directors.

The IC has had no effect on the application development backlog. This is due to the nature of the IC tasks and the size and nature of application development projects.

One of the specific benefits of the IC is the attitude of the IC manager. "It takes a strong will to change a traditional approach to DP," he notes, "but the productivity results make it worth sticking to your guns." He believes that timely access to data not only is cost-effective but also provides gains to end user productivity.

Another benefit is the presence of the IC as a marketing tool. The IC manager believes there is a growing need for companies to be able to gain assistance in developing information centers, and ETC's experience with its IC gives it a marketing edge. He expects that future ETC plans will include the ability to provide a turnkey installation of an information center, much as they do with their present products.

J. C. PENNEY LIFE INSURANCE COMPANY

> J. C. Penney Company, Inc., is a major retailer, with stores in all 50 states, Puerto Rico, and Belgium. The dominant portion of the Company's business consists of providing merchandise and services to consumers through stores, including catalog operations. The Company markets family apparel, home furnishings, leisure lines, drug store merchandise, and insurance, with total sales of $12,000 million.
>
> Annual Report

J. C. Penney Company, Inc., entered the financial services sector in the late 1960s with offerings from JCP Life Insurance Company of life and health and from JCP Casualty Company with auto and homeowner's insurance through direct marketing. Income from premiums and investments was $253 million. J. C. Penney Life, the focus of this case, has a staff of about 400 employees at its office in Richardson, Texas.

Like most retail and insurance companies, J. C. Penney Company, Inc., and J. C. Penney Life and Casualty Insurance companies have used computers as a course of business for decades. The parent company has seven data centers nationwide with an extensive communications network. This communications ability is so extensive that it leases time to other companies. In addition to the data centers, the Financial Services Division has two IBM 308X mainframe installations.

Penney Life Information Center

The information center of Penney Life is supported by a dedicated IBM Model

308X mainframe in the Park Central complex in Dallas, Texas. The division uses IBM Model 3178 and 3278/9 video display terminals via landline communications to the division office buildings. The IC concept is entirely mainframe-based, with no personal computers yet supported.

The primary language of the information center is FOCUS. FOCUS runs only on the IC mainframe, not on any of the data center mainframes. Users obtain their terminals by asking the IC manager, and the IC maintains only one terminal and one printer for common use. The IC manager believes that shared resources are of little value since an employee will seldom walk far from his or her desk for access.

The information center was opened in April 1982 without announcement or ceremony. It had only one staff member at that time, the present IC manager, and about six users. It presently has two product specialists who consult and train in addition to other DP duties. There are presently 160 users, 30 to 40 percent of whom are considered active, from a total population of 400 employees. Neither training nor certification is required for access to the IC. The staff conducts scheduled classes in three levels of FOCUS and has taught 136 users since the beginning of 1983. The accounting and marketing departments account for 80 percent of IC use, with data processing and human resources using most of the remaining capability. During the first quarter of its second year of operation, some 8,400 hours of timeshare connect time were recorded, of which 3,000 involved use of electronic mail. About 3 million resource units were charged direct to the users for a total first-quarter cost of $47,000. The IC computer budget for that year was $500,000, more than five times the funds budgeted and used in the previous year.

Penney Life has IBM PROFS office automation software and uses it exclusively for the electronic mail capability. PROFS is supported by the IC and used with great success. The executive level accounted for 300 of the 3,000 hours recorded for electronic mail during the quarter and noted enhanced communications. Of further note is the absence of the use of PROFS or SCRIPT for word processing. This service is supported by an entirely non-IC capability.

The information center is the result of the need to apply computer technology to a specific manual effort. The accounting department was spending a great amount of effort in data collection for an annual budget process requiring some outside timeshare and a lot of coordination, corrections, and data manipulation. The FOCUS language was used and resulted in a documented saving of $1.3 million and the formal beginning of the information center. Due to this success and its visibility, many satisfied users, and the creation of departmental experts, no marketing of the information center has been necessary.

As indicated previously, one of the primary reasons for the IC was the systems development backlog and the need to get an application created. However, as the IC has become established and over 100 small systems have been developed, the backlog has not been reduced because the jobs put on the IC were not in the backlog.

The information center at Penney Life follows the IBM model well. It is a mainframe-based environment with no strong consideration of PCs. It is completely internal-timeshare-based. The advent of the IC had basically no effect on the use of external timeshare services because of the very low level of use of this capability. The IC manager attended an IBM class on IC structure and has seen little need to vary from the model. The one exception from the classic IC model is the IC manager's agreement to do programming for users, a practice that IBM and others advise against.

The terminals are remote from the single mainframe with adequate communications. Access to production data is well supported, and presently only extract copies are accessed, and these are provided via tape.

Long-term plans call for extract to DASD, with continued production and ad hoc extracting.

The installation of the information center has had little effect on the use of data resources. The primary language also houses the IC DBMS, whereas the production DBMS is IBM's IMS, using CICS for communications. Of note is the way the language and the IC DBMS are used. Only 10 percent of the effort is for personal tasks, while 70 percent is for projects that affect several departments across the division.

The information center provides resources and charges basically like the rest of data services. The user must have a computer account number and network authorization prior to access of the IC or DP applications. Whereas DP has direct charges for development, the IC will help develop at no cost. However, the IC does charge directly for system changes and maintenance. This is where direct charging stops in the IC; the general services and training are added into computer overhead.

Security is not a sensitive issue at Penney Life. Users are responsible for their own data. The intent of the IC is to share data, not to control it. Thus only the few sensitive files concerning marketing and compensation data have any overt security. Although there is no specific training for security practices, the IC staff does make spot checks and encourages read passwords and encryption. The IC manager believes that the IC presents no unusual security problems as long as it is mainframe-based. He believes that "with PCs there is no control."

Data proliferation and integrity are not considered to be problem areas. In fact, the IC has helped improve integrity. Improvement occurred when end users employed the edit rules indicated for production files and found invalid data. Use of the IC, FOCUS, and easy data access have made data use very user-friendly.

There are no formal guidelines for defining projects that are appropriate for IC resource use. This is largely due to the rapid turnaround time experienced in the IC. However, the user is requested to fill out a form showing the intent of the project and the expected benefits. When quarterly charges are presented to the users, they are asked if the benefits were achieved. The value of the IC is then left to the user. The IC is used to prototype small and medium-sized systems as well as to build these applications. The IC manager has raised a question as to the ability to distinguish between what capabilities should be on the IC and what should go through formal IS control. Thus he approves of the use of the IC for motivating users to meet their information needs without extensive control.

Data services continues to question the user projects. The IC manager believes that DP doubts the data integrity and the correctness of the operation of the system. The IC manager feels that users tend to do as good a job of program implementation and testing as DP in most cases.

The users and management are pleased with the results of the Penney Life information center, as noted in the fivefold increase in budget and in letters of thanks. One project showed a hard return of $1.3 million on an investment of $35,000, but the successes based on intangibles are of equal value. The primary objective of the IC is to allow end users to meet their own business information needs; the primary benefits have been (1) the raising of the level of computer literacy, (2) reduction of computer fear, and (3) increased motivation to get the job done with the use of technology. The IC manager indicates that user productivity is a perceived benefit, but no attempt has been made to measure this variable.

Plans for the future include support of PCs and PC products and the creation of a local area network as an alternative to the mainframe communication network.

7

Implication of the Information Center

Until now we have been following the scheme recommended in recent literature and supported by interviews with managers of existing information centers. This chapter presents a discussion of the implications of findings from the study. These implications will be discussed in such a way as to allow the development of specific contentions for the development and use of an information center. Attention will be given to the creation of an information center or continuance of an existing one. All 20 cases in the study are considered successful instances of ICs. Therefore, implication of study findings are used to suggest the appropriate process for addressing specific IC issues and options.

IMPLEMENTATION OF AN INFORMATION CENTER

Signs of Need for an IC

We have noted two phenomena that preceded and supported the demand for an IC: (1) a significant backlog of requests for data services and (2) the existence of informal end user computing. The presence of a backlog would signal the pressure buildup, especially when it is realized that the invisible backlog is significantly larger than the official queue. The emergence of informal end user computing, though not easy to detect, indicates an existing user community that is (1) willing and able to accept computer-based responsibilities, (2) should be controlled, and (3) can be supported by an IC. The interviews with IC managers indicate that the expectations of the initiation of an IC is to control end user computing internally and externally (use of outside timeshare services), halt the proliferation of personal computers, support the user, and reduce the backlog.

> Backlogs of formal requests and the presence of informal end user computing are symptoms of a need for an information center.

Nature of the Company

There is no indication that there is any specific set of characteristics for a company that would cause or limit the installation of an information center. No comments during the interviews or data from the study point to conditions under which an IC would not work. The one characteristic of the companies studied and others contacted that seems to be an indicator as to the ability to install an IC is company size, probably not measured by level of sales but by the size of the data services department or operations. It appears that a data services contingent of reasonable size is required before adequate resources are available for the formal support of end user computing. Once the decision is made to initiate an IC, size of the data services staff does not determine the size of the IC staff.

> The only company characteristic that is required to establish an information center is willingness. This happens in many companies only after data services has reached a critical size large enough to permit the use of part of this resource for the IC. This is a matter of convenience, not a requirement.

Initiation of an IC

Contrary to some beliefs, the creation of an IC does not require lengthy planning and is generally not the result of a study or a cost-benefit analysis. For the most part, the direction of an IC is not one of formal policy and procedures. The decision to initiate an IC seems to be one of discovery and the evolution of a process—conditions arise that cannot be resolved by other means. Thus a company with a dedicated administrative or technical staff that is somewhat computer-literate, feels the pressure for improved methods of decision support, and realizes the potential of using technology in the resolution of the situation is a fertile environment for the installation and use of an information center. On the other side of the decision, the primary characteristics required for potential IC staff members are a willingness to assist the users on their own terms, reasonable technical expertise in one or more high-level computer capabilities, and the support of data services and user management. The final two ingredients required for the initiation of an IC are hardware resources and a champion to organize, direct, and lead the IC.

As indicated previously, the type of computer environment and the makeup of the firm's personnel will directly affect the pressure for IC initiation and its resultant growth pattern. Clerical personnel may be users of production applications but tend not to be heavy users of IC capabilities. The existence of a large professional staff is the most significant indicator. These professionals are able and willing to implement technology to be more effective and productive. The IC is an organized method of support.

The creation of an information center does not require lengthy planning or cost-benefit analysis. The primary requirements are pressure for better decision support, a willingness to commit resources, and a champion to organize the effort.

Information Center Style

The IC is involved in the operations of the firm and has a planning horizon in the range of three to six months. This is in keeping with the types of requests that the IC supports. It is also consistent with characteristics that are important to a successful IC: flexibility, creativity, brief objectives, and willingness to change. The IC management style is considered unique in its need to possess a short lead time and an unstructured perspective. IC managers of maturing installations indicate that the life of the IC may be as short as three years, at which time the concept will be reevaluated and its purpose looked at anew. With the apparent high cost of user processing comes management control. This implies the need for longer-term planning not presently found in the firms studied.

Information centers are operational and work with a short planning horizon. They, like their champions, must be flexible and creative.

PREMISES

IC Manager

The IC manager should have a combination DP and non-DP background. That is to say that although this person generally reports to the data services organization, he or she should be able to address the technical issues of the IC and its relation to data services while communicating easily with users and upper management. Part of all conversations will be the selling of the IC idea and its impact on the firm. This requires abilities in salesmanship as well as interpersonal skills, flexibility, patience, persistence, and a DP generalist attitude.

Data from the IC managers indicate that the position of IC manager does not have to entail only IC duties in order to ensure success. However, the data does infer that the presence of other responsibilities tends to produce a lower level of support to the users and slower IC growth. The concentration of all of the efforts of the IC manager has a greater impact on the IC support than does the initial staff size. The information center concept is such that requiring the IC manager to plan and direct its initiation and growth along with other duties is quite limiting.

IC managers tend to be males over 30 with DP backgrounds. This may well be a default selection process as opposed to an overt method. That is to say, none of these characteristics is deemed vital to IC success as long as other traits are present. IC managers can come from a variety of sources, both inside and outside the firm. Some firms search for a special person outside the company, while others use available personnel from data services and non-DP sources alike.

The IC manager is the champion of the concept. He or she must have DP skills yet able to communicate with and sell ideas to upper management. The IC will evolve best when the IC manager has no added (non-IC) responsibilities.

IC Staff

The size of the IC staff, beyond the IC manager, will generally be determined by management's willingness to allocate this resource and incur the attendant expense. However, size should be determined by the potential user population, training required, and the IC promotion effort. As noted in existing ICs, staff size is the principal limiting factor to growth because growth without adequate support implies impending IC failure. Thus the IC manager must be able to requisition and attract a size of staff that can train and support the user population before promotion begins. Numerically, the size of the IC should be kept to one consultant or product specialist for each 20 or fewer users until the growth and maturity of the user population has stabilized and user department specialists are in place to assist fellow users. (See Figure 4-1, p. 97, for more specific recommendations.)

The growth potential of the information center is dependent on the number of staff members in relation to the user community. A limited staff implies limited growth and service.

Present IC staffs include both male and female members, there is no preference for either sex. Nor is the age of the IC staff member critical. The background of IC staff members is presently three-to-two in favor of DP backgrounds. This may be a default condition as opposed to a true preference, and the use of non-DP personnel may well increase in the future, especially with a continued shortage of DP-trained personnel. All IC managers were quick to comment on the need for IC staff members to possess certain characteristics that cannot be taught, such as orientation, personality, and attitude.

IC staffs have been selected from DP backgrounds, but this is not a requirement and will likely change as new resources are added. Neither the age nor sex of staff members is critical.

The IC staff has developed good interaction with the users and has provided data services with a bettering of relations with the users. However, IC managers believe that the users distinguish between the IC and other data services staffs, with the other staffs still viewed with reservation. If the IC does become the primary interface point with the users, and the programmers and analysts digress to having little contact with the users, user-DP relations may continue to improve overall.

> The acceptance of the IC staff is helping improve the users' view of all of data services. This is due to the addition of a customer service function not normally part of data services.

A note of caution is in order. ICs are attracting highly capable people. In addition, the IC staff positions are being demonstrated as an especially viable career for women in or wanting to join data services. At the same time, the career paths within and beyond the IC staff positions are not clear. Thus the IC may attract creative and talented people to this new area of data services but lose them due to lack of opportunities.

> The information center is attracting competent creative people but has an unclear career potential.

IC Capabilities

Even though the languages and capabilities provided by the IC may initially be determined by default, that is, by what is presently available, users will ultimately request additional support in the form of added software. Two factors will affect the decision concerning the number and specification of packages acquired. The first is the familiarity of the user population with packages on the market. Individuals tend to want to use the application with which they have experience. The second factor is the exposure of the users to new offerings through advertisements and seminars by vendors. In the final analysis, few companies can afford to provide all software on the market, nor would they want to. Our interviews indicate that four major software packages are usually sufficient. Even then, the nature of the output should be the main factor in determining what packages to acquire and support.

Formal and informal comments by the IC managers indicate that availability of and access to company data was an objective and is a prime IC benefit in the firms questioned. This ability to provide computer-resident data to users will affect the selection of the IC capabilities. If data is not available, the software simply has to accommodate manual input and storage as well as manipulation and reporting. With access to copies of company data, more manipulation, analysis, and reporting will tend to take place, requiring better support in the form of the software and training.

> The IC capabilities provided will be determined by staff size, user preferences, and access to the corporate data resource.

Training

Any new capability requires the training of users so that the capability can be employed in an effective and productive manner. The primary methodology is classroom training by the IC staff for mainframe capabilities and private study or micro-based tutorial for PC capabilities. Although use of the IC staff for training is quite important, it reduces staff members' availability to users for problem resolution, software evaluation, and IC promotion. Vendor training is an available alternative.

As with PC training, the future of mainframe training is most likely to be in the form of computer-based training and videotapes. Many IC managers plan on these methods for future support. The advantages are self-paced instruction for the users, minimal interruption of the IC staff, and variety and number of courses. Basic courses are sufficient only for new users; maturing ICs require advanced training capabilities.

> Training is a very important but time-consuming function of the IC staff. Computer-based training, videotapes, and vendor training are acceptable alternatives.

Data Availability

The use of data includes knowledge of data sources and permission to address the data as well as the technical aspects of access. In this realm, the IC staff member must aid the user in determining the existence of the data, its owner, its availability, and, finally, gaining technical access. The IC staff member becomes an intermediary between the user, the owner, and the computer security staff. This function can make data a shared resource and improve the quality of decision making.

> A valuable service provided by the IC staff is to aid in discovering the existence, location, and ownership of required data.

DP OPTIONS

Growth

An information center can take many forms along a continuum. At one end is the concentration of physical IC facilities with staff offices, readily available hardware such as terminals and printers, training rooms, and administrative support. At the other end of the continuum is the IC staff cubicle and training in a convenient conference room. The configuration that a firm chooses will be dependent on the resources it is willing to allocate, the present computer facilities, and the user community.

A firm that presently has on-line applications and distributed terminals will find limited use for a physical IC with sharable facilities due to the existing user hardware. Space for training and IC staff offices will be the primary need. Significant pressure for IC staff support will build once initial training and IC promotion begin. On the other hand, a firm with basically batch operations and limited terminal access and experience will find the use of a physical IC with available resources of greater value. The pressure for rapid growth in either case will depend on the nature of the user community and other factors. The present hardware complement and the willingness of management to acquire equipment and staff will have a direct impact on the acceptance, use, growth, and ultimate value of the IC.

> The choice of concentrated physical IC facilities is dependent on existing computer hardware and management's willingness to allocate resources. Once promotion and training begin, pressure will build for additional staff and IC capabilities. The level of support will directly determine the value of the IC and end user computing.

Computer Environment

Information centers are installed in primarily shared IBM computer environments, usually with some PC support. Thus the environment with the highest probability of success is either a combination of an IBM mainframe and personal computers or a very strong IBM mainframe environment. Use of non-IBM mainframes has a limited future due to the lower availability of high-level (user-oriented) software. Complementing a non-IBM mainframe with IBM PCs can provide a reasonable environment. Ignoring or trying to prevent the acquisition of PCs will tend to be futile unless a viable mainframe alternative is provided.

 End user processing does not have to be in an interactive mode. Although most computer installations offer on-line capabilities, they should be reserved for creation of data and command files with final processing in a batch mode. This lowers the system requirements, resource use, and cost while providing a reasonably responsive environment. Users should be trained to use the appropriate mode—interactive processing when the decision environment requires an immediate response or sequential query, batch processing to make better use of resources without degrading access.

> Batch processing with interactive creation of files is a satisfactory low-cost mode. Interactive processing is appropriate for time-critical and sequential query activities.

Data Administration and Access

Access to stored data requires that the users know of the existence of the data, its locations, its owner, and methods of access. In a database environment, a data dictionary is of great assistance. Of even greater aid in any environment is a data administrator. This person is of significant value to the user in seeking and accessing the required data. Once mainframe data is found, it is often best to make an extract copy and address this copied file, preferably with a user-oriented database management system. This environment provides three advantages for the user: (1) search assistance, (2) access on the user's own terms, and (3) a tool for access. The functions of data administration and DBMS assistance may both be handled by an IC staff member.

> Data administration is an important function for helping users find needed computer-resident data. A user-oriented DBMS will greatly assist the users in access and use of the found data.

Effect of the IC on Computer Resources

Companies are finding that user processing is becoming a significant part of the total activity on the mainframe. With more IC staff provided, more users can be trained to gain access to the IC, and mainframe and resource usage will increase further. Thus the IC can have a significant impact on resource use, cost, and acquisitions. This requires DP resource planning that is more dynamic than that based on production applications. It also means that the IC must have upper-management endorsement in order to support the expenditures. As one IC manager indicated, this requires that the IC constantly show that it is of value to upper management in order to ensure survival, in the form of hard savings of cost avoidance and soft benefits such as productivity improvements and enhanced decision making.

> Adequate support of end user computing via the information center will result in increased use of the computer and the data resource. To survive, ICs must document their value as to hard cost savings and soft benefits to the decision environment.

MANAGEMENT ISSUES

DP Contact Point

One function that many IC managers see as desirable but not presently exploited is that the IC staff is the first point of contact for all user MIS problems and a clearinghouse for all requests for data services. The point-of-contact concept requires the interpersonal skills present in the IC staff, while the IC staff performing a clearinghouse function appears to be pragmatic. Both concepts seem to be a function of desires of data services, management, and the review committee as opposed to IC staff size. The intentions of the majority of IC managers interviewed to have these functions indicates an evolving trend in the DP-user interface.

> The IC staff is a logical first point of contact for all MIS-related problems. It is a practical clearinghouse for all requests for data services.

Data Access

Access to company data is very important to the IC user community and a primary benefit of the IC. Data management and administration is not presently oriented to the user. Thus the IC staff and other data services personnel must support the users in gaining knowledge of and access to the data they require. Direct read-only access to operational data by users is an appropriate and low-cost method of assuring data integrity. Extract copies may or may not be effective and efficient, depending on the environment, data use, and the dynamic nature of the data.

> Access to computer-resident data is important for user decision processes and productivity. The IC can be highly instrumental in helping users gain proper access.

Chargeback for Services

Charging for computer use is a management matter, and the IC will most likely follow the policies of production applications. The IC need not affect the method of accountability, but management must be comfortable with IC expenditures and believe that the company is getting its money's worth. It has been demonstrated that the IC can reduce expenditures for computer services outside the firm. It has also been shown that holding users responsible for computer charges is neither universal nor necessary.

> Charging for IC services will likely follow the trend in the production environment.

Security

Even with the high use of personal computers, security in an IC environment can be maintained and data and equipment can be protected. Though the users of the IC are not particularly well versed in security matters, use of the IC is not unlike ordinary paperwork. That is to say, methods to protect paperwork can often suffice in a user environment. Meanwhile, the production computer environment provides reasonable protection for production data. Many IC managers believe that the IC adds no new threats to security and continue to depend on the firm's employees to provide basic security.

> The basis of end user computing security is the nature of the users and the training they are given.

Marketing and Promoting of the IC

The important point about promotion of the IC is the potential for disaster. Present IC managers are aware of the pitfalls of marketing what cannot be delivered. As the IC staff size grows and the user community matures and stabilizes, the IC can afford to market more. Until these conditions materialize, the marketing effort must be kept at a cautious level.

> Marketing what the IC cannot deliver is a quick path to disaster. Promote in haste, repent at leisure.

Change in the Nature of Jobs

The objective of the creation of the IC and its major benefit now is that the users, primarily the professional group, can get their job done. This indicates that the IC has a direct effect on the nature of the jobs of the professionals and on data services personnel. That is to say, access to data and IC resources not only allows the professionals to do a job differently, via computer-based methods, but it also requires them to possess or gain the skills and apply different techniques to the job methodology. Thus it changes the nature of the professionals' job.

The impact on the jobs of data services departments will be twofold. First, by removing a category of job from the DP request queue, the IC allows DP professionals to concentrate on the larger, more complex tasks. This will change the jobs of programmers and systems analysts to some degree as they work more autonomously. When communication with users of large systems is required, these DP professionals may find communications more difficult because they are less frequent and based on a potentially poorer knowledge of the user's environment. The second effect is the creation of the new category of DP jobs, the IC staff positions. Even though the IC staff does not have to draw exclusively on data services members, these positions presently rely heavily on DP-trained personnel but require characteristics different from those possessed by many programmers and analysts. The creation of these jobs draws programmers away from large-system creation, thereby making the programmer shortage more acute. However, IC positions are attracting non-DP personnel, giving relief to application development. Thus the IC may be either a plus or a minus for data services.

> The use of end user computing will change the nature of the job performed by the users and data services personnel.

BENEFITS

Information centers are seen as beneficial in that they support effective, efficient, and productive use of company resources. Even though some of the effectiveness may be in bypassing backlogs and roadblocks seemingly required by formal development, the user gains are viewed as justifying the methods. There is little attempt to measure and quantify benefits, which may be an error as the need arises to justify growth or continuance of the ICs.

Primary Objective: End User Support

IC managers indicate that information centers are created with specific objectives and anticipated benefits in mind. These generally have to do with reduced expenditures for outside timeshare and control of the proliferation of personal computers. ICs have been successful in doing both. However, the real benefit of end user computing and the information center is the effect on user productivity. More productive users making better decisions is the desired result. Other benefits of the information center are a user view that data services is more responsive, better information quality and use, and enhanced users.

> Information centers affect user productivity. This is more important than a decrease in costs.

Future of Existing Information Centers

IC managers have a positive view of the IC and its future and have plans for expansion of support to users. Where the IC is mature, the thrust is to seek out users on their own turf and learn their business. In ICs that have yet to expand to meet the potential user community, the plan is to do so. The concept is being proved daily, and individual ICs are expanding to meet their potential.

> IC managers see the IC as a successful concept and plan on further expansions of the idea.

SUMMARY

1. DP size is the only company characteristic that influences the initiation of an IC.
2. A dedicated IC manager is important to the success of an IC.
3. Only minimal planning and analysis are required prior to setting up an IC.
4. Particular company policies will determine if justification or cost-benefit analysis will be required in the creation of an IC.
5. The following situations indicate a potential for the initiation of an IC:
   a. Existence of informal end user computing
   b. A significant backlog of DP requests
   c. Heavy pressure for the acquisition of personal computers
   d. Heavy use and visible cost of outside timeshare services
   e. A poor user–data services relationship
6. The support of a highly placed executive within data services greatly helps the success of IC initiation.

7. An IC champion is often found where IC growth is great.

8. IC support by upper management is effective for IC growth.

9. The heaviest users of IC capabilities are the professional and staff personnel. Clerical personnel use production applications or IC systems created by other people.

10. The department of highest use is determined by existing capabilities. However, accounting and finance are potential early adopters.

11. Reports are the primary output of the IC. This may change with maturity of users and capabilities provided.

Premises

12. The size and nature of the IC staff affects the growth of the IC.

13. There is a desirable user–to–IC staff ratio that depends on the characteristics of the user population.

14. Training is important to the IC. Vendors can help in this area.

15. Classroom and PC-based tutorials are the primary methods of training. Computer-based and videotape training have great potential.

16. Training prior to IC access is not necessarily required but offers advantages.

17. IC managers report to other data services managers or higher.

18. Knowledge of and access to company data is vital.

19. The IC staff generally assists the users in gaining access to the system and to data, but not in acquiring resources.

20. Age and sex are irrelevant in selecting IC managers and staff.

21. IC managers generally have a technical background. Other important characteristics include a generalist attitude, ability to sell ideas, patience, creativity, and the ability to relate to data services and users.

22. IC staff duties concentrate on user support.

23. IC staff members are well respected, but their career paths are not well defined.

24. Administrative support is the exception in ICs and is generally provided only in larger, mature ICs.

25. ICs generally affect an increased use of company data without an attendant view of increased data proliferation or loss of data integrity.

DP Options

26. The IC concept is generally installed in an IBM mainframe environment in combination with personal computers. Use of non-IBM mainframes requires PCs due to a lack of IC software for non-IBM mainframes.

27. A physical IC is not vital; easy access to on-line terminals is.

28. Interactive processing is not necessary. Batch processing is adequate if turnaround is reasonable.

29. The particular IC capabilities are company- and use-dependent. The acquisition of up to four capabilities is desirable.

30. Data management and data administration are not generally user-oriented, requiring the IC staff to assist users in finding and accessing data.

31. Most companies with ICs also have PCs. The PCs are generally supported by the IC. The quantity of PCs in a company varies greatly and is still low.

32. Most companies have limited PC-to-host communications or none at all.

33. ICs are effective in reducing the use of outside timeshare services.

Management Issues

34. The use of the IC as a clearinghouse for MIS projects is not widespread but is viewed by IC managers as valuable.

35. The planning horizon of the IC is three to six months, but this must be extended to ensure the survivability of the concept.

36. Certain management characteristics lead to a successful IC. The primary one is a user orientation. A unique characteristic is strategy.

37. The IC adds a concern for security but no new tasks.

38. Security can be assured in an IC with existing security practices. This includes the area of personal computers.

39. Direct read-only access to production data is appropriate and adds no security problems.

40. The decision for direct access or periodic extraction is dependent on the use of the data.

41. Chargeback of computer costs is not universal. Users tend not to be sensitive to costs, regardless of methodology.

42. Few companies provide free accounts for computer access for new IC users.

43. Charging for training is unusual but occurs in order to instill discipline.

44. The advent of the IC generally increases computer use and costs.

45. IC marketing and promotion are usually at a low level until the IC staff and user community mature.

46. The IC is well received, and the IC staff enjoys a better relationship with users than the rest of data services does. The users' view of the data services department is helped by the existence of the IC.

47. Half the IC managers interviewed viewed downloading of data from the mainframe to the PC as a potential problem. However, all believed the problem was containable.

48. Few firms allow direct upload of data to the source database or file.

49. Only one out of three IC staffs has an active role in PC acquisition.

50. The existence of an IC generally does not cause special problems.

51. PCs are considered to raise more problems than ICs.

52. Most companies do not have guidelines for IC projects.
53. Most companies use IC capabilities sometimes to circumvent problems associated with formal MIS development. This is done with user management approval.

Benefits

54. The primary objective of ICs is to support end users.
55. Most companies do not formally measure IC benefits.
56. The primary benefits of the ICs are:
    a. Improved productivity
    b. Enhanced view of data services
    c. Better information quality and use
    d. More competent users
57. IC managers have a positive view of the IC and its future and have plans to expand support to users.

DISCUSSION QUESTIONS

1. Operational management deals with day-to-day tasks and is data-oriented. Management control (tactical level of management) deals with resource acquisition and is information-oriented. Strategic management is planning- and decision-oriented. Describe the place of the IC in each of the three forms of management.
2. Discuss the importance of strategy for the IC. Since ICs operate in a time frame of three to six months, what type of strategy would one have?
3. What is meant by the style of the IC and its manager?
4. Name four sources for an IC manager and six for IC staff personnel.
5. We named eight basic EUC tasks but indicate that only four IC capabilities are required. Discuss.
6. Name the factors that will likely cause the demise of an IC, and place them in order of importance. What strategy would you use to counter each?
7. Since the installation of an IC to support EUC increases mainframe usage, is it not just a way for IBM to sell more computers? Would it not be better for the firm not to recognize EUC and save money?

CASE STUDIES

TEXAS INSTRUMENTS, INC.

Texas Instruments (TI) is a leader in the fields of semiconductor components, electronic systems, calculators, government electronics, geophysical services, and professional and business computers. Worldwide in scope, it is headquartered in Dallas, Texas. TI is one of the world's largest producers of semiconductors, with sales approaching $5 billion. The present employment level is 80,700 people.

The use of technology is widespread at TI, as indicated by the internal use of its own computer products. Some 18,000 of TI's professional and management personnel have TI Professional Computers (TI PCs) at their desks. TI has a communications network that can achieve five second computer response at almost any of its 48 plant locations in 18 countries. It uses this net and its TI PCs for electronic mail, central filing of data, and access to production files.

Texas Instrument's Information Center

Like its home state of Texas, TI does things in a big way. The company started end user computing in 1969 with a mainframe IMS-based electronic mail capability. It added a spreadsheet and electronic filing in 1970 and 1977, respectively, before IBM announced the IC concept. These capabilities were developed in house and were formally supported, but much like a third-party vendor. That is, end user computing was recognized, but support for a product was more like making a call to an outside vendor than phoning an IC consultant. It was not until 1983 that the TI IC was initiated and the TI PC was distributed on a wide scale.

A major factor that resulted in the formal IC in February 1983 was a review of TI's DP capabilities and the subsequent recommendations presented to upper management by James Martin, a well-known author and consultant in the MIS field. He made a strong point that end user computing should be less structured and there should be greater use of fourth-generation languages. This resulted in the full support of the information center concept by the board of directors, and planning began for the formal IC. TI currently has 25 physical IC locations with a total of 30 staff members, who support more than 14,000 people.

The largest group of end users can be categorized as professionals. These are the financial, engineering, manufacturing, and administrative analysts who were doing jobs manually and saw a significant benefit and productivity potential in the IC and TI PC with tools like the Lotus 1-2-3 spreadsheet or the FOCUS language for mainframe or PC data access and/or manipulation. Initially the applications were created to support their personal needs, but as the users matured, the applications tended to change to support departmental needs and multidepartmental or even companywide applications.

The 30 IC staff members and a separate training staff perform a significant amount of training. Although their specialty is in the classroom, much of the training is via videotapes. Part of this is due to the distributed nature of the IC, with 20 ICs away from the main Dallas complex. Thus the videotapes are used effectively at all ICs and other sites. The average course has a duration of eight hours, and TI offers some 50 courses. Most classes are conducted by non-IC training staff, with IC members providing support as required.

Part of the process of supporting end user computing has been supporting the introduction of technology in the form of the Texas Instruments Professional Computer TI PC as a standard workstation. Its use is so widespread (placing 18,000 units in 4 years) that there are almost no 3270-type terminals in use in a predominantly IBM IC environment. The intent of the IC manager has been to introduce and support products that work in the TI corporate environment. Thus the IC has had a great influence on the positive proliferation of the TI PC, and the TI PC has been very instrumental in the use of the IC.

Along with this equipment environment and the satellite-based communications network is a data access environment that was unequaled in the other companies studied. The production environment is TSO/IMS-based, with some 350 active databases available for FOCUS reporting. The methodology is to have the IC staff help establish the definition of the extract and the user create and initiate the batch job as required, usually weekly or monthly. Thus a significant amount of data is available to the users in a FOCUS environment. The idea of distributed data, in the form of replicated databases, has been considered, but communications are sufficient not to require it. In addition to the FOCUS data environment, some users have direct read-only access to the active IMS databases using PC-based products. Uploading of data from the PC to the mainframe is allowed, but not to the source databases.

Of special note is the high use of batch processing as opposed to on-line processing. All of the initial work with FOCUS and other applications is established on-line, but 60 percent of the actual processing is accomplished in batch mode. This is significant in the reduced use of resources as well as for cost reduction, which is an issue.

Getting a TI PC is primarily a question for departmental management. The IC TI PC "company store" obtains the devices in bulk quantities and provides them to users at cost plus markup. This price is still less than retail, and most departments have had sufficient funds to acquire PCs. To gain access to the TSO environment, the user needs only to take any mainframe training course, or to call or visit the IC and request access. Once the logon ID and password are issued, the user has access to most data in the FOCUS environment. TI has an extensive internally developed security system, so little data is secured by the TSO password.

The user departments must forecast and budget for computer usage. The users are charged for use, with costs of the IC being added into the computer-use overhead. At present, TI does not charge directly for IC services through the PC purchase. However, the IC manager believes this would be appropriate and if TI does charge users, it will be the only company studied that allocates part of the IC cost to the fixed-cost PC environment. Also, TI is one of only three companies in the study to charge for in-house training. Its fee is about $100 per student per course-day.

The IC has been actively promoted since its inception. TI has an IC newsletter with 17,000 readers, a user's guide, a computer-based electronic bulletin board, seminars for users and data services alike, and high management visibility and support. The proactive marketing approach, especially presentations to data services personnel, and user acceptance have been responsible for avoiding conflict with application programming and for improving the MIS image.

The original motive in starting the TI IC was to increase the productivity of people whose cost was increasing, the professionals. TI's continuing objective is to increase productivity by increasing the ease of use of products and to decrease the training and learning required for IC use. TI has noted that most fourth-generation products are not user-friendly, and the IC is actively involved in addressing this. TI has projects in progress using artificial-intelligence natural-language technology that "front-ends" the products so that users see a form that is much easier to learn, use, and tolerate. The continuation of this type effort to provide a better environment for users is considered very important at TI.

The major benefit received to date from the IC is the excellent return on the financial and professional investment. Surveys have been taken every year to receive comments; selective audits of the noted benefits have been made, with results verified. The 1986 survey results showed an average of $21,000 cost reduction or avoidance for each of the 3,400 respondents, with a total of $70 million reported in savings during a one-year time span. The second benefit noted by the IC manager is that "the DP stock has increased greatly in the eyes of management and the users." Though there has been no reduction in the (official) backlog, and none was expected, the relations between users and the DP staff have improved.

Future plans call for physical information centers at all major TI sites worldwide, increased functionality and user-friendliness of the environment and products, and increased marketing of the IC concept.

UPDATE

The TI information center (IC) has changed slowly but substantially during the four years since the initial study. All major statistical categories have increased during the period as the IC concept furthered the TI end user computing thrust. A significant number of TI employees are involved in using a wide array of end user computing tools, as reflected in the number of IC customers, the annual benefit survey response, the installed PC base, and the user specialists.

Three new IC services or substrategies have emerged during the period. Each reflects an area where the IC is endeavoring to support and endorse TI end users' productivity.

The artificial intelligence area consists of a two-person lab that is currently concentrating on building several significant AI tools using the TI Personal Consultant tool (PC-based). The AI thrust is also directing a companywide program to make all TI employees aware of AI tools (especially the PC-based ones) and their possible applications at TI.

Technical information supports the entire corporate requirement to access, obtain, and maintain technical information. Book acquisition and cataloging, micrographic filming, laboratory notebooks, technical literature awareness, and on-line information services are the cornerstones of this effort. The Information Systems and Services Library, supporting all the technical literature needs of the IS community, is the newest part of this thrust.

New technologies have always been a part of the IC, but the rapid advancement of desktop publishing, CBT, and other tools required that the IC establish a "point" person to augment IC involvement at the earliest possible stage. Early involvement results in the IC's keeping ahead of user knowledge and skills, enabling the IC to formalize its approach based on actual experience with the tool or technology. Currently, desktop publishing and CBT and presentation development tools dominate the new technology research.

Changes to existing services or substrategies have also occurred during the maturing years. Modest changes have taken place in all services, but three have undergone the greatest evolution.

Training has maintained its lean staff approach (one person) with the main role of ensuring that TI end user training stays on target and that the IC-supported classes maintain their high level of integrity. CBT training and development have entered the picture, establishing the IC as perhaps the only expert in the CBT methodology field.

The consulting activity has gone forward in a strong position and sought "high impact" end user projects where IC effort can result in significant savings to the corporation (often in the millions of dollars). This has enhanced the IC image with corporate leaders while accomplishing feats that average users would not have the time or possibly skills for. The risks of this "we will

TEXAS INSTRUMENTS UPDATE

Statistical fact sheet

	1984	1987
Installed TI PCs	11,000	18,000
IC staff (worldwide)	33	30
IC sites (worldwide)	19	25
IC customers	1,000	13,000
Files defined for FOCUS	45	328
User specialists	0	300
Benefit survey respondents	170	3,398
Total reported benefits	$10 million	$70 million
Average benefits per respondent	$59,000	$21,000

IC Services/Substrategies

Category	1984	1987
Product selection	Full-support tier Basic-support tier	Full-support tier Basic-support tier
Consulting	User assistance Some ease-of-use tools	User assistance Major ease-of-use tools Significant projects User specialists
Training	Classroom Video (FOCUS)	Classroom Video (FOCUS) CBT methodology class CBT model building
Data access	FOCUS file definitions	FOCUS file definitions
Marketing	Growth IC emphasis Awareness Products/services	Mature IC emphasis New services Business skills
Artificial intelligence		AI lab AI application development Corporate AI awareness
Technical information		Awareness/on-line services Acquisition Achieving Library services
New technologies		Desktop publishing CBT/presentation development Product evaluations

do it for you'' approach have been offset by a drive to recruit, train, and acknowledge user specialists (experts) in the various departments throughout this worldwide corporation. Each user specialist becomes his or her department's first line of support— literally an annex to the IC—a local franchise of the TI IC concept. This gives the department faster, controllable, and sensitized support from a person who is in direct and frequent communication with the IC. It gives the IC a virtual staff of substantial measure. During the period, the consulting activity has also aggressively increased its role in the support and building of ease-of-use tools via a TI-developed natural-language product. The goal is to make computer service access easier for end users while simultaneously reducing overall training time and cost requirements. The overall impact of these natural-language tool applications is intended to provide the corporation with a significant competitive advantage through the productivity improvements experienced by the professional staff.

The marketing service or substrategy has changed along with the IC. During the early years, there was a marked concentration on establishing product and service awareness and encouraging TI employees to use their IC to get help with solutions to their computing problems. Marketing was a concentrated function. Once this awareness push was completed, marketing was slowly redirected to help define the new services and determine how the IC would implement or distribute them to TI's internal and possibly some external markets. Central marketing through one office was modified over time to an effort where each key individual, responsible for his or her service or substrategy, was capable of developing and executing his or her own marketing plans.

Non-Dallas IC sites had always worked in this fashion. The gradual change in the marketing approach of the Dallas services was and still is supported by the marketing staff (one person) while continuing to pursue

and endorse the new products, services, and technologies that the IC needs for the future. Marketing has changed from an informing skill or service to one of viewing and preparing the IC for the future. It works hand in hand with other new services and substrategies (as well as the traditional ones) to make sure that the TI IC stays on track in supporting TI business needs.

The growth of the TI IC was probably accelerated by the large number of PCs available to end users and the fact that the corporation had been involved in various forms of end user computing since the 1960s. The ability of the IC to respond to its rapid-changing marketplace has not been fully measured. Current efforts to bring in artificial intelligence, ease-of-use tools, and other new technologies are efforts in the right direction. The final accounting will be in the IC's ability to make a continuing positive contribution to the TI business environment.

THE CITY OF DALLAS, TEXAS

Dallas, Texas, a physically large city with a population approaching 1 million people, has a city budget of approximately $1 billion and employs 14,000 people. Dallas has used the computer since the late 1960s and is very computer-intense at present. Many of the 31 departments in the city structure use the computer for daily tasks, accounting for part of the annual DP budget in excess of $8 million.

One aspect of this city management structure that has far-reaching effects is the fiscal budgeting cycle. Most financial considerations must be budgeted in the current year for action during the next fiscal year. This setup is not found in ICs in private industries. That is, acquisition of computer resources, such as video display terminals, for firms appears to be on an as-needed basis, whereas users in the City of Dallas organizations have to plan ahead in accordance with the budget process.

Information Center for the
City of Dallas

The IC for Dallas is the result of informal end user computing that began in 1979. In the late 1970s, college-trained and self-taught users began to find ways to gain access to the computer and use the FORTRAN language. This continued until 1982, when it became apparent that formal support was required. The users had developed a habit of going to the systems programming staff for assistance. The information center was created to handle this workload as it came to require a full-time position.

The IC staff presently consists of two employees. One came from the application programming division of data services, and the second was formerly an analyst-programmer in the Water Department. They report to the relatively new database administrator, who also oversees technical education for the data services department. All three are women, unusual in the corporate ICs. Another aspect that is somewhat unusual in this structure, but not in any way problematic, is that the database administrator reports to the assistant director of DP technical support. IC managers in industry generally report to the application programming manager or to the head of data processing.

Besides supporting the SAS language, SPSS, and DYL280, the IC staff supports nonproduction use of FORTRAN, COBOL, and PL/1. This is also unusual for an IC but seems to work well and fits the users' backgrounds and needs. Due in large part to the procedural languages, processing is performed in a completely batch environment. The IC shares the single IBM 3083 processor with the rest of the city administration.

The most intense users of IC services are from middle management and first-line supervision, financial applications accounting for the heaviest use. These applications are evenly split between personal and departmental applications, and reports are by far the major product.

At the time of the interview, the data services department did not yet have a DBMS. Backup copies of the extensive files are made nightly. This provides the backup files accessed by the users, requires no extracting on the part of the IC staff, and gives the users direct access to tape images of production data that is less than 24 hours old.

About 20 percent of the city's data is considered sensitive, 30 percent is restricted, and 50 percent is in a category called open records or public data. The control of the first two categories is by the application programs.

The City of Dallas has 140 Texas Instruments personal computers. However, PCs are supported by a separate microcomputer center, which also reports to the assistant director of technical support. The database administrator sees no conflict in the two-group approach or with PC and mainframe usage. She believes that PC considerations of data proliferation and security can be controlled with proper planning.

The data services department and the IC charge back the cost of computer use to the departments. The user departments forecast their requirements, like their equipment needs, in the annual budgeting cycle. Charging is not used as a marketing ploy, nor are free account numbers granted to new users. There is no charge for training, which is presently classroom-style. The IC per se has no budget other than personnel, whose salaries are factored as overhead into the computer usage rates.

In addition to users' forecasts of equipment requirements and computer usage, new MIS projects must also be forecasted. This, by definition, precludes ad hoc, impromptu systems outside of an information center context.

This IC was the only one studied that had a written, formal, published staff selection criteria format, mission statement, and statement of IC services. The database administrator (an M.B.A. with a concentration in MIS) is very well versed in the DP operations and uses planning extensively.

The primary objective of the information center of the City of Dallas is to be more receptive to end users. This was the original goal and one of continuing importance. The primary benefit has been the realization of happier, less frustrated users.

Plans for the future include creation of user groups, more user training, and additional promotion and marketing of the IC. DP plans to acquire a DBMS, and it is believed that a user-friendly query language will be provided with the system.

Update

The user support function in the City of Dallas has increased significantly. The information center now publishes a monthly newsletter that is avidly read by the users. An IC library has been established that makes technical manuals, textbooks, periodicals, and self-training courses available for in-house reference or checkout. Average attendance at the monthly mainframe User's Forum meeting has grown from 25 in 1984 to 50 in 1987. The average number of user requests for assistance per month has grown from 212 in 1985 to 340 in 1987. Growing user interest in Strategic Systems' Planning and Geographic Information Systems has required some additional support. Two new courses for users have been added to the IC curriculum. It was hoped that more courses could be created, but the rising workload left little extra time.

ADR's DATACOM/DB was selected as the city's DBMS. It was installed in May 1985 along with several optional modules including a data dictionary, a fourth-generation language, a query language, an uploading and downloading facility, and a graphics capability. With these new tools and greatly expanded computer hardware, the city is quickly moving its data processing operations into the fourth generation. Two full-time people support the database management function. The learning curve was longer than expected due to the number of modules acquired and the changing hardware and system software environments. To date, nine applications have been developed on the database, including a massive customer information and billing system for Dallas Water Utilities.

The microcomputer center (four employees) and an office automation specialist were brought under the management of the database administration in October 1986. The microcomputer center offers assistance and classes to users. The lab provides a variety of microcomputer hardware and software for general city employee use. The staff also tests and evaluates technical innovations for city adoption. A user microcomputer interest group meets monthly. All microcomputer-related purchases by users must be approved by the micro center. The city standard supported hardware is the Texas Instruments Professional Computer and IBM-PC compatibles. Users can purchase whatever software they like; however, the micro center only supports and provides classes on Easywriter, dBase II and III, and Lotus 1-2-3. The office automation specialist coordinates vendor support for all city word processors, most of which are Wang.

It is hoped that in the near future, all of these divisions can be placed together in order to share resources such as a clerk, the library, training facilities, audiovisual equipment, and storage space more easily. As the technologies merge in the industry, these groups will work together more closely. They are already collaborating on the newsletter, the annual user survey of needs, downloading capabilities, a user handbook, and an internal on-line support system being developed using the new DBMS. The system will help the user support staff manage training records and track manuals and maintain user profiles and mailing lists. Users will be able to view upcoming course schedules, register for classes, and scan the IC library holdings.

In 1986, Texas suffered a sharp drop in the economic climate precipitated largely by decreasing oil prices. The City of Dallas was forced to make significant budget cuts. The information center lost a position that was vacant at the time that a hiring freeze was instituted. Plans to expand service have been put on hold until the economy improves; however, current service will be maintained through reassignment of personnel in the technical support group.

8

Problems Addressed by an Information Center

This chapter gives the user a more specific idea about how an information center can be of value. It features scenarios of problems that arise and shows how the IC staff can provide aid and assistance. The point is that the IC can be of specific help as well as of moral assistance. The areas to be addressed deal with resources, data, tools, at-hand support, quick reaction capabilities, the variety of solutions, and long-term solutions.

RESOURCES

The first specific way in which the IC and its staff can be of value to users is to aid and assist them not only in determining what computer-based capabilities can be of value but also in obtaining these capabilities. For example, a discussion with the IC staff about the user's business would lead the staff member to recommend *mainframe* and *microcomputer* resources that could be of value. Then the IC staff would take action to aid the user in acquiring these resources.

Mainframe

For the mainframe, getting resources means determining that there are capabilities on the mainframe of value to the user and then getting hardware to access the mainframe. Thus the IC staff member would (1) work with the user to determine need, (2) coordinate with technical services as to availability, (3) help the user plan for installation, and (4) upon installation, give the user in-area training.

Assume that the investigation uncovers the need to access the cost ledger in order to track expenditures for a series of projects. Further assume that on-line access is required due to the ad hoc nature of the inquiries. The first resources needed are a terminal and a local printer. The IC staff member would determine the types of terminals available that would be appropriate for the user, learn the requirements for running coaxial cables or using phone lines and modems, and work with technical services to ensure that there are access paths (ports) to the mainframe if the equipment is installed. Next, industrial engineering is contacted for placing the equipment and assurance that adequate and appropriate electrical power is supplied. Upon receipt, technical services and/or the IC staff brings the equipment to user's area, installs it, tests it, and demonstrates it to the user. The user is given appropriate documentation and in-area training in use of the equipment.

This support is in addition to classroom training in mainframe access and capabilities. Generally, this latter training is best done in a formal environment. However, if the need is urgent or the amount of training is small, an IC staff member might provide it to the user in his or her work area on the problem at hand.

Mainframe equipment acquisition tasks	User	IC staff	Other
Determine need	•	•	
Determine computer access			• Technical services
Plan for installation	•		• Industrial engineering
Determine placement and power	•		• Industrial engineering
Install equipment		•	• Technical services
Provide documentation		•	
In-area training		•	

Microcomputer

An example for microcomputer users would be when a user determines that a PC could be of value and approaches the IC for help in determining just what to do. Let us assume that the user and IC staff member reach agreement on the PC software capabilities and now want to obtain hardware. The IC staff would offer aid by (1) helping the user determine what is needed, (2) aiding in selecting specific hardware, (3) assisting in filling out paperwork, (4) helping the user install equipment, (5) locating the documentation, and (6) providing initial hardware training.

The IC staff member, after understanding the nature of the user's tasks, would recommend a complement of equipment for a PC system. This would include the PC and its floppy or hard disk drives, monochrome or color monitor, printer, and any ancillary capabilities. Then the two individuals would either visit the IC computer store or local computer store or look up equipment in a catalog or discount computer service advertisement and then select the equipment specified. The IC staff member would then aid the user in filling out the required paperwork, such as internal documentation for authorization, justification to support the authorization, other data services and company forms, and, finally, the order blanks at the place of purchase. The IC would act as the overseer of the process and make sure that the order was correct, complete, and in accordance with company guidelines.

Upon receipt of the equipment, the IC staff member would uncrate it and assemble the PC system for the user. The accompanying documentation would be explained to the user. Finally, the IC staff member would provide initial hardware training, such as equipment power on, disk format, and printer check. If the user requires further training, as for use of normal PC capabilities and for the software in question, this should be arranged via scheduled IC classes.

Microcomputer equipment acquisition tasks	User	IC staff	Other
Determine need	•	•	
Select specific hardware		•	
Complete paperwork, order	•	•	
Install equipment		•	
Find, explain documentation		•	
In-area training	•	•	

DATA

When a user wants to include specific data in an analysis or report and the data is updated often or of a large volume, it is most helpful to be able to access the data directly on the mainframe or download it to the PC. This method is quite preferable to keying the data manually into the terminal or PC each time it is used. To get and use such data, the user will need assistance in (1) use of data dictionaries, (2) assistance with periodic reports, and (3) determining the owner and obtaining permission to use the data. Only then can the user and IC staff member address the mainframe or microcomputer considerations in data use.

The first task is often finding the data. This entails use of data dictionaries or other data management capabilities to find the data or just looking through periodic reports. Often the user has a copy of a report and the task is determining the source of the report and the file or database used for it. Once that has been achieved, the owner of the data is found and requested to allow this user access and use of the data. This latter task may not be trivial, as owners may have left the company and the records may not be adequate to determine the department of ownership quickly. Once the owner is found, it may be necessary to get permission in writing. Finally, the data can be accessed on the mainframe, with the aid of the IC staff.

General data location tasks	User	IC staff	Other
Review data need	•	•	
Check data dictionary		•	• Data administration
Locate report source	•	•	• Application development
Locate data source	•	•	
Locate data owner	•	•	
Permission to use data	•	•	• Data owner

Mainframe

Having determined where the data is physically located, the user requests the password from the owner. Then the IC staff member works with the mainframe security monitor either to link the appropriate disks, databases, or files to the user or to write a rule so that the computer will allow access. When this is accomplished, the IC staff member ensures that the user has proper account numbers and logon procedures and signs on to the computer application that is to be used for the data query and accesses the data. This is, in effect, providing the user with access training. The user will generally want a copy of the data, so the IC staff member creates a command file that makes the extract copy. The purpose of the command file is so the user can make this extraction in the future. Thus the user ends up with the data he or she needs and training in how to get to it.

Mainframe data determination and use tasks	User	IC staff	Other
Get password from owner	•	•	• Data owner
Security links to files/DB		•	• Data security
Create security rule		•	• Data security
Test access to data		•	
Access/extract data		•	
Train user in access/extract	•	•	
Provide user documentation	•	•	

Microcomputer

When the user wishes to use mainframe data on the microcomputer, the same process is followed as on the mainframe, except that a capability is needed to download or copy the data to a PC storage medium. This generally entails a software capability on the PC that converts the PC to a terminal and copies the file "from the screen" as it is listed on the mainframe or actually activates mainframe software and receives the files on the PC. In either case, the user will need training in these capabilities as well as documentation. If the software does not exist, the IC staff member will have to acquire it for the user.

In either the mainframe or microcomputer case, the aid from the IC does not stop with the access described. Training or emphasis is required in two areas: data security and data integrity. Since the user now has the data in his or her possession, the possibility of a breach of security is increased. The user should be cautioned about storage or destruction of paper copies of the data, copies on flexible or hard disks, or copies in a nonprotected area of the mainframe. In the case of the PC, the user's copy may be on a flexible disk and require physical safety as well as data security considerations. That is, the user must understand dangers to the media and not treat floppy disks with disregard.

The second concern with copies of data is that they be current. With the assumption that the user can only read and copy data and cannot change the source file, the user must ensure that the data is not used outside of the valid time frame of the data. Of final note is the use of the data after change as if it had come directly from the source file.

Microcomputer data determination and use tasks	User	IC staff	Other
Perform mainframe access task	•	•	• See 'mainframe determination and use tasks'.
Acquire download software		•	
Test download capability		•	
Train user in download	•	•	
Provide documentation		•	
Security and integrity training	•	•	

TOOLS

Tools consist of hardware, software, and possibly other items or procedures that will aid the user in accomplishing his or her task. We have already addressed hardware, so we will concentrate on software here, realizing that the potential exists for other types of tools as well as they become evident. The areas of concern will be (1) to determine the nature of the problem, (2) to determine the nature of the solution, (3) to help choose an appropriate tool, (4) to determine the level of training required, (5) to sign the user up for training, and (6) to assist, on request, in the use of the tool.

The determination of the problem, which leads to all other actions, is nontrivial. We addressed this subject in Appendix B of Chapter 1 and again in Chapter 3, giving a road map as to how the user progresses from problem to solution. One way to approach this task is for the user to write a white paper or IC problem definition report describing the nature of the problem and its environment. A white paper is a description of the area of concern and does not find fault. It, or the IC paperwork, should attempt to describe the situation that is to be corrected, the parties involved, and the data that might be needed. Once the nature of the problem has been considered, a second way to address the same subject is to describe what a solution might look like. Thus if you need a five-year budget, draw a mockup of a five-year budget and see if it fits well. In this process, the user, with the aid of the IC staff, is setting the goal toward which he or she will travel. The location of the goal is described as well as what it looks like.

Only after the problem and solution models have been described can an appropriate tool be selected. By use of this path, neither the user nor the IC staff member will assume that any given problem is really a spreadsheet or database problem looking for a solution. Define first and select the tool second. If the tool is readily available, the IC staff member simply aids the user, as appropriate, in using it. If not, the tool must be acquired. This is generally a task for the IC staff member and will involve tasks much as on p. 181 for microcomputer equipment.

After selection, the IC staff must help determine if training is required. The training can range from use of a tutorial, quick help at the terminal or PC by the IC staff member, or scheduled formal classes. If classes are required, the user will need to sign up for the training or enlist the aid of the IC staff member to act as a facilitator if the time pressure is too great to allow training time.

Tasks to acquire and use tools	User	IC staff	Other
Determine problem and solution	•	•	
Select appropriate tool	•	•	
Determine training required	•	•	
Schedule training		•	
Provide documentation		•	
Aid user on problem, as required		•	

AT-HAND SUPPORT

The IC staff aids and assists users in several ways. Formal, scheduled training is one way, but there are others, especially to provide quick answers. These include (1) telephone hotline service, (2) walk-in service in the IC, (3) user-group meetings, and (4) chat sessions and lunchtime seminars.

Telephone Hotline Service

Many references have been made to this form of support, and a number of organizations use this service. The point of this type service is that help is just a phone call away. The assumption is that the person answering the telephone is capable of providing adequate answers, or at least will know where to get an answer and provide the caller with the information. Although this sounds simple, some tasks are involved. For example, making arrangements to ensure that the phone is covered may take administrative personnel, facilities for busy lines, and ways to avoid playing telephone tag.

Each IC will handle the phone differently, using available resources. With the latest telephone capabilities, some of the problems disappear. For example, if the primary IC line is busy or unattended, the telephone automatically transfers the caller to another number. A further extension of this is to have a telephone answering machine as the transfer number, ensuring that the line is answered. In either case, the IC hears the caller. Nevertheless, telephone tag remains a problem and may be acute if the IC staff is small relative to the user community.

Telephone hotline service tasks	User	IC staff	Other
Establish primary phone number		•	• Phone group
Determine phone answering		•	
Provide for phone switching		•	
Provide answering machine		•	
Check up on follow-up		•	

Walk-in Service in the IC

A major appeal of an information center is access to consultants. Part of this is achieved via the telephone and part by walk-in service. If management has allocated adequate IC personnel, users will find a consultant quickly available in the physical IC. As in a barber shop, too long a wait will cause the customer to leave the premises. Thus, as with the barber shop, the IC needs to present a friendly, service-oriented environment. For example, if the wait will be long for a particular consultant or help in general, someone must take the user's name and tell the user that the consultant will call or come to see the user. This is action on the part of the IC staff.

Walk-in service in the IC	User	IC staff	Other
Provide adequate IC staff		• Manager	• Management
Friendly atmosphere		•	
User visit log		•	
Follow-up of user visit		•	

User Group Meetings

When the user community matures in the use of capabilities, users of specific tools will form groups, such as an SAS users group or a Lotus 1-2-3 club. These users will find meeting and discussing successes and failures with the specific tool of great interest and value. The IC can be the catalyst for such meetings, scheduling and hosting them in the IC. The meetings might be held during lunch, during working hours, or after hours. The host should take the responsibility to have an agenda, based on user requests and responses; possibly speakers; an open forum for the participants; and perhaps even a newsletter of results. Although an IC staff member is usually the host initially, this task will often later be assumed by a user, acting as an officer of the group.

User group meetings	User	IC staff	Other
Determine participants		•	• Department specialists
Schedule meeting, advertise		•	
Host meeting, prepare agenda	Leader	•	
Present topics of interest	•	•	
Encourage participation	•	•	
Follow-up on topics		•	

Chat Sessions and Lunchtime Seminars

As an extension of the user groups, semischeduled informal gatherings may attract users who shy away from formal groups or just don't have time for them. For example, many people like to bring lunch and eat while participating in an activity or sitting under a tree. When users know that the IC hosts informal gatherings during lunch on Tuesdays, say, at which on some days there is a low-key seminar on an announced subject of interest, people will wander in and not feel intimidated. After all, they are just there to eat lunch and see what's going on. The IC staff members take turns hosting the meetings and have a (hidden) agenda so as to provide some structure. However, the thrust is to let the meeting flow with the needs of the attendees.

Chat sessions and lunchtime seminars	User	IC staff	Other
Schedule and advertise meeting		•	
Arrange area for lunchtime		•	
Prepare tentative agenda		•	
Present seminar		•	
Guide discussion		•	
Follow-up on topics and needs		•	

QUICK REACTION CAPABILITY (QRC)

There are times when users, especially management- and executive-level users, will need analysis and reports quickly, and the best alternative is simply to ask an IC staff member to provide immediate assistance. The assistance will often be in the form of doing the work as the user sits by and directs. This can be an excellent public relations function and will, on occasion, be the greatest aid to user productivity. The areas of concern will be (1) requests of immediate assistance, (2) the search for data, (3) preliminary analysis and report, and (4) final analysis and report.

Let us assume that the manager of revenue management has been asked to present the recent history of cash management to the board of directors in two hours. The manager receives daily reports on activities and status and feels that the accounts are in good shape. The problem is to access the data from these reports, perform some analysis, and create a summary report quickly. The manager is not versed with the computer to the extent required for this task and needs someone expert in these actions immediately.

1. *Urgent Request*

The manager calls the IC manager and arranges for an IC staff member to provide immediate assistance, doing what is required to get the task done. (The call to the IC manager may or may not be required, depending on the resources available, other user requests, and the nature of the IC organization.) The IC staff member becomes the assistant to the manager for a short time and coordinates with anyone necessary for the task.

2. *Description and Solution Model*

The IC staff member has the manager describe the problem and an indication as to what the solution will look like. The location of data is provided, and the type of analysis is given.

3. *Data Acquisition, Preliminary Analysis, and Report*

The IC staff member accesses the data and prints a copy to be verified by the manager. The manager indicates the type of analysis to perform and the basics of the report layout. This indicates the tool for analysis. Preliminary data access, analysis, and report generation are performed, and the manager reviews the report for correctness and completeness, referring to daily reports.

4. *Changes and Final Report*

The objective of IC tools is to allow quick and easy changes. As the manager reviews the preliminary reports, he notices missing data items, defects in the analysis, and changes that are needed. These things are pointed out to the IC staff member, who makes them on the spot. A second analysis and report are run, reviewed, and changed. The final report is generated just in time for the start of the meeting of the board of directors. The manager leaves, makes the presentation, and returns later to relate how successful the presentation was. The manager returns to his or her normal business, and the IC staff member returns to the IC.

Quick reaction capability immediate assistance	User	IC staff	Other
Manager contacts IC for help	•		
IC staff member specified		Manager	
Problem and solution explained	•		
Data located and printed		•	• Data security
Analysis tool selected		•	
Preliminary analysis and report	•		
Changes made	•	•	
Final analysis and report	•	•	

VARIETY OF SOLUTIONS

The situation of direct, immediate, and concentrated aid to a manager is one example from a variety of services provided in an information center. In this case, the general rule of assisting users in doing their own work was set aside for an immediate problem. Other ways of increasing the variety of services offered include (1) assisting with the quality and volume of reports, (2) discussing the use of summary and exception reporting, (3) explaining the use of microfiche, (4) demonstrating graphics and plotting, and (5) discussing the use of executive information systems, decision support systems, and knowledge-based (expert) systems.

Assistance with Reports

Users will find a variety of report methods of value. Executives will value summary reports and reports by exception, which show out-of-bound conditions. Often the user will not be familiar with features in the IC tools that provide for exception reporting and summarization of data. Each of these conditions reduces the volume of reports and generally increases information content. In all cases, the quality of the report is important. Users may require help in ensuring that the quality of the output device is maintained and in creating reports that are informative and pleasing to their audience. Finally, occasions arise when a large volume of reporting is required, and special care must be taken to ensure that all goes well. For example, large reports may be placed at the end of a queue, delaying their creation. The user may think that the volume is required because of a lack of knowledge, which refers to summary and exception reporting. There are a number of printing devices, such as impact printers and laser printers, each producing a different quality. These considerations require experience to maintain quality and ensure production.

Assistance with Output Media

As there are alternatives for printers for output, there are choices for the medium of the output. Often the preliminary reports and test runs of analysis need only to be viewed for errors and then discarded. Printing can take time, especially during the evolution of an initial solution. An alternative to hard-copy output is to output to a disk file and view the result on screen. This reduces paper use, time, and expense and allows the thought process to proceed faster. In the case where a permanent copy is desired, especially of a large volume of output, microfiche can be used to good advantage. These small (3- by 5-inch) film records hold several hundred pages of print. Use of either disk or microfiche often requires aid from the IC.

Alternatives to printing are the use of graphics on the terminal, and subsequent screen printing and plotting of the output. Both capabilities transform numeric data into pictures, generally reducing the data content and increasing the information content. Each capability requires some knowledge and possibly special equipment. The IC can provide both.

Alternative Systems

So far we have been discussing the use of data from transaction processing systems (TPS) and the analysis and reporting attendant in management information systems (MIS). As users mature and as the level of decision making increases, alternative methods of approaching problems are often required. The use of executive information systems for the executive is proving to be quite valuable and can be end user-developed. With support, an executive's assistant can create and update those special screens that allow the executive to be current with a minimum of effort.

At the executive and middle-management levels, decision support systems can be of significant value. Generally, DSS require access to databases, model bases, and user-oriented dialog systems for control. The IC staff can aid the user with a DSS need, helping to access the data, find or create the model, and create the dialog subsystem wherein the system is accessed and controlled. Finally, an extension of DSS is its enhancement with knowledge bases and expert heuristics. Again, the IC can aid in the creation and operation of such systems.

Information centers and their staffs increase their worth by expanding the variety of services offered. This requires education and training for the IC staff and continued training and assistance for the user community. This effort is part of the charter of the mature information center.

Variety of solutions	User	IC staff	Other
Review user projects	•	•	
Help assure quality printing	•	•	• Operations
Explain use of disk output		•	• Technical services
Suggest summary/exception		•	
Find volume printing source		•	• Operations
Explain microfiche output		•	• Operations
Support graphics output		•	• Operations
Support plotting		•	• Operations
Explain EIS, DDS, and KBS		•	• Application development
Follow-up on user projects	•	•	

LONG-TERM SOLUTION

An objective of the information center manager and staff is to change the environment of the corporation. This includes increasing user computer literacy, constantly upgrading the tools complement, and generally applying computer-based solutions to problems. These activities require continuing efforts on the part of the IC staff. The areas of concern are (1) training, (2) software and hardware evaluation, and (3) technology infusion.

Training

Training involves three phases: (1) scheduling, (2) providing, and (3) follow-up. The IC needs to acquire sufficient staff so that adequate training can be provided without sacrificing consultation services. The way this is determined is a combination of the number of courses, the duration of each course, and the frequency of classes. Generally, training for any particular capability will require a number of offerings of the basic level of training, a few offerings of an advanced course, and an occasional class at the expert level. The more a capability is in demand, the more classes at any given level will be required. Once the type, number, duration, and frequency of classes are decided, the IC can begin advertising classes and providing training.

Assuming that an IC has adequate resources to support the user community, advertising courses is vital to the training effort. The schedule of training should be easy to find, should contain a variety of courses, should be taught at frequent intervals, and should provide one-on-one support as required. A number of short classes will interfere less with daily work routines, and one-on-one reinforcement and follow-up will ensure the highest level of learning. Finally, just as the training should be advertised, so should training successes.

Software and Hardware Evaluation

One function of the information center is evaluation of software and hardware. Part of this task, if not its primary reason, is to limit the large number of available capabilities to a small set that will be of greatest value for the cost incurred, can be supported, and will provide useful capabilities. As the user community matures, users will have use for a greater variety of offerings, and each capability will potentially have a smaller following. Evaluation of capabilities will be required to keep compatibility high. Added to this evaluation is the knowledge of users of new software who can be resources for others. Thus part of the evaluation process is being a databank of knowledgeable users and uses for a capability.

Technology Infusion

Technology changes what we do and the way we do it. The information center has been a harbinger of change by introducing and supporting technology that was new to many people. The introduction and infusion of technology are part of the charter of the IC staff. As they understand their users, the IC staff can review and introduce new technology and new methods. This preserves the value of the IC and the challenge for the IC staff.

Long-term solutions	User	IC staff	Other
Schedule training		•	
Advertise training schedules		•	
Follow-up on training	•	•	
Review new software		•	• Vendors
Review new hardware		•	• Technical services
Recommend new methods to users		•	• Management
Continue to infuse technology	•	•	• Management
Follow-up with users	•	•	

SUMMARY

- Information centers are of greatest value when they are flexible and offer a variety of services.
- Mainframes and microcomputers have different uses and requirements, and the IC staff and user must address them differently. However, data always has the same need for security and integrity.
- Data services is seldom the owner of the data, more often the custodian. Only owners, not custodians, can give permission to use data.
- Mainframe data is a primary resource for microcomputer users. Download capabilities may seem awkward but are very valuable. Data outside of the mainframe environment is always at more risk.
- A telephone is a valuable tool for the IC and the user. A busy or unanswered telephone is a source of frustration.
- User groups are fun and provide a resource for all.
- Providing a quick reaction capability (QRC) for management is good public relations and can foster continuance. It is very productive for this group of users.
- Quality output always makes the task of greater value; volume seldom does. If volume is required, choose microfiche, summarize, make a report by exception, or use disk output.
- The long-term objective of the information center is to support change.

Key Terms

Determine need	Facilities planning
Paperwork	Documentation
Download of data	Telephone switching
User log	User follow-up
User group	Seminar agenda
Quick reaction capability (QRC)	Output to disk
Microfiche	Plotted output
Executive information system (EIS)	Decision support system
Knowledge-based system (KBS)	Technology infusion
Software and hardware evaluation	

DISCUSSION QUESTIONS

1. What is involved in planning for a significant amount of new hardware in the user's area? Who are the participants, and what does each do?

2. For what use is hardware documentation?

3. What special care is required for a microcomputer system?

4. How do you know what report you are using?

5. Why get the file password from the user? Why not from data security?

6. What should you do with data and its storage medium after downloading?

7. What do you think of using a telephone answering device in an IC for calls when staff members are busy or away from their desks?

8. How long would you wait for service in an IC? Would you come back if you left without assistance?

9. How would you organize and advertise a users' group?

10. Certain information centers apply the rule "Never do programming." The QRC service says, "Do what the customer requires." Are these rules in conflict?

11. Describe a situation in which you would use disk, fiche, or plot output.

CASE STUDIES

ZALE CORPORATION

Zale Corporation, established as a jewelry retailer in 1924 in Wichita Falls, Texas, is today the world's largest retailer of fine jewelry and one of the nation's dominant specialty retail organizations. The Zale's jewelry stores serve Middle America in 793 stores, while another 328 carriage-trade jewelry stores nationally identified as Bailey, Banks, and Biddle jewelers, operate in a number of local markets. The company also operates leased jewelry departments in major department stores nationwide. In total, there are more than 1,300 outlets worldwide.

Zale is now headquartered in Irving, Texas, and in 1986 had sales of $1 billion. Zale employs 1,000 people at its corporate headquarters in Irving and an additional 7,000 in the stores and regional credit centers nationwide. The company began business in 1924 and introduced the use of computers into accounting in the 1950s. The present computer support is a quad-processor IBM Model 3090, supporting a 100 percent batch environment for end user processing, which is to say that computer use beyond file creation and editing is in batch mode.

There are more than 400 IBM Model 3178 video display terminals in the corporate headquarters, providing access to production applications, plus a small number of personal computers. Each department operates on a monthly profit-and-loss (P&L) statement, and any expenditures are well thought out. Personal computers and video terminals are expenses on the P&L statements and are therefore brought into the firm on a one-at-a-time basis.

Zale's Information Center

The introduction of personal computers began in 1978, when it appeared that proliferation might be commencing in spite of the P&L statement considerations. In addition, there was some informal end user computing in process with the use of SAS and DYL280. MIS viewed the PC introduction rate with concern, and it appeared that an IC could be a way to keep control of the environment, avoid the problems attendant with PC proliferation, and provide official suppport to end users. In addition, Zale was spending a significant amount on outside timeshare ($200,000 per year). To control all of these situations, System W was purchased, after extensive evaluation of several products. The actual IC was instituted soon afterward in January 1983. A specific objective and benefit projected was through the use of a consistent approach to PC hardware and mainframe software acquisition and use.

The Zale's IC continues to have only one staff member, the original IC manager. For this reason, much support is limited. For example, PC training is provided via tutorial software on the PCs and from outside firms. However, a specific thrust of the IC manager is to interject planning and policy in the area of end user computing. The small size has not stopped the support of the user and the bettering of relations with MIS.

The primary users of the information center are the business professionals. These are the departmental group members rather than specialized staff members or management. Middle management comprises the next largest group, departmentwide applications being the principle type of use. Reports and analysis are the primary output.

There are 13 IBM, 10 Apple, and 9 Radio Shack PCs. All of these brands are acceptable in the corporate policy guidelines; however, IBM is the preferred vendor and the only one supported by the IC. As noted, the PC must be cost-justified, and the acquisition rate is low by design. The basic configuration is now the IBM Model 3270/PC, which communicates with the mainframe via coaxial cable.

There is no central control point for data, and the user may have to go to the application programmer in MIS, a hard-copy report, or a CICS screen to find the data he or she needs. If extract-copying a file is appropriate, the user generally does the task from backup tapes.

The IC manager emphasizes the need for business analysis skills as well as communication and interpersonal skills for a successful IC. To these skills, he adds a good background in DP as requirements for IC staff members. He is very sensitive to the need for being able to relate to the business of the firm, not just work out problems.

Downloading of data to PCs is being discouraged until the IBM 3270/PC is in general use. However, even then data upload will be highly restricted. At present, upload is possible only via standard data entry.

Data security is a major concern at Zale and is controlled on the mainframe via ACF2 software. Control is at logon, with the user first requesting access to the computer region where the desired application processes. If the user requests logon to the region containing a secured application such as credit application and he or she is not authorized credit access, the logon will fail. Once the user gains access to a region, there is further security by application.

Chargeback is on the basis of artificial units, in many cases, at the users' request. For example, a SAS run carries a fixed charge of $35, a CICS transaction has a specific charge, and some departments' applications charge by their own basic units, such as number of checks written. The IC manager believes that this will change eventually to use true resource units as the basis of chargeback.

The primary objective of the IC is to provide guidance in the area of end user computing in two directions: (1) MIS management of desirable avenues of use and (2) assistance to the users in solving their own business problems. Although access to data is no easier, use of data is easier. The success of the IC has been demonstrated by the conversion of manual to computer-based systems and the use of IC capabilities after hours for company business.

The primary benefits are increased productivity in the user community (clearly evidenced but not measured) and the view of MIS in a better role, as a centralized contact for problems and providing more responsive service. Future plans call for more staff, better support for mainframe products, better balance of PC and mainframe products, and use of graphics.

Update

In September 1984, a staff member was added to the information center. The primary role of this person was to provide support for System W and other mainframe products. This individual was selected from the user community due to her excellent communication skills, previous analysis background, and skills in the use of mainframe products at Zale.

In February 1985, the information center was relocated to a more spacious location, away from its MIS parent and deep in the middle of the user departments, where it remains today. At the time of its move, the IC added a second PC for walk-in users. There are now three PC systems available on a first-come, first-served basis, each with a well-rounded assortment of business software loaded and available through an easy-to-use in-house-developed menu system.

Late in 1984, an office automation pilot project was begun at Zale to determine the potential value in the use of PCs with word processing software. Included in this project was the strategy to incorporate mainframe-based electronic mail. The information center manager was brought into the project as an internal consultant. When the IC relocated in February, the office automation staff of two joined it in the new office and later moved under the direct control of the IC manager. This project was responsible for the installation of 45 Model 3270 PCs.

In a follow-up study, the users reported an average 45 percent internal rate of return based on productivity gains. The electronic mail products were later dropped from the project, although a personal appointment and telephone message package was retained.

In the summer of 1985, another staff member was added, bringing the total staff to five. This new staff member was a recent college graduate with a B.S. degree in business systems and previous experience with personal computer systems.

At around the same time, the information center hosted visiting data processing management teams from Italy and Finland. The IC manager was invited to speak to IBM in Raleigh, North Carolina, on the topic of acquisition controls and establishing a positive user environment.

The office automation project was extended to the company's New York office in January 1986. A team of two IC staff members went to New York to install six 3270 PC systems and conduct training on the hardware and software.

In late 1986, the IC guided a user group in the installation of 15 PC systems in field offices around the country. The equipment displaced dumb terminals connected to leased lines out of the Dallas office. The primary justification for PC equipment was economic: PCs could be leased more cheaply than terminals!

The information center kicked off a quarterly newsletter in the fall of 1986. It includes software tips, product announcements, and maintenance information.

The population of PCs has grown to almost 150. Only IBM and approved compatibles have been acquired since this program started in 1983. Only major brands of equipment are allowed; "clone" PCs are not purchased. The acquisition policy has not changed substantially since 1983, except to become more comprehensive and clearly defined.

The information center provides complete turnkey services in the PC acquisition process, from business problem analysis and assistance with cost justification to system purchase and installation. Vendor negotiations and contacts are likewise managed by the center and not the purchasing department. Most add-on purchases are also handled by the IC as a convenience for the users; this also allows the center to keep up with what the users are doing. Routine postimplementation support and consulting are a natural extension of the services available.

During this time, budget has not been made available for formalized training. Consequently, the IC staff is called upon to provide more basic levels of assistance than it would prefer.

Today, the information center continues to maintain high visibility in the corporate structure. There is regular contact with all levels of management and staff. The IC is active in a group known as the Dallas Office Automation Roundtable, which includes members from many large firms in the Dallas area. Another corporate roundtable has just started, with the Zale IC as an early member. The IC manager just concluded $2\frac{1}{2}$ years as vice-chairman and later chairman of the North American System W Users Group.

Internally, the emphasis of the IC continues to be user effectiveness and productivity. Additional products for the mainframe are being researched, all of the application development and fourth-generation-language type. The corporate mainframe has grown to an IBM 3090-200, running MVS/XA. File transfer is available for PC users. Research and evaluation of new PC software and hardware are always under way. The IC is expanding its role by starting to develop small PC-based application systems for its users.

Pier 1 Imports, Inc.

Pier 1 Imports, a specialty retailer, presents unusual imported items at affordable prices to adventurous customers. The merchandise focus is on home furnishings. The company owns and operates 252 stores in the United States and Canada. It is the nation's top import chain.

Headquartered in Forth Worth, Texas, Pier 1 had 1987 sales of $262 million. It employs 4,000 people, 400 of whom are in the corporate office. The firm is expanding its operations and plans to add 152 retail stores by the end of 1990.

Due to the expansion of business, the limits of the existing NCR computer equipment and application aids, and a shortage of NCR-oriented programmers, Pier 1 is converting to IBM hardware and replacing and upgrading all of its software. The firm is able to acquire most of the financial, general ledger, and payroll packages that it requires. (Major packages, such as Payroll, Human Resources and Project Tracking, General Ledger, and Accounts Payable, are being obtained from Management Science America, Inc.) It was originally believed that the applications for merchandising, inventory, and distribution would have to be re-created internally due to unique features required. To ease the burden, the DP department used a model created by IBM and purchased database structures from an outside firm. This is estimated to have saved two years of effort and allowed the transition from all-batch to interactive database operations. As work continued, however, it was determined that these three functions could be effectively purchased after all.

Pier 1 was founded in the mid-1960s, began using computers in the early 1970s, and is presently computer-intensive. The on-line systems will allow all buyers and other corporate staff to access much of the company data via 3270-type terminals on their desks.

Two problems cropped up during the batch-to-on-line transition period, both related to support of users of DP services. The first problem was that only one person was available for maintenance or changes to the old systems. These applications are modified only if a positive return on the investment can be identified. This environment left no one to support end user-requested services. The second problem was that the application backlog lengthened and the pressure from the user increased. Realizing the impact of this environment, the purchase of Radio Shack TRS-80 microcomputers began in July 1982 for the purpose of satisfying the immediate needs of the end users via VisiCalc. The one individual designated to support maintenance also supports the micros where possible, with training being left up to the user. This was considered a reasonable alternative initially and was the beginning of the formal support of end user computing and the information center at Pier 1. Also, a hotline was instituted whereby any end user could phone a single number for any problem related to computer software or hardware. The hotline has proved highly successful.

Mainframe support commenced in August 1984 with the advent of on-line systems and the opening up of Easytrieve to more users. One staff member was recruited from a user area to work with end users in any way possible. A specific objective and benefit of the IC staff and the hotline has been the positive effect on IS-user relations. The IC manager believes he has seen users change their views of what DP can and will do.

Pier 1 originally used an internally developed mainframe data security capability. It secures data to the database or file only and not to lower levels. Logon IDs and passwords are controlled by the database administrator. With the changeover of computer environments, IMS is being eliminated, and ACF2 has become the security software. There is extensive PC-to-host connectivity planned and in progress.

In the early stage of on-line services, chargeback was for batch processing only, via an account number system in the batch job control language. This gave the early on-line users a free ride. With the maturing of the timeshare environment, all chargeback was eliminated.

An early objective in the introduction of on-line services was to provide services on the mainframe that will satisfy the user community and avoid PC proliferation. The IC manager believed that the mainframe environment could be made more secure with less effort and provide advantages to the user that the PC environment did not have. However, in early 1986, the information center concept and installation changed. The new charter was to control the acquisition of microcomputer hardware and software and to provide user education on their use. The microcomputers currently supported are IBM and Compac units. The supported packages are Lotus 1-2-3, Multimate Advantage word processing, and dBase III Plus. Two microcomputers are dedicated to training and use

multimedia training packages. The company is phasing out the last of the TRS-80s.

In light of the dynamic changeover in progress, the need to educate users concerning data processing practices, and the need to train them in the use of the mainframe applications, the IC manager originally took a wait-and-see attitude on IC marketing. With the change in practice, an IC newsletter was created, and a survey is in progress on desktop publishing.

The objective of the information center now is to be a focal point for PC utilization at Pier 1 Imports. Future plans call for controlled flexibility through the use of PCs, increased user awareness of data processing, increased communications and decreased backlogs, and increased productivity of DP and user personnel.

9

Building (or Rebuilding) an Information Center

If your company presently has an information center, chances are that you are concerned about (1) ensuring that it is proper and adequate for your environment, (2) achieving the desired end result, and (3) being as effective as presently possible, given normal resource constraints. On the other hand, if you do not have an IC, you may well be on the market for one. This chapter will be a discussion of how to initiate an information center, presented so that the model can be compared with existing ICs. From the model, one should be able to build a new information center of great value to the firm or evaluate and renovate an existing IC.

As indicated in the early chapters, pressure for the creation of an IC can come from several sources. One is "users' pull," significant user activity such as informal end user computing or an outcry due to large backlogs of systems development work. "Data services push" occurs when that organization sees no relief from the overload condition and moves to initiate this new form of delivery of services. Both responses are reactions to bad and worsening conditions. An alternative reason to encourage end user computing via the formal support environment of the information center is a change of management attitude. The community of knowledge workers is a valuable resource that can be more effective and productive when supported by the capital and resource investment of the information center. This realization may be enough for management to take positive action and create an IC. James Martin recommended this at Texas Instruments, and the board of directors took positive action.

CONSIDERATIONS FOR CREATING AN INFORMATION CENTER

The 20 IC managers interviewed told stories of creating information centers that were unlike anything found in management texts. For the most part, the creation exercise was reactionary, at the direct request of a corporate executive, to solve a specific, short-term problem. There was little intent, in many of the firms, to create what is now the formal support environment for end user computing. The intent was to solve an urgent problem and to do it quickly. The task was successful, the immediate problem was solved, and, in the process, it was realized that an entity had been created and demonstrated to be of great value. At that point, the information center was officially recognized as a desirable concept.

If you are in the process of overtly creating an information center, you can take one of two tacks. The first is reactionary. The second, recommended method involves planning and coordination. The reactionary model is presented first for emphasis.

Reactive Support Model for Data Services

Figure 9-1 shows the chronology of a reactive support effort for end user computing. It starts with a realization of an out-of-control condition and seeks immediately to impose needed control. Management is made aware of the true nature and size of the backlogs, and data services acts quickly to become part of the process. The result is a realization that planning is in order, and the outcome is the beginning of end user computing support.

Figure 9-1 describes two concepts: an early rush to do something and eventual recognition of the need for management in the process. The initial intent may have been to support the idea, making sure the bases were covered, and wait until the idea died. However, as the idea lived, the support evolved until a managed concept was installed.

It was noted earlier that few of the 20 information centers studied involved significant amounts of preplanning or support justification. Generally, the ICs developed quickly due to an urgent need. If your firm is in such a predicament, follow suit. However, whether pressed for time or having the luxury of slow development, some planning should be done for any new venture, and an IC is no exception. The experience of many ICs is that a planning period of one to three months is adequate and will provide sufficient structure and coordination. During this time period, the following agenda will be in order:

- Management approval of the information center
- Organization of the IC team
- Planning for the IC
- Continuous review of the concept

Management Approval of the Information Center

To initiate an information center, company management and/or data services must first take what would appear to be obvious steps: They must (1) agree to initiate the information center, (2) select the IC manager (the champion), and (3) establish management support.

1. Initial response
    A. Control issues
        i. Control outside timeshare expenditures
        ii. Control proliferation of PCs
        iii. Control in-house uses of the computer
    B. Management of resources issues
        i. Address both backlogs
        ii. Add resources to work on backlogs
        iii. Recharter review committee
    C. Data services management issues
        i. Insulate programmers from interruptions
        ii. Allocate personnel better
        iii. Acknowledge users
        iv. Maintain security
2. Intermediate or stopgap support
    A. Inventory of data services resources
    B. Allocation of customer support personnel
    C. User access to programming languages
    D. Inventory of present user accesses
    E. More active data administration function
    F. Establishment of PC consultant
3. Initiation of formal support
    A. Information center manager named
    B. IC staffing level determined
    C. Official list of supported user capabilities
    D. Basic training schedules established
    E. Physical IC facilities created
    F. Assistance to user-acquiring resources
4. Multitiered support
    A. Emphasis of departmental specialists
    B. Additional training
        i. Advanced classes
        ii. Vendor-conducted training
        iii. Computer-based training
    C. Management support
        i. All processing is to support management
        ii. EUC and formal development are both viable
        iii. Management assists users in acquisitions
    D. Data services support
        i. Separate processors
        ii. Accessible data or extract copies
        iii. Distributed IC staffs and analysts
        iv. Career path for IC staff

Figure 9-1   Chronology of a reactive user-support effort

The agreement to establish the IC can be in the form of a memo or a simple order. However, the determination of management support is not necessarily contained therein. Thus the champion—the person who will take the challenge of the IC and carry it forward day after day—once identified, must ensure that executive management does indeed provide its personal and professional support. One form of support was provided at Texas Instruments in Dallas, where the board of directors took an active interest and an IC staff group was established to aid these people directly. Not only did the board give the go-ahead to initiate the concept, but it also provided some of the first clients. This had a dramatic effect on acceptance of the idea.

New ideas require forces to ensure their survival. For some ideas, masses gather to support the concept, seeming without a leader. However, this is unusual; more often, success is tied to the emergence of a champion. The term *champion* is well chosen, because just as a Knight of the Round Table would champion his king or lady, the IC manager champions the information center concept. The manager must ward off attackers and keep the idea from folding under doubts, paperwork, and apathy. Though the IC manager will not wear the armor of a knight, he or she must have armor-thick skin for protection against defenders of the status quo. The manager is the unflagging advocate for the idea.

IC manager candidates can come from many sources. While almost half come from application programming and thus have an understanding of the formal systems development process, others come from non-DP sources inside and outside the firm and occasionally from other areas of data services. It is undoubtedly more important for the candidate to possess certain characteristics than to come from a particular background. These characteristics, noted in Table 9-1, center on technical skills coupled with an outgoing nature, persistence, and the ability to gain the confidence of data services and company management. The individual must be able to understand and discuss MIS and the user's business. In

TABLE 9-1   CHARACTERISTICS THAT CONTRIBUTED TO THE SELECTION OF THE IC MANAGER

Computer or technical background
Background in technology implementation

Outgoing, friendly nature
Teaching experience
Sales background
Communication skills
User orientation

Leader of group that became IC
Experience with user tools

Promotion
Display of interest

fact, a business background is of great value but must temper and be supported by technical skills.

The research that supports this book indicates that the IC manager is vital to the success of the information center, more important than the size of the staff, the capabilities provided, or the shining glory of the physical facilities. Quite simply, a champion is required. Find one, give him or her the support of data services and user management, and you are well on your way to success.

In reality, the information center idea is not hard to protect, once the initial succcess stories begin to be heard. However, the champion cannot rest on minor successes but must continue to sell the concept. The catalytic nature of the IC is so great that it deserves to be hailed, far and wide as one of the greatest productivity tools available. This is the charter of the IC manager, to champion the IC. The word may be spread via presentations to management and executive meetings, training seminars, lunchtime open forums and marketing show-and-tell lectures, talks with data services, and MBWA ("marketing by walking around").

The form of management approval and support seems to be embodied in the IC manager, the champion. When such a person is selected and designated to be successful, management approval and support are evident. Until this person is in place, the concept is just another idea. Thus it is vital for the champion to be found, selected, and appointed.

> *To ensure the success of IC creation, tell all employees of your intent. Then find a champion and provide him or her with full support.*

Organizing the Team

Once the word has been given to initiate an information center and the IC manager has been selected, a team should be organized to guide the creation of the IC. This team, with the IC manager as the head, should include members from data services, potential user departments, and possibly an outside consultant and/or an IBM staff member. These groups have different views, agendas, objectives, and benefits to be gained and need to interact in the early stages of the creation effort.

The *IC manager*, as the champion, guides the process but does not dictate it. He or she must be sensitive to the views and goals of the other participants. From this leadership should come an integration of ideas in such a way that all feel a part of the process. Specifically, the users will want total access, and data services will want to retain security and control. Experience has shown that a compromise can be reached, with both parties gaining over what was in place before the IC. The IC manager must guide and direct, negotiate, and never let the process die or get bogged down.

Since the information center has the computer and resident data as its center, *data services* will be sensitive to what it does and how. Therefore, the team should have representatives from application development, data administration, and technical services. *Application development* will be a likely source of the first IC staff members, and the IC will take over, or originate, the customer service function possibly found in this department. Without an understanding of the tasks and responsibilities of the IC and formal development groups, stress could develop between the two groups. With an appreciation of the logical separation of duties, application development should quickly value the new organization.

Access to data is vital to the success of the IC, and *data administration* knows where the data is located, who owns it, and how it can be accessed. Data administration will have a natural fear of hordes of end users accessing the data, affecting data integrity, and violating all security. However, the fears are generally due to a lack of understanding. Involvement in the team will give data administration an appreciation of the value of the data resource to the users and the need for ready but protected access. Extract copies and read-only access eliminate most of the fears, and a management policy on use of downloaded files will address other important concerns.

The last group of data services normally involved is *technical services* because they will be the ones to control user interference with production processing. They also will have a natural fear of the effect of large numbers of untrained users accessing the processing power and storage of the computer. Many of their fears can be resolved with standard security measures, separate mainframe processors and/or personal computers, and an understanding of the level of processing required. Technical services, like the other members of data services, can be opponents or supporters of end user computing; it all depends on their involvement and understanding.

The involvement of *potential user departments* will take two forms. If there is presently informal end user computing, these present users are natural candidates for the team. They understand the need for the support concept and will be willing participants in a team that will provide what they know is needed. If the company does not have active users, likely candidates must be found. These must be visionaries who can see the value of a process they have not tried. In either case, it is best to have seasoned employees with ties and loyalties in the organization, as opposed to new college graduates. These representatives will likely be the first departmental specialists and the local champions of the IC concept. Their appointment is not intended for appeasement; they are included as active clients who will be instrumental in the initial success of the idea.

The final member of the team may well be overlooked but is a valuable addition. The *outside consultant or IBM representative* can bring to the organization and the team the experience required to avoid early mistakes and make the team's efforts highly productive. IBM brings the corporate view of the concept. Consultants may bring a variety of experiences. Both are temporary members who have the view of a disinterested party and wish to aid without political ties. They have seen the mistakes and successes, the trials and the triumphs, the feuds and the understanding necessary for resolution. Although this will involve an out-of-pocket expense, the up-front money should be very productive for the team's efforts.

Planning for the IC

Once the concept has been inaugurated, the IC manager selected, and the team organized, the task at hand is to address these five issues:

- Indication of objectives and charter
- Anticipated benefits
- Capabilities and ground rules
- Implementation cost
- Timetable of events

The *indication of objectives and charter* sets out what is to be achieved by the information center and formulates the initial mission statement under which it will operate. At this point, the user community should be determined to establish the degree of maturity of the early users and the level of immediate assistance that will be required. From this will come an indication of the early levels of training, consultation, and even direct programming assistance. The result of this review will be the mission statement used to guide the actions of the IC staff. If direct programming assistance is deemed desirable, it can be so stated in the charter and resources acquired to accommodate this task. If this specific level of support is deemed undesirable, the charter can give protection to the staff as they guide the users to do their own work.

The verbalizing and listing of *anticipated benefits* will provide a target at which the IC staff can aim as they begin to support the user community. ICs are often established to control the expense of outside timeshare and the internal proliferation of personal computers. If the benefits relate to these two phenomena, the IC must provide alternatives in the form of capabilities and support. If, however, the objective is to introduce end user computing to the firm, the benefits may be stated as less tangible. Each organization will anticipate somewhat different benefits from the IC, and noting them will give an idea of the direction of the new support group and resources required.

With the specification of objectives and benefits will come an indication of the *capabilities* to be provided and the *ground rules* under which the IC will operate. The capabilities range from IC staff to computer equipment. Ground rules, as possibly part of the charter and mission statement, will indicate what support will be provided and what will not be furnished. Thus the objectives and anticipated benefits will produce a list of capabilities and ground rules that will give rise to a charter and mission statement.

Determining the capabilities to be provided represents the physical aspects of the IC. This collection will tend to start with a list of the computer applications presently available that are appropriate for end users and evolve from there. Added to this will be the requirements for IC staff personnel, common facilities, data access, security, and considerations of charging and promotion.

Since many information centers will be established using existing distributed capabilities—that is, the users will access them via existing remote devices—the *IC staff* will be the first order of consideration. That is to say, a staff will in many cases be more important than common facilities. In all cases, these people will advise, consult, troubleshoot, train, and console, whether in the physical IC, on the phone, or in the user's area. Thus the IC planning team must address the level of support to be provided as embodied in the number and capability of the IC staff members. Other than the consideration of management support and the selection of the champion, the number and capability of the

IC staff will be the most important deliberation of the IC planning team. If management agrees to the IC concept and then fails to allocate adequate staff, the IC will be significantly limited.

Specifically, the team must determine from the objectives, charter, and user population the number of staff members, their qualities, and their duties. The initial user-to-staff ratio for a nontechnically oriented user community should be near 20 to 1, with most staff personnel performing the duties of consultant and trainer. (Refer to Figure 4-1, p. 97, for detailed recommendations.) With time, the supported user population will change in that early users tend to be more innovative and technically oriented, whereas the next group of users requires significantly more aid and assistance. Thus the supported population will change over time, and the number and capabilities of the staff will generally evolve with the users.

The question of *physical IC facilities* addresses two primary issues: (1) the extensive use of microcomputers versus a dependence on mainframe capabilities and (2) the dedication of a mainframe to support end user computing. The second concern considers the need for separate facilities for the users but will be decided to a large extent by the level of resources available. Will management obtain or allocate a mainframe to the IC? The answer is difficult because of the need for easy access to production data versus the advisability of separation of environments.

Additional concerns for physical facilities, other than the common IC office space and openly available equipment, are for the use of microcomputers (PCs). As noted, many ICs have been initiated to control PCs, and the use and support of these devices will be implied. However, support of PCs is not automatic when the pre-IC environment is main-frame-intensive. Thus the team must determine the environment and how it should evolve to serve the charter of the IC. If support of PCs is part of the mission, hardware and software evaluation will be more intense than in a mainframe environment, and there will be a specific need to indicate those capabilities officially supported by the IC.

Part of the physical facilities of an information center will be the office and training area for the IC staff. If the IC concept is basically a distributed hotline support group, these centralized facilities may be minimal. However, in many cases a significant training, consulting, administrative, and open-access equipment facility is desirable and thus must be specified by the IC planning team. The environment will entail offices, work areas, training rooms, training computers or terminals, and supply rooms.

The *tools supported* will relate to the physical facilities. For both mainframe and PC environments, the planning team must address hardware and software support. This means number, kinds, access methods, need for public availability and checkout, and self-instruction or formal training. If the equipment and software are acquired by the IC and provided to the users, methods of requisition, acquisition, and installation must be considered. If the users must get their own hardware and software, procedures must be established. The question of official and unofficial (nonsupported) PC equipment and software must also be considered.

Even though the production environment may be a database medium, users often need a database management system that is more suited to their tasks and methods. Whether data access is direct read-only or involves extract copies, the IC may best support data use by a user-oriented database management system. The planning team must not assume that production capabilities are adequate for the users.

Training has been mentioned and deserves additional review. Training is a prime task of the IC staff and will produce major benefits. The planning team must determine the training needs of the users in relation to their backgrounds, the capabilities provided, the physical facilities, and the speed with which management wishes to pursue end user development. IC staff members involved with training are not available for user consultation and will affect the number of staff members required for any given level of user support.

Data availability and access have also been mentioned as considerations. Early users of the IC may find they can do without computer-resident data, but it takes only a few months until the data becomes the most important part of the process. The planning team must take into account the data needs of the users along with data services needs for *security and control*. The existence of a user DBMS in the IC with periodic extracting of production data is a conscious decision point for the planning team that can have excellent results. This early decision can resolve potential problems and concerns in the minds of data services team members.

Charging, promotion, and marketing of the information center will relate to the charter, anticipated benefits, growth rate, and other considerations. Marketing and promotion efforts must be tied directly to the staffing levels and the IC's ability to support large numbers of users. The concept of charging is a management issue, and the IC may be the instrument to change the view of this allocation method. Charging, promotion, and marketing revolve around the charter and management expectations. If they are not in synch, the results can be unpleasant.

From the planning team will come an indication of the *implementation cost* and a *timetable of events*. This would include the actual out-of-pocket budgets required for purchases, the costs of the physical facilities, and the costs of the IC staff and manager. Even though this may involve a transfer cost, the estimation of these budgets will be of value in determining the cost-versus-benefit figures that may be required. Many ICs studied did not develop a detailed estimation of the cost of installing an IC. Even if this is not a firm requirement, the creation of these costs will be a good exercise in anticipation of addressing a change in method of providing computer services.

Along with the costs will come a need for a timetable of when staff, facilities, capabilities, and training will be available. Training will tend to be an early requirement, along with equipment and software purchase. The first few months will be hectic as the new concept is established, and a plan for implementation will be of great aid.

Continuous Review of the Concept

The need for review and reevaluation does not stop when planning for the information center is complete and the IC is installed. Startup is always characterized by an atmosphere of great excitement in planning the facility, hiring the staff, acquiring new capabilities, and starting the training. However, with time, the concept becomes commonplace, even though encouraging results are received every month. To support the continuance of the IC concept, the IC manager must address the following:

- Survey of users for costs and benefits
- Acquisition of adequate staff
- Career paths for IC personnel
- Promotion to encompass all users
- Support of the concept for continuance

To determine the continuing benefit of the IC, a *survey of users* should be conducted periodically. On a semiannual basis, survey forms should be sent to users who have completed tasks during that time period, as determined by the End User Developed Project Description Form (to be introduced in Chapter 10). The surveys will allow the users to indicate the value of end user computing and the tangible and intangible savings achieved. These benefits can be compared with the IC costs to show the return on investment generated by the support of end user computing via the information center. This survey to show cost avoidance will be important to the continuance of the IC. As use of its services increases, so will costs. As with use of production services, there will be a tendency to control the costs of EUC. Thus it will be vital to be able to show the benefits of these expenditures. The surveys provide this data.

The supported user community will grow with time. The characteristics of these users will change as more timid users avail themselves of the IC services. Keeping track of the number and characteristics of users and ensuring a proper user-to-staff ratio will be important. This means acquiring staff as the supported community grows and staff members leave for other opportunities. The information center assignment should be viewed as a temporary situation for the staff, and plans should be made for turnover of these valuable employees. The IC staff members have high visibility, and, as motivated personnel, they will want to pursue their own career paths. The IC manager should welcome the movement of staff personnel and overtly consider *career paths for the IC staff*. With the experience achieved in the IC, staff members will become some of the most valuable and sought-after employees in the company and, as such, are ready candidates for promotion. To deny this natural tendency is to deny the nature of the IC.

With adequate staff, *marketing and promotion to encompass all potential users* should be undertaken. As noted, the early users are more technically oriented and competent but are few in number. Great productivity can be achieved by supporting the less technically competent but more numerous personnel. Promotion to these people will have great returns.

The everyday job of the IC manager is to remain the champion of the IC concept. Time will dull the brightness of the concept unless the champion is ever mindful of keeping the story and benefits in front of users and management alike. *Continuous support of the IC concept* will be necessary to ensure the continued receipt of benefits and will reap rich rewards.

IC Creation Checklist

Figure 9-2 is a composite checklist of the duties and tasks needed in setting up an information center. This can be used as the IC team's itinerary, a guide for their actions.

Building a Centralized Information Center

One aspect of the IC that the team will address is that of a physical center. If the choices are limited, the team will make best use of what is available. Given the availability of funds and the ability to build IC quarters or refurbish existing facilities, the team might choose to create an IC based on the two models shown in Figures 9-3 and 9-4. Figure 9-3 shows the placement of all the resources we have discussed. There is room for con-

---

1. Management approval of the information center
   A. Agreement to initiate IC
   B. Memo or direction
   C. Selection of IC manager (champion)
2. Organization of the IC team
   A. Announcement of IC manager, team leader
   B. Data services participants
   C. User department members
   D. Consultant or IBM representative
3. Planning for the IC
   A. Indication of objectives
   B. Anticipated benefits
   C. Determination of user population and characteristics
   D. Capabilities and ground rules
       i. EUC mainframe computer facilities
       ii. Personal computer support
       iii. EUC software
       iv. IC staff
       v. Common facilities
       vi. Data sources and access
       vii. Data extraction
       viii. Programming support
       ix. Security
       x. Training required
       xi. Training methods and facilities
       xii. Charging procedures
       xiii. EUC equipment acquisition
       xiv. Promotion
       xv. IC charter
       xvi. Mission statement
   E. Implementation cost
   F. Timetable of events
4. Continuous review of concept
   A. Survey of users for cost and benefit
   B. Acquisition of adequate staff
   C. Career paths for IC personnel
   D. IC promotion to encompass all users
   E. Support of the concept for continuance

Figure 9-2   IC creation checklist

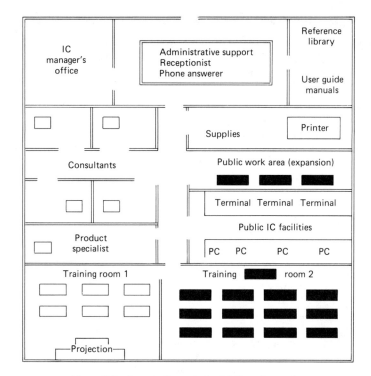

Figure 9-3 Layout of a centralized information center

sultation, training, supplies, administration, and management. Following this building plan exactly is not critical, but providing for the various resources will be. Figure 9-4 is a somewhat more modest center, requiring only one room. It provides space for a single consultant and readily accessible facilities.

Characteristics of a Successful IC

Managers of ongoing ICs were asked about management characteristics that lead to a successful information center. Tables 9-2, 9-3, and 9-4 show their responses. Table 9-2 gives a summary list of management characteristics; Table 9-3 provides a detailed list of

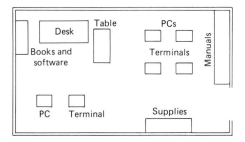

Figure 9-4 Layout of a small IC

TABLE 9-2 MANAGEMENT CHARACTERISTICS THAT LEAD
TO A SUCCESSFUL IC

Characteristics	Number of responses	Percentage of companies
Orientation	23	36%
Be user-oriented		
Treat user as a customer		
Be sympathetic/empathetic to user		
Try to understand user's business		
Treat user as sophisticated		
Personal characteristics	12	19%
Be patient		
Be flexible		
Be creative		
Possess communications skills		
Strategy	11	17%
Have brief objectives		
Be willing to change		
Market carefully		
Let users lead		
Background	10	15%
Possess technical skills		
Have a generalist, not a technical view		
Have a broad view of the firm		
Have a business understanding		
Have a political understanding		
Attitudes	8	13%
Be honest with users		
Be willing to change DP		
Take the initiative		
Be persistent		
Be aggressive		
Be self-confident		
Be resourceful		

TABLE 9-3 MANAGEMENT CHARACTERISTICS THAT LEAD
TO A SUCCESSFUL IC—DETAILED RESPONSES

Characteristics
Personal characteristics
Patience (a primary trait)
Ability to listen
Effectiveness
Flexibility
Creativity
Six-minute manager skills

TABLE 9-3   (*Continued*)

Characteristics

Strong communication skills
People skills
Attention to detail

Attitude
Honesty with users
Ability to sell ideas
Willingness to attempt to change the traditional DP process
Persistence in trying to change processes
Aggressiveness and self-confidence
Initiative and resourcefulness; knowing where to get answers
Top-level management commitment and support

Background
General DB background
Generalist characteristics—nontechnical
A broad view of the firm
Understanding of the business climate
Good applications background
Systems analysis skills
Understanding of the political environment
Competent technical skills in products
Product knowledge

Orientation
Keep objectives brief
Define objectives—don't detail
Market carefully
Distribute hardware and software—don't control materials
Optimize people with hardware—hardware is cheap in comparison to people
Change perspective frequently
Change strategy as necessary—environment is dynamic
Provide option to users—show costs, let users choose
Let users institute control through cost
Organize and control end user computing

User orientation
Be more user-oriented than DP-oriented
Provide response and answers to users
Remember that the IC requires people interfaces (where MIS is isolated)
Remember that a dictatorial, non-customer prospective will not work
Treat the user as a customer
Believe that the customer is right
Get along well with people
Try to understand where users are coming from
Be people-oriented
Be sympathetic/empathetic with user. Don't look down on user
Let the users approach the task on their own level
Learn to understand the user's business
Deal well with the users
Learn to understand user frustrations
Be nice

TABLE 9-3   (*Continued*)

Characteristics

Determine what you can do to get users to buy more from you
Be able to communicate on user level
Look at what customers are doing and don't automatically be defensive
Accept the users as being sophisticated, as are their methods
Place yourself in the role of wanting to help user
Accept the user's "off the wall" desires as tasks
Understand that you are in a service business; service clients

TABLE 9-4   UNIQUE MANAGEMENT CONSIDERATIONS FOR AN IC

Characteristics	Number of responses	Percentage of companies
Strategic	11	35%
Short lead time		
Unstructured aspect		
Non-technician orientation		
Personal	8	26%
Outgoing and energetic manager		
Self-starting staff		
Concepts-oriented manager		
Adaptive, changeable manager		
Orientation	8	26%
User and DP orientation		
User empathy		
Other		
No unique qualities	4	13%

responses from the 20 IC managers (from which the summary list was created) to show more of the flavor of the responses. Table 9-4 lists management characteristics considered unique for an IC.

SUMMARY

- An IC requires special people, the most special of whom is the IC manager, referred to as a champion of the concept.
- An IC can be installed in almost any firm, but the best results will be obtained with a moderate amount of planning.
- An information center is an investment, and a return on investment should be expected. Planning is a way to specify requirements, estimate costs, and plan for benefits.

Key Terms

Knowledge workers	Anticipated benefits
Reaction	Career path
Champion	Centralized
Consultant	Distributed
Timetable of events	Decentralized

DISCUSSION QUESTIONS

1. Write a memo from management announcing the creation of an information center. What wording will demonstrate that the concept has executive support?

2. Write an advertisement for a major newspaper that describes the IC manager you wish to hire.

3. Where should the IC creation team meet? How often?

4. Select class members to take on the roles of IC creation team members and act out a meeting. What problems do you see arising during meetings of the IC creation team?

5. Design an alternate layout for a physical information center. On what do you base the differences between the model in the book and your model?

CASE STUDY

POTATO-TEX, INC.

The Potato-Tex company began in the late 1920s and presently has annual sales in excess of $2 billion. Potato-Tex employs 28,000 people. The company began using computers around 1965 with services purchased from a service bureau. Management brought the computer applications in house in 1970 into an IBM environment and makes extensive use of this environment today. Since that time, outside timeshare has not been a major consideration except for external database access.

Potato-Tex's Information Center

In late 1981, the vice-president of data services noticed PCs in various parts of the company and began to receive calls concerning PCs from other interested departments. The VP believed that DP should be coordinating the PC environment in order to be of service to the users, provide a consistent policy, and allow for a smooth expansion into the mainframe environment. Around this time, IBM was beginning to market the information center concept. A task force was formed in early 1982 to study how the IC concept might be applied at Potato-Tex as a way to support both PC use and existing mainframe-based informal end user computing. The result of this study was a capital acquisition request in February 1982 for initial IC expenses. The information center was informally inaugurated in September of that year. The three-person staff began immediately to organize the training and facilities, and the formal opening of the IC took place in January 1983.

The Potato-Tex IC has had physical facilities, including an extensive training area, since its beginning. The staff has grown to nine full-time members and one part-time. The IC has always supported PC

and mainframe products and training. The user community has grown from 25 to about 600, about 60 percent of whom use PCs.

The IC was the result of a firm belief held by the VP of data services. This senior manager could envision such benefits from the IC as the reduction of the MIS applications backlog, quicker response to user requests, increased system accuracy due to user involvement, increased control of data, and an improved view of management services on the part of users. The concept has received significant upper-management support and has a very high level of acceptance among users. The extent of user acceptance of the facilities, concept, and staff is evidenced by career movement of IC staff members to positions in the user areas.

The largest category of users of the IC are the professional staff, primarily from the departments of accounting, finance, manufacturing, marketing, sales, and engineering. Data manipulation and reports are the most frequent tasks, with word processing capabilities also experiencing significant use and growth. The records of the IC indicate that each of the seven consultant-analysts is supporting 24 users. Potato-Tex was the only company studied that profiled the support staff in this manner, providing a way for staff expansion to parallel end user growth.

The IC shares one of the two Potato-Tex mainframes. This machine supports all development activities, and no production work runs on it. The two machines communicate, so IC users can access extracted copies of production data. Though there are some 200 mainframe video display terminals in use, end user processing is 60 percent batch, using primarily SAS, FOCUS, IFPS, and APL.

The support of PCs, an initial goal of the IC, continues today. Potato-Tex has some 600 IBM PCs in place, and training is active and continuous. The PC training room includes large-screen (48-inch) projection from the instructor's PC for ease of viewing by the entire class. As in most firms studied, Lotus 1-2-3 was the most used PC software application.

Beginning in 1983, data services has charged a fixed fee of $4,095 per user logon ID per year. For this fee the user has unlimited use of the computer, with the exception of disk storage space. A benefit of this method of cost allocation to the user departments is knowing what computer services will cost for the year and that it is low but not free. This appears to be a good alternative to simple end-of-the-year chargeback for services.

More than half the staff of the Potato-Tex IC comes from a non-DP background. This is unusually high among the companies studied. What's more, the IC manager was also from a user area, which was atypical. This non-DP background, the use of administrative support, and an attractive and well-thought-out physical facility created an excellent end user-computing support concept.

The IC manager made an interesting comment on the security issue of having PCs in use in the IC environment. "It is no easier to copy data to a PC disk and remove it from the office than it is to make a copy of data on paper for theft and removal." Both considerations are related to personnel selection and management.

The primary objective of the Potato-Tex IC is to support the users in order to increase their productivity. In the words of the IC brochure:

> The Information Resource Center is a place where you can learn to apply "user friendly" computer tools to help you do certain parts of your job faster and easier. Center personnel will help you learn these new skills and Center equipment will be available for limited use. Once you're familiar with the tools, you'll be able to find answers to certain questions without direct Data Services intervention. Quicker answers will allow additional analysis of variables and thus, better business decisions. Your increased ability to access and manipulate data will improve your effectiveness in making decisions and allow Data Services' personnel to concentrate on major development projects.

Future plans call for (1) use of mainframe computer-based training, (2) use of videotapes for training and taping of training sessions for use away from the IC, (3) increased emphasis on language-specific user groups such as the FOCUS users group, (4) the upgrade of present courses and development of new training courses, and (5) the evaluation of hardware and software. Of note is the future need for multiple IC locations due to the pending relocation of some of the departments. This is a concept already followed by Texas Instruments because of its many separate locations.

REFERENCE

9-1.   Peters, Thomas J., and Robert H. Waterman, *In Search of Excellence*, New York: Harper and Row (1982).

10

Control in the Information Center

Information centers have been created, at one end of a continuum, to solve a problem that could not otherwise be resolved. In this situation, an individual or small staff was designated to produce a report, break a bottleneck, or provide support to a user product. Preplanning was minimal, on occasion lasting only a day. The results of such an exercise were excellent, and the service continued under the name *information center*.

The other end of the continuum seems to be the origination of an IC to control activities that were costly, such as outside timeshare, or were believed to be out of control or heading in that direction. The latter environment deals with the proliferation of personal computers and/or informal unsupported end user computing. The IC was initiated to control and support.

INFORMATION CENTER MODELS

With such models for IC origination, the question arises as to how an information center should be developed to receive the greatest benefit. There could be several models for the installation of an IC. One such model would have loose organization, reactive support, with no overt control to formal organization. The other end of choices would be one with specific control of end users and end user computing. These are discussed briefly before a compromise model is presented.

216

Reactive-Support Model

It would seem to make sense to begin this discussion with the formal organization model, because the literature indicates that such must be the case. However, the most prevalent model for initiation is that of loose, reactive customer service and support. Where the organization is constructed for and provides support in an environment of "customer first, last, and always, regardless of the formal organization," end users see a possibility of success. Users are accustomed to formal organization, formal development, and formal time delays. Thus this reactive model indicates that a formal organization of control is the last thing desired. Only an outwardly reactive organization will be of benefit to the users.

The fact that the most used model is the least organized would not give support to continuing this practice. If you have the time, why not organize properly? The answer to this will develop in the following discussion, as the narrative progresses to a compromise model.

Orderly Organization, Minimum-Control Model

An organization closer to formal control but containing elements desired by the users would be an IC that has elements of orderliness but presses for minimum control of the users. Such an organization would have a charter outlining basic functions and objectives, a one-year plan of resource development, a continuously updated training schedule, and a hierarchy of IC staff duties. This seems quite formal but in reality is considered orderly only because the formality is not allowed to get in the way of productivity. The charter is to inform, not to constrain. For example, the mission statement in the charter might say, "The information center is presented to assist the users in developing their own computer-based systems, reports, and analyses," but the staff would not hesitate at doing some of the programming to get the user started or over a hurdle.

Such an organization would schedule and pay for the training requirements of the users and react to the users' changing needs. Thus training and the resource plan would be a combined tactical plan. Training would provide education and skills for existing resources, while surveys and discussions would determine added needs and resources not presented. Surveys of users would not only determine what had been accomplished with specific projects but would also ask about resource adequacy.

Formal-Organization, High-Control Model

Because we now have several years' experience with IC development and operation, history would indicate the desirability and need of providing an environment of formal organization and control. Even in supporting end users, there would be no reason for letting the situation get out of hand and letting the users run helter-skelter. With control should come better management and a greater return on the IC investment.

The beginning of control would be a formal mission statement and IC charter that is followed. Such might delineate responsibilities of the IC as training, capabilities evolution, and consultation, but no actual programming or systems development. The statement would also indicate that all user projects will be described and reviewed prior to work and that the IC staff has the duty and responsibility to pass complex tasks on to data services for formal development, as appropriate. Requests for additional user resources, such as terminals and personal computers, would be formally requested and justified. Only authorized software would be supported or ordered by the IC staff. The object is to control the end user computing environment and to ensure proper use of the resources.

Good management practices and the literature seem to demand this form of organization. With experience should come the knowledge of better administration and, ultimately, control for best usage. However, as we indicated previously, control scares the users away and tends to stifle end user development. I contend that a compromise model is the most appropriate.

A Compromise Model

To ensure the best return on the total corporate or organizational investment, support *on the user's terms* is essential. Just as the object of the IC at IBM-Canada in 1976 was to provide data and computer access on the user's terms, so should formal support. This might imply anarchy as the users run over the support staff, indicating at every attempt at control that the rules are getting in the way of the use. The fear of anarchy and suspicion of the users' demand for total control both come from various past experiences. It is the past that we are trying to change—or at least the organizations of the past.

The compromise that seems in order is between control on the part of data services and freedom on the part of the users, all while providing the support users need. There must be a blending of orderliness, support, friendliness, and productivity. This can be achieved with the proper view of the true objective of the information center: orderly,

YOUR LOCAL NEIGHBORHOOD INFORMATION CENTER

We provide training, consulting, access, aid, and support: no cost, no justifiction, no hassle.

We ask you to give us an indication of each project: no justification, no approval or disapproval.

We ask for a final report on each project to show benefit: no justification of results, no approval.

We ask that you complete surveys of value or benefit of the IC: no criticism, no justification, just show needed resources.

In order to be of greatest assistance to you, we find it prudent to support a select set of hardware and software resources. You may use others, but at your own risk.

Finally, for your sake and ours, we ask that you attend a security seminar. We will teach you how to protect the corporate data, your data, and the equipment.

Figure 10-1   Sample abbreviated IC mission statement

productive support of valuable resources. A very abbreviated mission statement of such an organization would be as shown in Figure 10-1.

INFORMATION CENTER STRUCTURES

Figure 10-1 will be well received by the users, but some additional information should be conveyed to them. The formal mission statement should include this added information. It should be accompanied by the information center guidelines and user's manual, initial project description form, and follow-up project form. Desirable training for the users would be a security seminar, preferably conducted in two sessions.

IC Documentation

To show the users what is provided and expected, four items are presented: (1) a sample mission statement, (2) an outline of an IC guideline and user's manual, (3) an end user-developed project description form, and (4) an information center project evaluation form. The object of these instruments is to provide an environment of order and a level of control in an atmosphere of service.

Mission statement.   The mission statement in Figure 10-2 is more specific than the one in Figure 10-1.

Information center guidelines and user's manual.   The users who take advantage of the information center will need documentation that explains the facilities and services. A user's manual can be created to include just that information. It should be user-oriented and available for users to keep for ready reference.

Figure 10-3 contains an outline, actually a table of contents, of an IC guide that is also a user's manual. The document would serve three purposes: (1) provide a model for services in the information center, (2) provide a reference for the IC staff, and (3) guide the users in services, responsibilities, and actions. By delineating the specific areas of service and the separation of responsibilities, the guide should make the users feel comfortable by knowing what they can ask for and what they must do. It provides the IC staff with a basis for their actions and activities and gives authority for denying support outside a given area. This is not meant to provide excuses for the staff not to work for the users; it is intended to protect the staff from unusual requests.

End user-developed project description form.   In our compromise model of the IC, we want to have an integration of user freedom and control. One document that will do this is a form by which the user informs the IC of a pending task. The intent is not to block user activity but to allow the IC staff to be knowledgeable of these activities. In filling out the form, the user is asked to think through the task, the resources required, and the required completion date. When this is done, the user and the IC staff will be in a better position to determine the level of support required by the user and whether the task is appropriate for end user or formal development.

SAMPLE MISSION STATEMENT

The purpose of the information center is to support the end user computing environment. To this end, IC staff members are available to all personnel to consult on problems and opportunities where computer-based resources can be of value. Services provided are as follows:

- Personal consulting on

  Data: sources, permission, and acquisition
  Supported software and hardware
  Language syntax, JCL, and references

- Training on all supported resources, including

  Mainframe access and JCL
  Data security, access, and downloading
  Microcomputer use and operating systems
  Supported software, basic and advanced operations

- Software and hardware evaluation for possible incorporation
- Equipment ordering, receipt, setup, and instruction

There is no charge for these services and no specific training requirements. However, users are encouraged to obtain training prior to resource usage to ensure proper utilization and the highest productivity. You are also requested to attend a security seminar to ensure that data and equipment are used safely. Consult an IC staff member about your needs. Advanced users are eligible for extended training so as to be able to take on the duty of departmental specialist, thereby providing in-area support for functional areas.

Figure 10-2 Sample IC mission statement

Information Center Guidelines and User's Manual

1. Introduction
   1.1. IC charter and mission statement
   1.2. IC organization chart
   1.3. Definitions
   1.4. User registration
2. Information center capabilities
   2.1. Mainframe capabilities
       2.1.1. Supported software
       2.1.2. Supported hardware
       2.1.3. Disk storage
       2.1.4. Database management systems
       2.1.5. Extract copy of data

Figure 10-3 Information center guidelines and user's manual table of contents

2.2. Microcomputer capabilities
    2.2.1. Supported software
    2.2.2. Supported hardware
    2.2.3. Supplies
    2.2.4. Manuals
3. Direct assistance
    3.1. Consultation
    3.2. Data search and access
    3.3. Advanced consultation
    3.4. IC services not offered
4. User training
    4.1. List and schedule of courses and seminars offered
        a. Classroom
        b. Videotapes
        c. Computer-based training
        d. Vendor courses
    4.2. Student enrollment
    4.3. Seminar checklist
5. Technical support
    5.1. User-related
        5.1.1. Trouble-shooting
        5.1.2. Coordination with data services
    5.2. System-related
        5.2.1. Testing procedures for new products and releases
        5.2.2. System migration
6. Resource planning, evaluation and control, and justification
    6.1. Best location determination
    6.2. User-developed capability methodology
    6.3. User-developed project description form
    6.4. Other planning worksheets
    6.5. Resources monitoring procedures
    6.6. User benefit worksheets and evaluation form
7. Security
    7.1. Mainframe
        7.1.1. User responsibilities
        7.1.2. IC responsibilities
        7.1.3. Data services security systems
    7.2. Microcomputer
        7.2.1. User responsibilities
        7.2.2. IC responsibilities
    7.3. Training
8. Data services operations
    8.1. Database backup and restore procedures
    8.2. System backup procedures
    8.3. Printing and plotting capabilities
9. Data services interface
    9.1. System programming
    9.2. Operations
    9.3. Telecommunications

FIGURE 10-3   (*Continued*)

10. Administration
    10.1. Mainframe
        10.1.1. User profiles
        10.1.2. Setting up user IDs
        10.1.3. Job accounting
        10.1.4. List of internal IC reports
        10.1.5. Terminal booking at the IC
    10.2. Microcomputer
        10.2.1. Ordering hardware
        10.2.2. Ordering software
    10.3. Common
        10.3.1. Internal contact list
        10.3.2. Ordering manuals
11. Promotion of the information center
    11.1. List of demonstrations and presentations
    11.2. User groups
12. Product evaluation
    12.1. New product review format
    12.2. Cost-benefit analysis
13. Operational procedures for end user products
    13.1. Mainframe
        13.1.1. Standards
        13.1.2. Establishing job accounting
        13.1.3. Submitting a job
        13.1.4. Retrieving a job
        13.1.5. Priority considerations
        13.1.6. Backup
        13.1.7. Operations interface
        13.1.8. Terminal logon procedures
        13.1.9. Database / general workspace access
    13.2. Microcomputer
        13.2.1. Registration
        13.2.2. Program documentation
        13.2.3. User documentation
14. Mainframe program maintenance procedures
    14.1. Program structure
    14.2. Program documentation
    14.3. Program registration

FIGURE 10-3 (*Continued*)

Figure 10-4 shows a form that would be used by users to communicate to the IC staff the nature of user-developed projects. This would serve three purposes: (1) The users indicate projects, their nature, cost, benefit, risk, and needed completion dates; (2) the IC keeps track of user activity and reviews projects for IC staff and data services support; and (3) the IC staff has a reference for surveys and cost-benefit analyses.

END USER-DEVELOPED PROJECT DESCRIPTION FORM

The purpose of this form is to describe the end user task to be addressed. The process, resources, costs, benefits, and risks will be reviewed by the information center staff only to the extent necessary to assist the end user in the timely completion of the project. Should the IC staff member determine that the project is of such magnitude that it will require significant resources, will have a long useful lifetime, or will be of benefit to several individuals or organizations, the IC staff will consult with the user as to the desirability of formal data services assistance and/or development. Otherwise, the purpose of this form is to communicate the goals, resources required, anticipated benefits, and risks of the subject project for informational purposes.

Name of developer: _____ Department: _____

Name of project: _____

Date to start development: _____ Date of completion: _____

Date capability needed: _____ Date capability too late: _____

Hardware to be used: [ ] mainframe   [ ] microcomputer   [ ] other

Software to be used: _____ _____ _____

IC staff assistance anticipated: [ ] likely   [ ] unlikely

Access to privately owned data: [ ] likely   [ ] unlikely

Data services assistance anticipated: [ ] likely   [ ] unlikely

Out-of-pocket resources needed: [ ] likely   [ ] unlikely

What is the penalty of not having this capability developed? _____

_____

What will be the cost of development? _____ hours of your time
_____ computer units _____ hours of IC staff time _____ hours of DS aid

What is the probability that you can complete the task? _____%

What risk do you see in your developing the capability as opposed to formal development by data services? _____

Who else might benefit from this capability? _____

What benefits, tangible or intangible, will result from this development? _____

_____

Figure 10-4 Sample end user-developed project description form

Evaluation of User Projects after Completion

We indicated earlier the value of continuous review of user and IC activities. Thus it is appropriate to survey the user after completion of each project. Using the end user-developed project description form, plus informal knowledge by the IC staff as to undocumented projects, the staff would send the form in Figure 10-5 to appropriate users and request

INFORMATION CENTER PROJECT EVALUATION FORM

The purpose of this form is to review a user-developed project and evaluate the success, benefits, and costs associated with the project. When the project began, you were asked to indicate certain aspects of the project, such as assistance needed, risk involved, benefits anticipated, and cost. We now ask that you review the project and look at these items again.

Name of developer: _____ Department: _____

Name of project: _____

Start date: _____ Anticipated completion: _____

Actual completion date: _____

	Not very						Very
	1	*2*	*3*	*4*	*5*	*6*	*7*
How successful do YOU consider the project?	+ --- + --- + --- + --- + --- + --- +
How successful does YOUR BOSS consider it?	+ --- + --- + --- + --- + --- + --- +
Did the task change much as you did it?	+ --- + --- + --- + --- + --- + --- +
Will the product be useful to others?	+ --- + --- + --- + --- + --- + --- +
Did the project take more of your time than you anticipated?	+ --- + --- + --- + --- + --- + --- +
Did the project cost more in real dollars than you anticipated?	+ --- + --- + --- + --- + --- + --- +
Was the IC staff involved in the project?	+ --- + --- + --- + --- + --- + --- +
Were other data services personnel involved?	+ --- + --- + --- + --- + --- + --- +
Was the data required easy to find?	+ --- + --- + --- + --- + --- + --- +
to access?	+ --- + --- + --- + --- + --- + --- +
to use?	+ --- + --- + --- + --- + --- + --- +
Was additional training required?	+ --- + --- + --- + --- + --- + --- +
Did you use the software originally planned?	+ --- + --- + --- + --- + --- + --- +
Would MIS programmers have done a better job?	+ --- + --- + --- + --- + --- + --- +

Costs: Hours of labor by your _____, IC staff _____, other DS _____

Other dollars expended: _____

Benefits: Dollars saved or costs avoided: _____

Intangible benefits: _____

Your overall feelings about this project: _____

Have you given the IC documentation on this project: ___ Yes ___ No

Figure 10-5 Sample information center project evaluation form

feedback on their projects. This form should be easy for the user to complete, should be nonthreatening, and should show the degree of involvement by the parties, level of expenditures in time and monies, and benefits derived.

Security Training for IC Users

Part of the concern for control in an end user environment is the question of security. This means a user awareness for safety of his or her own data and safeguards for any data accessed, copied, or used. It is quite desirable to provide user training in these areas, but couched in a view of safety, not "Big Brother is watching." Figure 10-6 presents an outline for an IC seminar that all users would be requested, or required, to take. It includes instruction in the areas of safety and safeguards, as well as cautions as to actions on the user's part.

The seminar is designed to be completed in two phases. The first phase realizes that many users have limited knowledge of the computer and may not internalize the information presented at the time of the seminar. However, it is important to provide security information early to protect corporate and personal data and equipment. The follow-up seminar readdresses the subjects after a period of use. The users should then be more aware of the cautions presented and be more comfortable with the various subjects.

Security Seminar to End Users

1. Ground rules
   A. Two meetings, 45 minutes each, held often
   B. Session 1 before using IC
   C. Session 2 four to six weeks later
2. Introduction to the information center
   A. Staff is here to assist all interested parties
   B. We offer personal consulting, trouble-shooting, aid
   C. Call our hotline
   D. See our training schedules
   E. See the user's guide for all our services
3. Seminar 1
   A. Job security: Don't copy copyrighted software
      i. The copyright symbol means that the owner is granted protection
      ii. You are not the owner
      iii. Company policy: Violation of copyright = termination
      iv. Software provides for multiple users, one at a time
      v. Additional copies can be ordered if required
   B. Belt and suspenders: Disaster protection—protect your data
      i. Make a copy of hard disk files to floppy or tape
      ii. Have two copies of all files concurrently
      iii. Act as if the hard disk will crash within 20 minutes
      iv. Store floppy disks in a safe place
   C. Data protection: Protect organizational data
      i. Disk files can be copied if available
      ii. Hard disks cannot usually be protected
      iii. Once data is out of the mainframe, you are its custodian
      iv. Use encryption if necessary

Figure 10-6 Security seminars for end users

D. Foot insurance: Don't shoot yourself
    i. FORMAT destroys ALL data
    ii. ERASE removes from directory but can be recovered
    iii. Use subdirectories to keep control
E. Memory aids: Document what you do
    i. Register your capabilities with the IC staff
    ii. Write up documentation about each capability
        a. Who did the program
        b. What capability does—generically, specifically
        c. Where it is located
4. Seminar 2
  A. Review of Seminar 1
    i. Job security: Don't copy copyrighted software
    ii. Disaster protection: Protect your data; back up often
    iii. Data protection: Protect organizational data
    iv. Foot insurance: Don't shoot yourself
  B. Discussion of mainframe data
    i. Sources
    ii. Ownership
    iii. Direct access and extract copies
    iv. Downloading
  C. Discussion of hard-disk security
    i. Backup to floppy or tape
    ii. Encryption
    iii. Archiving
  D. Discussions of documentation
    i. Write up documentation about each capability
    ii. Register your capabilities with the IC staff
  E. General discussion
    i. User groups by product
    ii. Interesting projects
    iii. New resources
    iv. General problems
    v. How to save money and be more productive

FIGURE 10-6   (*Continued*)

DIFFERENCES BETWEEN FORMAL AND USER DEVELOPMENT

There are specific differences in the creation of capabilities via formal procedures and end user development methodologies. The processes differ by characteristics, methodology, and imposed methodology and control. The objectives differ, the guidelines and levels of control differ, time frames differ, and uses of the resultant products differ. The realization of these differences will aid in knowing which is appropriate for any given task. The considerations of formal and end user development are outlined in Figure 10-7. A direct discussion will tie these topics together.

FIGURE 10-7　DIFFERENCES BETWEEN FORMAL AND USER DEVELOPMENTS

1. Characteristics
   A. SDLC for formal development
      i. Systems development starts with the feasibility study
      ii. The analysis phase produces a requirements specification
      iii. The design phase determines structure before development
      iv. The system is built and tested in isolation unless a prototype is used
      v. The system is user-tested through implementation
      vi. The system has a good structure and proper documentation
      vii. The process is not responsive to change
      viii. The maintenance phase supports the system during a long life
   B. Development for end user computing
      i. The capabilities have a brief time frame for development and a short useful lifetime
      ii. The capabilities are difficult to justify as to cost-benefit
      iii. A single person or department is the ultimate user
      iv. The system is developed by an individual as opposed to a team
      v. The feasibility phase may be taken for granted
      vi. The process iterates through analysis, design, construction, testing, and implementation phases
      vii. There is no initial specification—just an idea
      viii. The system evolves with the user's concept and with hands-on use
      ix. There is little or no documentation
      x. This developmental methodology has no maintenance phase
2. Methodology
   A. Formal development
      i. The work starts with a formal work request for the system
      ii. A formal review is required before proceeding
      iii. An MIS team is formed
      iv. The feasibility and analysis phases are performed, creating a specification of desired capability
      v. The make-or-buy decision is made at the end of the analysis phase
      vi. The system is purchased or created
      vii. The system is tested according to a test plan
      viii. The system is installed and user documentation is provided
      ix. The system becomes operational
      x. The maintenance and change phase is initiated and continues for the life of the system.
   B. End user developments
      i. The user sees a need for a new capability
      ii. The user thinks about cost versus benefits (feasibility phase)
      iii. The user selects the tool for creation from those available
      iv. The user develops an abbreviated working model
      v. The user expands and changes the model based on use
      vi. The capability is used
      vii. The user goes to other tasks—documentation is neglected
      viii. Other users may benefit from the system
      ix. The user-creator performs maintenance and change as required
3. Imposed methodology and control
   A. Formal development (requirements)
      i. Formal request
      ii. Review committee

FIGURE 10-7 (Continued)

      iii. MIS team
      iv. Project management
      v. Phased development
      vi. Formal documentation
  B. End user developments (recommendations)
      i. Project description
      ii. Clearinghouse function
      iii. Project follow-up
      iv. Documentation requirement
      v. Completion survey

Characteristics

The purpose of the environment and methodologies of *formal development* is to provide a managed process by which a system or capability will be created that will meet the intended need and have a long and useful lifetime. The phases of analysis, design, development, testing, and implementation are designed to provide an excellent product that can then be maintained and kept up-to-date. The evidence is that the period of support after implementation will be long and ease of maintenance is critical due to the large number of programs in this phase. The programs that are developed in this mode are important for the firm in the long run and require good construction and documentation. They are stable and respond poorly to changes other than small additions and deviations, such as added reports.

    Contrary to these characteristics for formal development, the environment for user development needs to address the short time frame for development, short lifetime of use, and necessity to evolve the product from the very beginning. Whereas formal development takes as much as 30 percent of the time and resources for analysis and design, the user-developed effort will iterate through the phases of analysis, design, development, testing, and implementation over and over. Each cycle will improve the developer's ideas and the resultant product. Flexibility and change are the keys to development. Even though these capabilities have a longer useful lifetime than originally anticipated, therefore requiring documentation, there is no overt maintenance phase. Thus the emphasis is one of discovery in iterative development, reasonable documentation as to intent and method, and progression to the next need.

Methodology

Formal development is achieved through formal paperwork, teamwork, specifications, review, and coordination by a number of people. There are milestones to be achieved and documented during the phases. Since a number of people are involved, meetings, minutes, and memos are required. This is all preceded by a feasibility analysis and review board approval. The result is a well-coordinated product that requires time, talent, and resources.

By contrast, few people are involved in *user-developed projects*, which thus require few meetings, fewer memos, and little coordination. The user often develops the system as an evolving prototype model and uses that model to learn and communicate. There is no written specification, and no formal reviews are conducted other than by the user.

CONCLUSION

End user computing is the result of past high levels of control and lack of resources. In supporting the end user, the information center should present an atmosphere of order without overt control. An attitude of "We're here to help you and we try to keep the place and procedures tidy" is orderly support; "Sign up, shape up, and cough up" is control. The former will attract users, whereas the latter will repel them.

SUMMARY

- Users are accustomed to and wary of high levels of organizational control. Keep the information center organized, but keep the focus squarely on user service.
- Tell the users of your service orientation in the mission statement; then practice it.
- Create an information center guide and user's manual to guide the IC and help the users understand their role.
- Keep enough records of the user's activities to aid in resource acquisition and cost-benefit analysis.
- Hold informative security seminars often. Help the users protect themselves as well as valuable resources.
- There are differences in formal development and user development. They have different objectives, tasks, methodologies, outcomes, and appropriate methods of control. Don't confuse them.

Key Terms

Control	Compromise
Integration	Justification
Approval	Documentation
User manual	IC guidelines
Responsibilities	Project description form
User survey	Project completion survey
Security seminar	

DISCUSSION QUESTIONS

1. Discuss the wording and content of Figure 10-1. Is it practical?

2. What has been omitted from the information center guidelines and user's manual outline (Figure 10-3)?

3. What would IC staff members do with end user-developed project description forms (Figure 10-4)?

4. Are users likely to complete the evaluation form (Figure 10-5) if not harassed to do so?

5. Do you think that two 45-minute security seminars will be adequate? How might this be done using computer-based training or videotapes?

6. How can the IC determine when users need refresher security seminars?

7. List some elements of control that are intuitively distasteful and repelling.

8. Cite elements of control that must be tolerated to avoid real problems.

CASE STUDIES

AMERICAN AIRLINES

American Airlines (AA) is one of the leading air passenger carriers in the United States. AA is the major operating unit of AMR Corporation. AMR's total revenue in 1986 was $6.2 billion, of which $5.0 billion was from airline passenger revenue. Other operating units, which have access to the AA information center, are AA Training and Sky Chefs catering. The American Airlines headquarters are in Forth Worth, Texas.

AA began to use computers for decision assistance in the early 1960s, when AA and IBM combined in a joint project to develop the SABRE computer-assisted airline reservation system. This was the forerunner of real-time systems.

American Airline's Information Center

Beginning in the mid-1970s, there was a growing use of outside timeshare at AA. There were many vendors, but the primary product used was the APL language. In 1976, the cost of timeshare was significant (over $2 million per year before volume discount) and increasing rapidly. Management became concerned and made the decision to support timeshare via an internal environment in order to decrease cost and gain control of this use of computing. Internal timeshare became an environment for end user computing and required significant management attention. There were problems initially with internal timeshare as its use grew rapidly. The need for support and control of EUC became apparent. It was soon obvious that users wanted access to more than just APL. Users wanted access to corporate data as well as other computer resources. IBM was beginning to advertise the

information center at this time (early 1980s), and it seemed appropriate to investigate the concept at AA.

AA had started a timeshare support group as early as 1977. The initial product supported was APL, and the manager of the group at the time it was decided to implement the IC concept was the person who became the IC manager in May 1981. The IC staff had four people at the beginning and has grown to nine, two of whom are located in Tulsa, Oklahoma. During this time period, the user base, which started with APL timeshare, has grown to over 700. As an indication of support to the end users, the IC staff in Texas is logging 800 to 1,000 user contacts per month, including phone calls, personal consulting, and training.

The primary use of the IC is for queries and reports, with the classification of projects fairly evenly spread among personal, department, and corporate applications. Supporting this, the IC provides SAS, GDDM, APL, BASIC, and the AA-developed AAIMS data access system. Seventy percent of the IC processing is on-line due primarily to the APL language. The AA IC has a dedicated Amdahl Model V8 processor, which is accessed by 3270-type terminals and IBM PCs. AA supports a physical IC facility in Forth Worth, Texas, with seven cubicles, five terminals, two PCs, and a training room with additional terminals. This is augmented by a small IC facility in Tulsa, Oklahoma.

The IC provides mainframe and PC training. The two primary courses in APL are 24 hours each. Other courses cover VSPC (the primary user environment), BASIC, MARK IV, SAS, and the AA-developed AAIMS data access capability.

The development of the internal timeshare support group and the IC came at a time of deregulation in the airline industry. Thus the environment in which the firm operates has become very dynamic. Access to corporate data by management and the use of modeling and "what if?" exercises have become vital. This has led to high reliance on the IC.

In comparison with the other firms studied, AA was unusual with respect to career development of the IC staff members. Thanks to high visibility, several of the IC staff members have been promoted to positions in user departments. However, they are often viewed as technicians. This is perceived by the staff as growth-limiting and has resulted in some members' choosing to return to data services.

The American Airlines IC supports both mainframe use and personal computers. It has adopted the IBM PC as the standard, with the XT model as the basic configuration. There are PC-to-mainframe communications at a 1,200-baud rate, and downloading of data is a practice. The IC does support PC acquisition with consulting and receives and installs the hardware when it arrives. As with most companies studied, the user pays for all PC equipment.

Even with the installed information center and the use of personal computers, use of outside timeshare services remains significant ($800,000 per year). Much of the activity is in accessing specialized databases.

AA has a data administration function and a data dictionary for DP use. At present, the data dictionary is not user-oriented. Most of the user-accessed data is not secured, and the IC becomes the interface for user data. Most data is accessed via extract files, with repetitive extracting initiated by the user.

The user of AA data services and the IC have computer account numbers, although chargeback for services occurs only in subsidiaries. To internal AA users, the services are essentially free. There is no forecasting for IC resources and no consequences for high usage. The only consideration of high use is that the IC staff will watch for this condition and consult with the

users to promote efficient use. Monitoring for efficient use is the only audit performed in the IC.

Most nonproduction data is not secured, and users can give other users access to personal files. The RACF capability is used for security control, but security is not an issue in the IC environment. On the other hand, corporate data is considered more sensitive and more secure.

AA considers the IC a valuable resource and a potential problem. The use of the computer and of data has increased with the IC, which has merit and drawbacks. The high use of resources can cause resource forecasting problems, and the high data usage is causing data proliferation. However, deterioration of data integrity has not occurred.

The AA IC kept a low profile initially, and its growth rate was low also. Once marketing and promotion of the IC began, use mushroomed. As in most companies studied, marketing the IC can be very successful in gaining a significant amount of new use. If the IC is not ready for the increase, it can spell disaster. AA has succeeded in avoiding disaster.

The primary objectives and benefits of the AA IC are (1) self-sufficiency of users to develop applications and (2) enhanced response to management for data in a dynamic environment. The IC has received high visibility with upper management by providing data that was not available prior to the installation of the IC. Future plans for the AA IC include acquisition of additional fourth-generation languages, supporting the spread of PCs, and the development of the integrated end user environment.

To achieve a viable information center, the IC manager indicates that the staff must have significant patience. Another important characteristic is the ability to align with both the user and data services. The lack of patience and of dual alignment leads to reduced effectiveness.

FEDERAL RESERVE BANK OF DALLAS

The Federal Reserve Bank of Dallas, which is one of 12 regional Federal Reserve Banks in the United States, serves the Eleventh Federal Reserve District. The Federal Reserve system is the central banking system of the United States with the basic purpose of providing a flow of money and credit that will foster orderly economic growth and a stable dollar. In addition to the major function, Federal Reserve Banks issue Federal Reserve notes and hold deposits of and make loans to financial institutions. Reserve Banks also perform various services for financial institutions, act as Fiscal Agent for the United States, regulate and supervise banks, and assemble, analyze and distribute economic and banking data.

Annual Report

The Federal Reserve Bank of Dallas, Texas, was created by the Federal Reserve Act of 1913 as a private industry operating in the public interest. It has 1,500 employees, operates over an area of approximately 335,000 square miles, and had revenues in 1986 of $157 million, mainly from interest on government securities.

Four Texas locations support the Eleventh District: Houston, El Paso, San Antonio, and Dallas, Dallas being the major facility. The Bank provides three primary services: (1) regulatory services to evaluate conditions of financial institutions in the district (100 people), (2) monetary policy services to study the economic environment for the board of governors in Washington, D.C. (100 people), and (3) a service department to provide services to financial institutions, transfer funds, and process checks (1,150 people). The Dallas office houses all computer facilities and provides processing and programming support to the other three sites.

Dallas Federal Reserve's Information Center

In 1980 and 1981, the assistance vice-president for DP application development,

supervisor of 55 programmers and 12 database administration personnel, saw a need to distribute the power of the computer to the users and give some relief to the backlog problem. (One budget program had been on the official backlog for ten years.) He attended an IBM seminar, learned of the IC concept, and started a project in August 1981 to define the IC concept in the Bank's environment and install formal support for end user computing. He assigned a new manager this responsibility. After talking extensively with companies around the country about the IC concept, the new manager presented the idea to DP and Bank management. Until this time, all DP resources were tightly controlled. Thus there was no informal end user computing to act as a base for the idea. In December 1981, he presented his recommendations of an IC implementation plan to Bank management, DP management, and the users, all of whom were a little skeptical.

The IC began operations in December 1981. It was first tried as a pilot project in one department using the SAS language for a user who definitely needed help. The project was to supplant a card-oriented batch application that was not adequate. The existing system was so constrained that the users would run the month-end reports and make corrections with correction fluid and typewriters before publication. The next reporting date was six months away, and there were no DP resources to apply to the project. The user department would have to do the work.

Early in the pilot, the FOCUS language was acquired for developing the budgeting system to be built by DP programmers and maintained subsequently by users. The budget system replacement project (estimated at six worker-years using traditional methods) was completed by three DP staff members in 35 worker-days. At that time, SAS was abandoned by the pilot IC user as the primary novice and user tool in favor of the more user-friendly FOCUS 4GL/DBMS.

The resulting FOCUS-based solution was very well received as the system was completely replaced by the user before the next reporting period. A series of successful end user applications were subsequently developed in other departments, and FOCUS use expanded in the pilot department. The third project was a prototype of a marketing system that documented a $65,000 saving over the intended IMS application. The FOCUS-based prototype has since been implemented as a production system.

This initial activity is considered contrary to the suggested IC modus operandi— make the pilot cases guaranteed successes in a way that is not time-critical. The Bank IC started with a very visible, time-critical budget project. The initial successes were achieved under trying conditions and adequately demonstrated the power of the information center.

At the time that this was occurring, the Monetary Control Act was implemented, requiring the Bank to make revenue equal to cost. This required a significant budgeting effort, an effort that could not be achieved through formal development methods. The users learned FOCUS quickly and became advocates of the new methodology.

The IC staff has grown during this time from three to ten, and support now encompasses mainframe activity, personal computers, office automation, and executive information services. The object of the Federal Reserve Bank information center is to be a focal point for the integration of computing, office automation, and executive information services and to support users in being more effective. The optional user base is 700, of whom 325 have received training in one of these areas.

The Federal Reserve Bank of Dallas was one of the firms studied with a significant formal physical information center. The IC manager was quite proud of the consultants' cubicles, the open area with eight user-accessible mainframe terminals, personal computers, the training and conference

room, and the plans to add video projection in the future. One feature of the Bank that supports this concentration of IC facilities is that all of the Dallas employees work in one building.

The IC shares the Bank's IBM Model 3084 mainframe computer. There are also six IBM Model 8100 distributed processors for support of user communications. The Bank has 450 workstations in the district; 150 Model 8775 monochrome graphic, data, and text terminals; 10 Model 3279 color graphic terminals; 80 PCs; and 210 Model 3278 monochrome data terminals.

The IC acts as the focal point for data access, which is controlled by ACF2 security software. All data is secured, and the IC staff assists users in getting access permission and ACF2 rules written. The IMS databases are read directly by the users using FOCUS in batch mode. Batch mode is considered an excellent trade-off for the amount of disk space that would be required for extract copies. Program libraries and FOCUS database designs and definitions are controlled by the IC. Thus the IC performs the roles of production control and data management.

The users are charged for computer use, the primary measurement being CPU usage. No departmental forecasting is required, and thus the departments are not held accountable for actual cost. Of note is the practice of charging for training (by means of departmental funds transfer). The rate is about $50 per hour, not enough to affect the request level. PC purchases are made through the IC, with the user paying all costs. The PC is primarily used as an executive workstation rather than as a terminal replacement for staff and professional employees.

The IMS environment has no record-level security capability, so the FOCUS security capability is used extensively. Some users add security via encryption of data and programs. The security software in place does indicate unauthorized data access attempts. The primary objective of the information center is to provide access to information, not just data, so that it can be presented in some usable form to management. The intent is to improve the decision-making process. The benefits derived from the IC also result from better decisions.

The IC manager believes that the IC project has matured well and that the concept has progressed to a point where the prime interest is now concentrating on integrating the technologies of mainframe use, personal computers, and office automation. The object of this concentration is to support an effective business work environment.

11

The Future: Data Services, End User Development, and the IC

One way to view the future is to review features of the past and present and indicate how these characteristics have changed and will continue to change over time. As the time line in Figure 11-1 shows, the time to the future is much shorter than the time from the beginning of the use of computer resources. Just as the period of generation of knowledge (and its half-life) has decreased exponentially over the past five centuries, the rate of technological change has increased exponentially over the past several centuries, especially in the twentieth. As the rate of change has increased, the time of reaction to problems has decreased. There is no reason to believe this trend will slow.

THE PAST: FORMAL DEVELOPMENT

The value of a review of the past is primarily as a point of reference. We have discussed the DP shop, a centralized, closed facility, peopled by individuals speaking in strange languages, with a Merlinesque ability to effect results from the new and strange machine called the computer. The major characteristic of interest is that only large, costly, and direct cost-saving projects were appropriate for computer systems. Programmers were remote from the ultimate users of the programs. Systems were created from a frozen specification and had little tolerance to change. This was the age of transaction processing systems, a time of change from manual to computer-based methods. It was the beginning from which all modern systems evolved. This evolution has been dramatic and rapid.

	Past		Present	Future
Facilities:	Centralized		Accessible	Distributed
DP personnel:	Separate		Accessible	Co-located
Perspective:	DP shop		Mixed	Data services
Cost and time:	High, long		Lower	QRC
Flexibility:	None		Limited	Maximum
Type of system:	Large		Mixed	All
Participation:	None		Limited	Team effort

Figure 11-1   Data services, end user development, and the IC

THE PRESENT: FORMAL DEVELOPMENT VERSUS USER DEVELOPMENT

The past became the present during the 1970s. Part of the process was the acceptance of the computer resource as much more generally supportive of management decision processes than just collecting data. ''Computerization'' matured into management information systems, began to address decision support systems, and even acknowledged the users of the systems. The way formal systems were created changed, and the need for an alternative was recognized. The differences between the methodology of formal development and user development, each with strengths and weaknesses, are now clear. The data services organization has also changed and evolved, and its continued evolution will affect systems development methodologies.

Formal Development versus User Development

Application development will continue to be needed even when its methodology changes due to the addition of support technology. End user development is a vital alternative to formal development, but neither will negate the other. Each method has both advantages and attendant problems. Advantages have been addressed previously, so we will review and discuss problems with each that will extend into the future.

Problems attendant to formal development situations

Formal Development Conditions

  1. Shortage of analysts and programmers
  2. Management demands that analysts and programmers understand the business
  3. Replacement of aging software
  4. Software aids to formal development

---

1.   *Shortage of analysts and programmers.* The situation of having an adequate number of analysts and programmers is somewhat akin to that of telephone operators in

the 1920s. The projection was that all employable females would be telephone operators within a few decades. That did not happen due to the application of technology to that industry. However, analysis and programming have evolved slowly, and the application of technology (to be discussed later) has not significantly reduced the need for competent MIS professionals. It has been noted that the inability of businesses to apply computer technology to their domain is not the result of a lack of hardware but a lack of personnel with the appropriate capabilities.

We will discuss several forces that will add pressure to this problem and then address the influence of technology. The short term seems less than optimistic, but the long term is brighter.

2. *Management demands that analysts and programmers understand the business.* As with user-development tools, one of the problems with programming is the addiction of technology usage. Programming is fun and exciting; however, much more important is what is programmed. Thus analysis of the problem and solution is far more complex and valuable than the coding of the syntax for computer execution. Analysis requires an understanding of the environment of the problem, the business of the business. Users have never been very good at explaining problems and desired solutions. How can a programmer-analyst understand net present value implications when he or she does not understand net present value? Programmers and analysts are not mentally limited; they just have much to learn about technology and often prefer the domain of the computer to the environment of the business.

The days of sending a specification to programmers in application development and receiving an application in return are long gone. As business students are educated and trained in the value and use of technology, management is demanding that programmers and analysts understand better the business of the business. For example, a 100-employee department of a large corporation insisted that the six supporting analyst-programmers reside in the department and be immersed in the organization's day-to-day problems and activities. Only after two years could these MIS professionals begin to understand the business and contribute instead of react.

3. *Replacement of aging software.* Some organizations began to create computer-based applications in the 1950s. This software is now three decades old. Some of it is unchangeable, cumbersome, expensive to run, and out-of-date. The replacement cost for software created in the 1960's (two decades old) is estimated to be in the billions of dollars. (One corporation alone estimated it will cost more than $17 million to replace its aging software.) At present, more than 50 percent of the programmer-analysts are occupied in maintaining existing applications. Thus the need for replacement to update the capability clashes with a shortage of personnel available for the task.

Individual organizations confronted with significant costs for software replacement have two options, referred to as the make-or-buy decision: (1) make the new application or (2) purchase it. Software houses have been developing generalized applications, such as payroll, accounts receivable and payable, inventory management, and personnel systems. Thus organizations have the ability to purchase the replacement applications and have someone else maintain them, at a cost lower than that of creation. The tendency to resist purchase due to out-of-pocket costs, special needs of the firm, and NIH ("not invented here") must be fought.

When making the replacements, extensive user involvement will be a new force with which data services may not have previously dealt. As management insists that programmers and analysts be knowledgeable of the business of the business, they want the ultimate users to be involved in the development or purchase efforts of new and replacement capabilities. Data services will have a new partner in replacement efforts and a new way of doing business.

4. *Software aids to formal development.* As the purchase of applications will greatly affect the cost and time of implementation of new and replacement capabilities, so will advances in development technology. During the past two decades, timeshare has replaced batch programming with excellent productivity. Now PC-based programming that can be transferred to the mainframe is having an effect. The productivity center, an equivalent to the information center, is aiding MIS professionals in programming and testing. This is all applying the greater power of the machine to the task at hand but has not changed the way applications are designed.

A way that the power of software is being applied is through fourth-generation languages and application generators. This ranges from RAMIS and FOCUS languages, which are powerful database technologies, to PC-based tools providing for the creation of a data dictionary, data flow diagrams, and the resultant production of computer code.

As nonpower aids to development, project management tools are available to guide and track tasks and projects. Between the machine power and new methods of development, this is management of development. It is not to be taken lightly, as experience has indicated that most projects take longer and are significantly more complex and expensive than first estimated. Project management is an important aspect of creation and replacement.

As to changing methodology, there are a number of methods to document the task, but most are manual. We are just now seeing computer-based analysis and design aids appear to make the analyst more productive. The aid to programming is significant, but the aid to analysis is just beginning. The experienced analyst is still in high demand and limited supply.

Problems attendant to user development

User Development Conditions

1. Tendency to understudy and undertest
2. Longer life than expected and poor documentation
3. Need to communicate to others what has been done
4. Duplication of effort
5. User development of large systems
6. Inefficient use of user resources

1. *Tendency to understudy and undertest.* Whereas user development allows quick creation of short-lived applications, the very nature of development tends to ignore extensive up-front analysis. The heat of battle pushes for results, and tools allow creation in ways that overshadow investigation. Users tend to believe they have sufficient knowledge to overcome this, but education is in order to add the discipline of analysis. Pursuing the right problem is always an important issue, as is determination of alternatives and choice of the best one.

Like understudying, undertesting is a continuing problem. Testing is generally not considered as much fun as creation, and quick-and-dirty test methods often suffice. However, as with analysis, testing determines if a developer has created what was intended and whether the application will be reliable and useful. Testing, like analysis, is a discipline issue and must be instilled via education.

2. *Longer life than expected and poor documentation.* User-developed applications have longer lives than intended. This is not bad in that the investment will have even larger and longer-lived returns than originally anticipated. However, it is a problem when someone other than the developer tries to use or change the application. Application developers use a model of their own when creating a capability, and that model, thought process, or conceptualization may not be obvious to others. Thus documentation is needed by others from the beginning and throughout the life of the capability.

Like analysis and testing, documentation takes time and is often considered drudgery. Some languages are believed to be self-documenting, but the need remains for the developer to capture the model. Also, like analysis and testing, documentation is a concern for discipline that must be learned.

3. *Need to communicate to others what has been done.* Part of the value of the investment made in applications is the use of these creations by others. As with data, they cannot be used by others unless their existence is known. Thus there is a growing need for an applications library to store or at least list applications. Using something like the data administration function, an application administration function could be a common point of reference for the capabilities, house the documentation, and be a starting point in their use. This has a potential much like data administration in sharing costs and benefits.

4. *Duplication of effort.* Users work in isolation and may reinvent the wheel. Because of the ability to create applications easily and the pressure to meet time schedules, duplication of effort is likely. This may be inevitable, but the IC has a chance at least to inform the user community of like interests via newsletters and user groups. To enforce too high a level of management will stifle the very productivity that end user computing supports, but coordination can be of great value. Whereas analysis, testing, and documentation take education and discipline, the reduction of duplication of effort requires coordination and advertising.

5. *User development of large systems.* L. W. Hammond of IBM originally believed that the information center and end user computing were not to be used to develop large systems. As software increased in power and users became more capable with these tools, larger and larger capabilities were created with no more effort than was once required for

a report. At the same time, the definition of what is large and what is small has been evolving. Thus what may seem like a large system to an outsider may simply be the evolution of an idea that is well known to the user.

There remains a need for someone to be aware of what is being created and how it can be used. The coordination function will direct the more valuable, longer-lived applications to formal development and leave the shorter-lived, time-sensitive, ad hoc applications with end user development.

6. *Inefficient use of user resources*. IC managers note that high-level users spend their time programming spreadsheets or using the BASIC language. Learning and using user tools do take time, though it may be considered an investment. While this time may give the user a better understanding of the tool and technology-based process, it may also be quite costly. Thus there may be a type of position that is best supported by others as opposed to direct use of technology, until such technology requires less training and effort.

An Alternate View of the Information Center

An Alternate View of the Information Center

    1. Management functions: Planning, staffing, organizing, directing, and controlling

    2. Critical success factors

---

1. *Management functions*. The Hammond-IBM model of the information center has been presented as a viable support environment for end user computing. The IC is viewed as having premises, options, issues, and benefits. This is one aspect of the IC concept. Another even more important view is from the stance of general management. We must recognize that computer-based systems and computer-resident data are created and maintained ''for the pleasure of management.'' This somewhat unusual phrase is another way of saying at the direction and for the use of management. Thus we should always realize that computer-based capabilities have value only when supporting management in its effort to achieve the goals and objectives of the organization.

Specifically, the information center is a way of supporting the most important resource available to management, the personnel under the control of managers. We refer to this resource as the end users. The purpose of the IC is to enhance end user productivity, that is, to support an environment of creativity, effectiveness, and efficiency of effort. Thus we should expand the thoughts of the IC to the generally accepted functions of management that are used in the quest of goal achievement through productivity. These functions are (1) planning, (2) staffing, (3) organizing, (4) directing, and (5) controlling.

Planning relates to the up-front thinking, scheduling, and choice design activities that go on before an organization is created and continue throughout its life. In planning, management translates the goals and objectives of the organization into specific courses of action. While it is expected that medium- and long-term planning is in order for organizations, it has been found that there was little planning prior to the initiation of many ICs in the study and that the planning horizon for an IC tends to be between three and six months. Thus overt planning, especially of a tactical and strategic nature, seems to be supplanted by operational activity. This would appear to be a problem, not so much in the operation of an IC as with the integration of the IC with other forms of organizational support. Specifically, planning for the long-term goals of end user computing and the way the IC will support these goals could have an important effect on the continued success of the information center concept. This in turn will tend to affect global productivity of the total organization.

Staffing is the process by which managers acquire human resources with which they carry out the goals and objectives of the organization. This means hiring people with the appropriate skills and personality traits. With the advent of end user computing, computer-oriented skills have become more important than only a decade ago. A computer-literate individual joining the organization will be productive only to the extent of resource support. If the new employee does not have the necessary computer-related skills, training is required, and thus resources must be available. The information center is the organizational entity by which support can be maintained and training made available. Staffing the IC with a motivated manager and a reasonable number of personable, competent people will have a significant impact on end users' productivity. The present conflict as to the high value of the IC and the apparent lack of willingness to staff it at a reasonable level must be addressed. The failure to provide a career path for the IC staff must be considered in order to develop the IC positions as viable opportunities and to reward successful staff members for excellent performance.

Organizing is the means of creating the form of a functional unit, the structuring of resources. ICs have been successful in organizing support for end user computing. Though the specific level of support is often less than desired, the form and conduct of the support organization have been well received and highly productive. ICs have drawn from several sources for their staffs and have demonstrated the value of this new form of marketing for data services. The IC has been instrumental in improving relations between data services and the user departments. A very important part of this organizing process has been finding an IC champion, ready, willing, and able to interface with end users, managers, and members of data services. The single most important aspect of the IC organization is the person given the charge of developing the IC-user interface. Once established, this individual and the subsequent staff can be surprisingly effective.

Part of the success of the IC is the overt plan to organize and support the user-MIS interface. Some IC managers believe that the IC should be data service's primary user contact point, a dramatic departure from past practices. Part of the reason for the failure to recognize the importance of this interface has been a shortage of human resources on the part of data services. The IC has now been shown to be so effective in this interface role that it has a significant productivity effect on the rest of the data services organization by insulating it from day-to-day queries. The users are demanding support of their interface with data services, and the IC staff has shown their ability and willingness to provide this support.

Directing, or coordinating, is the process of communicating management's wishes and combines with the process of control to achieve the desired result. It is the execution of the plans made earlier in the management process. Management directs in order to forge a productive organization that uses its resources as efficiently as practicable. The IC supports the firm's management of the user departments. That is, the support provided by the IC allows end users to be more productive. Whereas direction of the staff is of concern to the IC manager, the support provided by the IC staff is a resource available to all of the firm's managers in realizing their functional unit goals. Thus the IC is a resource of many organizations.

Controlling organizational units is achieved by comparing actual performance with planned performance and initiating corrective action to remedy any negative variance or enhance any positive variance. This includes the actions of the human and machine resources. Another form of control relates to the use of resources. During the past decade, control has extended to the information resource as the cost of data and information, as well as their value, has been recognized. The IC supports the effective use of the information resource by providing access to the data, training in its use, and consultation in tools that provide analysis. Without the support provided by the information center staff, data may be just an expensive, idle asset. The IC staff assists in ensuring that the resource is secure, retains its integrity when accessed by end users, and trains the users in appropriate controls of data under their dominion.

2. *Critical success factors.* To operate an organizational unit, the person charged with this responsibility needs certain information. Several approaches have been advocated for identifying such information needs. The most recent of them is the critical success factors (CSF) method. CSFs are those few areas where "things must go right" for the organization to flourish. Some of the factors believed to be important for an IC include planning, data availability, organizational culture, services provided, and communication between users and information center staff. Formal studies on the information needs of information center managers reveal a substantial list of CSFs, but none has been designated as truly critical [11-1]. As with any level of management, the IC manager must be sensitive to a few areas. Present research is attempting to isolate these few areas where IC managers must be kept up-to-date to survive.

THE FUTURE: FORMAL DEVELOPMENT AND USER DEVELOPMENT

The question of the future relates to three areas: (1) the method of data services for the firm, (2) the data services organization, and (3) the nature, effect, and support of end-user computing. These three areas are interrelated and will interact as a system to address the total computer and data resources of the firm.

Provision of Data Services: Methods and Capabilities

As technology has evolved, so have the methods of providing data services. The first change came when engineers were allowed to use the computer directly in batch mode. This meant that people other than members of the DP organization were having direct access to the machine. The next change was from batch mode to timeshare. This allowed quicker changes and faster responses for existing users. Timeshare also allowed placing computer access devices in the user areas for direct use as opposed to writing data entry sheets. With the change from batch to timeshare and the ability to gain access came a general question of who could have access and by what means—end user computing. This brought pressure to bear on formal development and the general decentralization of resource access.

Methods and Capabilities

1. Growing influence of microcomputers
2. Centralized versus decentralized resources
3. Formal development versus end user development
4. Mainframe versus personal computers
5. File versus database technology
6. Purchased versus created applications

---

1. *Growing influence of microcomputers.* IBM introduced the Personal Computer in August 1981. This started a force of great proportion that shows no signs of subsiding. The advantages of PCs were discussed in earlier chapters, as were the problems. It is the subject of problems as well as the potential of the PC that makes the topic worth revisiting.

The microcomputer, as first introduced into the business world by Apple and Radio Shack, is evolving into the concept of a business workstation. In a workstation, the user will treat the computer as a normal part of the workday, like the telephone. It will be capable of communicating and working with data, text, video, voice, and graphics, alone or in concert with a mainframe. This workstation will constitute an environment, not just a tool.

Until the workstation becomes an organized part of the work environment, the continued proliferation of microcomputers will be a problem. They are expensive, somewhat fragile, seductive, and require care. Standardization of hardware and software is generally required in a multiunit environment. The IC can support, control, and organize this PC environment to the extent desired. The concept and force are here and must be supported and controlled, not constrained and controlled.

2. *Centralized versus decentralized resources.* The centralization of any resource is a question of power. Tight control means determining who can use the resource and for what purpose. Timeshare allows that question to be addressed directly in ways never envisioned with a batch environment. Microcomputers apply even greater pressure.

Management must address the question as to the purpose of computer power and computer-resident data as never before. The question of organizational efficiency by "computerizing" some clerical tasks, such as accounting, is far less important than the issues of competitive edge and organizational effectiveness made possible via proper data services. Data services must be part of the business for the business to be highly successful. Resources can still be controlled and maintained centrally, but they must be seen as organizational resources, available for organization uses.

3. *Formal development versus end user development.* As has been stated several times, formal and user development are two alternatives that must be considered and applied widely. Neither is intrinsically better, nor should either be ignored. End user development has just too much to offer to be constrained but must be adequately supported to provide the potential available. The IC staff is the logical resource to review and direct tasks from the users to the proper development area. As organizations learn to apply both methods, all resources will be applied more productively.

4. *Mainframe versus personal computers.* The personal computer of today is the mainframe of two decades ago. The PC has brought new capabilities and has changed the way organizations can operate. It is not an *either-or* situation, it is an *and* environment. To make the PC a part of the technology base, it must be part of the known resource and supported as such. Clandestine purchases solve immediate problems but create others. Management must realize the potential of the microcomputer workstation and provide it the support it deserves.

5. *File versus database technology.* Data sharing is a consideration of efficiency and effectiveness. A file-oriented organization has less potential for data sharing, will likely incur greater costs, and will probably fail to realize the potential possible with a common database information resource. The higher cost of database technology acquisition will be quickly returned by effectiveness of effort and efficiency of organizations.

Part of the discussion of database technology is the issue and practice of data administration and management. It is one thing to have data in a centralized facility and to support it technically. It is quite another to provide a librarian and management function for this resource, ensuring its reliability, integrity, and accessibility. Database technology and data administration are two powerful tools for the computer-resident data resource. However, it may be necessary to provide different facilities for production and end user needs.

6. *Purchased versus created applications.* The basic problem of creation and replacement of applications has been addressed. Data services must realize that NIH ("not invented here") is far less important and more costly than the alternative of purchase and outside maintenance. In this area, data services becomes a project manager, analyst, and implementer and leaves programming, especially maintenance, to others.

The DP Organization: Data Services

The DP Organization

1. Need for business-oriented management
2. Realization of "business within a business"
3. Investment rather than expense
4. Data as the lifeblood of the firm

DP organizations have existed for less than four decades. The technology they control has changed the nature of business. The data services organization has been slow to change, to evolve to the business within a business. This must happen for several reasons: (1) Technology for its own sake is very costly and of little value, (2) change is occurring at a very rapid rate and technology is needed to support it, and (3) the business environment needs technology on its own terms to be competitive. Data services has several issues to address internally.

1. *Need for business-oriented management.* The managers within data services have generally risen to their positions through technical paths. Often the director of MIS and manager of application development were once programmers in the same organization. Although the person may know the technical aspects of data services, what are now required are management and business skills. The direction of the computer room of hardware, with data libraries, data entry, and telecommunications, is now more management than technical, and the person in charge must understand people more than machines. Data services is an investment with the potential for establishing a competitive edge. All of data services management must understand this and be oriented to the larger goals of the parent organization.

2. *Realization of "business within a business."* Data services has all the features of the parent organization. It must be cost-conscious, profit-conscious, and people-oriented, develop and market products, and have a service perspective. With a business-oriented management team, data services will be a business organization.

3. *Investment rather than expense.* The budgets of data services have long been a cost. Data and information processing is as vital to organizations as people, capital, and machinery. DP budgets are an investment and must provide a return, like any investment. Computers are like drill presses, programmers are like financial analysts, and managers of data services are like managers of accounting and marketing departments. As the organization recognizes that data services supports the corporate effort, the view of data services will change. As data services realizes that they create not programs but technological underpinnings for the entire corporate process, the objectives and methods of this organization will change.

4. *Data as the lifeblood of the firm.* Information resource management means data administration and management for the entire company. This involves data quality, sharing, security, and accessibility. Data and information are not a function's resource any more than DP's resource. Data and information are the company's resource. If the resource is not available, it is useless and very expensive. With proper data, a firm can survive and be competitive. Without it, the future is significantly less certain. Data services is the custodian of the resource. What is more important, it becomes the comanager of the resource.

THE FUTURE OF THE INFORMATION CENTER

During an interview, the manager of a large information center ventured that the three-year mark was a special time in the life of an IC. He believed that after three years of existence, information centers face some form of threat or transition. The IC manager did not know what was in store for him as his IC approached the three-year mark, but he realized that its existence was at stake, and for that reason he gathered data continuously to be able to show the return on investment of his IC. He was prepared for the confrontation, for he continued to be the champion.

There are a variety of views of how to address the future of the information center. We shall examine several, ranging from considering the stages of growth of an IC to the general management tasks of planning, organizing, directing, controlling, and coordination (see Figure 11-2). Organizations change as they mature, and the IC is housed in a short-lived, technology-based, changing environment of data services. What happens to the IC concept is closely related to the future of data services, and vice versa.

Stages of Growth

Like a living organism, an information center is born, develops a level of organization and critical mass, expands, eventually arrives at a level of stability and maturity, and subsequently reevolves or dies. This pattern follows the familiar S curve of growth. Nolan first noted a growth curve for DP organizations and concluded that the life of such an organization was divided into four stages: (I) initiation, (II) expansion, (III) formalization, and (IV) maturity [11-2]. As noted in Figure 11-3, the growth of the DP expenditure curve is S-shaped, increasing at an increasing rate (stage II) as users realize the value and power of computer-based systems. In stage III, management exercises control due to runaway costs.

Information centers evolve into mature organizational units integrated with the rest of their organization. Typically, this evolution progresses through the same four stages as DP organizations (see Figure 11-4). The time in each stage varies greatly; the figure shows averages. However, the stage hypotheses do indicate that ICs evolve, confront different opportunities and problems in each stage, and finally arrive at a point of potential absorption [11-1].

The value of realizing the various stages of growth is that in each stage the IC will involve different users, management styles, and needs. The following describes the four stages of IC growth. This was used in a survey of over 300 IC managers.

> Compatibility of hardware and software is the primary goal at start-up (stage I), followed by diffusion of technology in stage II. The rapid, often runaway growth in the use of EUC technology leads to curbing this growth during stage III. As EUC activities spread throughout the organization the goal becomes one of coordinating these EUC activities.
>
> Planning is virtually nonexistent during stage I and is initiated only during stage II. By the time an IC evolves into stage III, planning procedures are well developed and eventually (stage IV) the IC plan becomes a part of the global corporate plan.
>
> Typically, ICs tend to be centralized during the early stages (I and II) and some functions become decentralized into the user departments during the later stages (III and IV). The centralized IC, if it still exists, takes on the role of coordinating the activities of the ICs in the user departments.
>
> The size of the IC staff is typically very small (mean = 5.8) during all stages; however, the skills, level of specialization, and need for supervisory and administrative functions increase as an IC evolves.

1. Stages of growth
   A. Initiation
   B. Expansion
   C. Formalization
   D. Maturity
2. Formal development versus user development
   A. Problems attendant to user development
      i. Tendency to understudy and undertest
      ii. Longer life than expected
      iii. Poor documentation
      iv. Need to communicate to others what has been done
      v. Duplication of effort
      vi. User development of large systems
   B. Formal development situations
      i. Shortage of analysts and programmers
      ii. Management demands that analysts understand business
      iii. Replacement of aging software
         a. Large replacement costs
         b. Make-or-buy decisions for new capabilities
         c. User involvement in replacing capabilities
      iv. Software aids to formal development
         a. Timeshare and productivity center
         b. Application generation languages
         c. Project management tools
         d. Computer-based analysis and design aids
3. Provision of data services
   A. Centralized versus decentralized resources
   B. Formal development versus end user development
   C. Mainframe versus personal computers
   D. File versus database technology
   E. Purchased versus created applications
4. DP evolution to data services
   A. Need for business-oriented management
   B. Realization of "business within a business"
   C. Investment rather than expense
   D. Data as lifeblood of firm
5. Reporting level
   A. Part of application development
   B. Manager below MIS director
   C. General manager
6. Distribution of the IC concept
   A. Multiple physical facilities
   B. Distribution of the IC staff to user areas
7. Influence of microcomputers
   A. Need for control
   B. Importance of communications and mainframe-PC link
   C. Workstation concept; data, text, voice, graphics
8. Alternate view of the information center
   A. Management functions: Planning, staffing, organizing, directing, controlling
   B. Critical success factors

Figure 11-2   Considerations for IC and data services

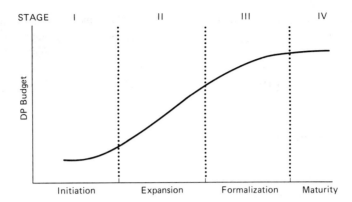

Figure 11-3   Stages of DP growth

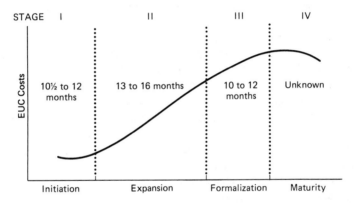

Figure 11-4   Stages of IC growth [11-1]

Initially, control is centralized with numerous control mechanisms aimed at curbing growth being initiated during stage III. Stage IV sees refinements of existing control mechanisms and an increased influence from the user departments. Priority criteria are based on a first-in-first-out basis changing to well-developed procedures during the later stages. Evaluation procedures are initiated only during stage II and are refined during the later stages.

With regard to training, a variety of methods are used during stage I and training is provided for limited hardware and software. Stage II sees a reduction of the training methods and an increase in the scope of such training. In the last stages, the training tends to be very specialized, perhaps computer-based.

Finally, in stage I, the users are typically self-motivated and place limited demands on the IC staff. With the goal of diffusion of technology, the user base expands, increasing the demand for IC services. Eventually, decentralized ICs serve the needs of the users from specific functional area. [11-1]

As stage III is reached, the informality of earlier stages gives way to more organization and control. Expenses are increasing and, as in stage III of DP growth, management will want to understand and control these costs. With stage IV comes a reevaluation of the IC charter. It is during stages III and IV that the availability of data supporting the value of the IC will be vital. The glamour will be gone, and the champion must, as always, show how this concept is very positively affecting the productivity of the organization. Survey data, project review forms, letters of comment, and diaries will be of great use in this task.

Reporting Level

Data services often started as a minor data processing function in the accounting department. As the value of data services increased and the person responsible for the DP function recognized the power involved, its position was elevated, eventually to a line position on a par with many executives, often reporting to the president or general manager. The director or vice-president of data services is now viewed as an important and powerful person in any firm.

The customer service function, if it existed, was a minor operation in application development. As end user computing has developed and been recognized, the information center evolved as a visible part of that function. With the increased importance of end user computing and the recognition of the differences between formal application development and user development, the IC may be moved out of application development to a position of equal power. An extreme position may indeed be a part of the information resource management function at an even higher level. In any case, the IC is being viewed as not just another function of application development. It is important in its own right and should take its proper place in the management hierarchy.

As an example of such a view of the IC, an electric utility firm in Atlanta, Georgia, has separated formal development and the IC and placed the latter in a new organizational entity called end user services. As shown in Figure 11-5, the new function reports to the manager of MIS on the same level of authority as formal development, technical services, and operations.

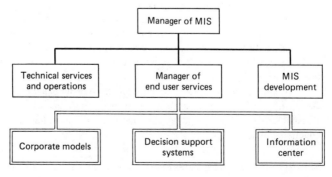

Figure 11-5   End user services placement of the IC

Distribution of the Information Center Concept

Several of the larger ICs studied for this book have sufficient responsibilities and scattered clients that more than one IC became desirable and necessary. This is in keeping with two views of the IC. One emphasizes centralization of resources—a place for people and things—and distribution of assets—separate the centralized facility to be closer to the user community. Distribution of the facilities to multiple sites will be of value for a large, scattered firm; for one that is more centralized, a single IC facility is in order.

The other view of distribution of resources is to break up the central IC facility and distribute the people and assets to functional areas. In other words, let the IC staff live in the user areas and support specified corporate entities. This process is happening to a limited degree with analysts and provides a way for the analyst to learn the business of the firm. This would be true of the IC staff's distribution but would take the core of expertise away from common access. Because of the dissolving of resources, it is unlikely that the IC staff will be so distributed in the near future.

SUMMARY

During its existence, the information center concept has demonstrated a new way to provide data services and overcome problems associated with formal MIS development. Most people knowledgeable of the information center concept, especially those in the study supporting this text, agree that the information center is a successful concept, one that can be very effective in supporting end user computing and enhancing end user productivity. And, as noted by Edelman, "End User Programming is 'inevitable' and will bring with it the need to change the data processing organization, if not the profession itself. End User Programming is coming, because it offers just too many benefits to end users" [11-3]. With such a force whose time has come has come the organization for support.

Key Terms

Stages of DP growth	Stages of IC growth
Initiation stage	Expansion stage
Formalization stage	Maturity stage
Documentation	Duplication of effort
Aging software	Planning
Staffing	Organizing
Directing	Critical success factors

DISCUSSION QUESTIONS

1. Why do DP costs continue to increase?
2. Should we expect production data service costs to decrease in proportion to the anticipated increase in EUC costs?

3. Design an EUC administrator's task description. Be careful to differentiate it from that of a data administrator.

4. How can we prevent users from developing what appear to be large systems—and should we?

5. What do you think will cause the apparent shortage of analysts and programmers to disappear? What is the time frame?

6. Since software does not wear out, what does "aging software" mean?

7. Discuss the office environment for the year 2000.

8. Discuss data services for the year 2000.

9. If data is the lifeblood of the firm, what is the backbone?

10. Develop a case for creating an organization answerable to the CEO that is headed by the chief information officer and has the functions of information resource management and EUC support.

11. Realizing the value of certain centralized IC resources, how would you distribute an IC?

CASE STUDY

THE SOUTEX COMPANY

The Soutex Company, which has headquarters in Central Texas, was started in the early 1940s as an oilfield services company. It had sales of $500 million in the middle 1980's and employed 4,500. The firm's sales follow the economics of the world oil exploration efforts, which are presently recovering from a depression.

Soutex Company's Information Center

The entry into the formal support of end user computing via the information center was partly the result of IBM's announcement of the concept and partly the result of a perceived need to support informal end user computing. In January 1983, data services organized a business systems development (BSD) group to provide a quick-reaction response within the MIS department. This was to be an alternative to the long delays and high cost of formal MIS development. The BSD group provided coding services and assisted the users in utilizing SAS, FOCUS, and Easytrieve. Meanwhile, some of the more sophisticated users were using SAS and Easytrieve on their own without support. During a reorganization of data services in March 1983, the quick-reaction group was divided, with one part becoming the information center. The IC had three full-time employees and one part-timer. Meanwhile, the user population has grown to about 50 people, with the growth rate presently following an exponential curve.

The purpose of establishing the quick-response group and the resultant IC was to provide a service that would allow data services to be responsive to users. Besides the benefits of response, cost reduction, and the better use of DP resources, an added benefit was the display to Soutex Company customers of the use of new methods and technology. This is considered important in the competitive market in which Soutex operates.

The IC is used primarily by the groups categorized as professionals and upper management. The departments of marketing, accounting, and finance are the principal users, for personal, departmental, and corporate applications, in that order. As in most of the companies studied, reports, queries, and analysis were the top uses of the IC capabilities. Atypically, word processing was also in great demand.

It is a specific objective of the IC manager to educate and train the higher levels of management in the IC capabilities, both to show that data services has capabilities that produce results and to have these people begin to use decision support tools. Soutex is sensitive to costs as well as contribution to income, and data services believes they must show that they are earning their budget. An example of both of these thoughts is the present test of the INTELLECT capability being offered by IBM, using Soutex company data. A presentation is being made to upper management to show how such a high-level capability might be usable for better and faster support of the decision making process.

Training is important and strongly supported at Soutex. The company has a large, dedicated training complex. This is where all IC training (except PC tutorial training) is accomplished. The IC offers a dozen courses, many of them in sequence to take a new user from the introduction to data processing through use of a language.

The IC support is provided via a single shared IBM Model 3033 mainframe. The user community has some 125 video display terminals for IC and application access. In addition, Soutex has 40 IBM PCs, many of which are connected to the mainframe. The primary mainframe languages are Easytrieve, SAS, IFPS, and FOCUS.

New computer accounts and data access are controlled by the IC staff. All data that is accessed by the end user is first extracted from production files and databases by the IC staff. The IC staff then assists the user in gaining permission from the owner to use the data and makes a Top Secret security system rule that allows access. All data except the user's personal files is secured by Top Secret, and no access to production data is allowed except via on-line terminals using a production application.

The users of IC services and DP applications alike are charged for use of the computer. The on-line charges are based on connect time only. The departments do forecast usage and are held accountable for costs. An interesting response to a question as to use of costing as an IC marketing ploy was that there is no charge for IC consulting but application development groups do charge for this consulting. This is a nonobvious use of costing to influence the use of the computer and departmental personnel.

Outside timeshare services were heavily used prior to the IC, and reduction of this cost was an objective of the IC installation. Some departments were experiencing timeshare charges in excess of $30,000 per month. Outside timeshare is now of very low volume, and its use, though allowed, is discouraged.

This IC manager believes that the existence of an IC does raise special problems. Specifically, programs developed by users are generally not documented. When the person leaves the department, continuation and maintenance of the program are difficult, at best. Unlike another firm's IC manager, who believes that users are at least as good as programmers at testing programs, this IC manager believes that the IC presents a much greater potential for the creation of inaccurate reports.

The primary objective of the Soutex Company information center is to promote the use of end user computing to improve decision making and contribute to revenue and profit. The IC manager believes that distributed data processing is very valuable and

that traditional DP methods are less productive than the IC and end user computing techniques. "The IC can make all the end users more efficient in doing their jobs," notes the IC manager.

The IC manager observes that information needs have a life of about three months. This is short compared with the time it takes for formal specification, analysis, design, programming, testing, and implementation via MIS techniques. Thus end user computing is required to be able to provide computer-based support for information needs during the short life of these needs. The end user computing methods are more timely and far less expensive to discard when the need ends.

Plans for the future include expanding the IC staff in order to be of more assistance to the end users, assimilating new technology and languages, and acquiring more effective and complete training methods and capabilities.

Update

The interviews with IC managers were completed at different times during the development of their respective information centers. Some time has passed since these interviews, and the question arises as to the effect of that time. To determine what a worse-case scenario would be for an IC, I called the IC manager at the Soutex as a follow-up. I chose this company because the oil industry continues to be in a dynamic and depressed state and because I knew that Soutex had had some difficulty. The IC manager at the time of the original interview was no longer with Soutex, so I spoke with the director of information services.

The information center at Soutex no longer officially exists. The former staff has been reduced to a single person who handles user requests two days per week. As the MIS director indicated, "If you need assistance, call on Tuesday or Wednesday." Beyond reactive support, there is no information center activity and none under consideration.

The environment in which the IC was disbanded was one of severe cost reduction for Soutex. During a short period of time, the company went from 4,200 to 1,800 employees, a 57 percent reduction. The MIS organization was also subject to a similar reduction, going from 75 to 33 employees, a loss of 56 percent of the work force. The director indicated that the MIS organization had the same reduction targets as the rest of the company but that it was also agreed that 33 was the minimum number of MIS professionals required to support Soutex's activities. While the MIS organization has executive support for the original 33 specific individuals, the director indicated that it was very difficult to receive authorization to replace one when a programmer or analyst left the firm.

As for the information center staff, what was the effect of reducing the support of the users? In this instance, the users being supported were the first reductions; thus the staff that supported individuals that were removed were themselves considered candidates for removal. The users that were employing end user computing were not the revenue-generating personnel of the company and were therefore expendable. They were the staff personnel, who seem to be less necessary in time of cost constraint. Thus the support staff for these people was also considered expendable for the same reason.

The one individual that remains provides reactive support. Thus, as in an IC that is just starting and has limited resources, the Soutex support person keeps a low profile. It is understood that there are both need and demand in the user areas, as before the creation of an IC, but there is no plan to surface or support this demand. The primary user language is now FOCUS, and the consultant generally provides aid to users in this capability. In some instances where there are no qualified users, the consultant will perform FOCUS programming for a requester.

The demise of the information center at Soutex is not an indicator of the fate of such organizations during hard times. Texas has many companies fighting for survival. When survival is at stake, the consideration is one of revenue generation and cost reduction. Other considerations seem of little consequence. If the organization is not fighting for survival, a different scenario will dominate. The IC permits organizational personnel to be productive and effective. These consultants act as an amplifier for the users and allow the remaining users to be the best they can be. One consultant can have a highly disproportionate effect on the organization. Thus the value of the information and the career of its staff will be recognized and will each have a positive and bright future.

REFERENCES

11-1. Magal, Simha R., Houston H. Carr, and Hugh J. Watson, "Critical Success Factors for Information Center Managers." Working Paper Series, *University of Georgia End User Computing Research Center Working Paper #21*.

11-2. Gibson, Cyrus F., and Richard L. Nolan, "Managing the Four Stages of EDP Growth." *Harvard Business Review* January–February 1974, pp. 76–88.

11-3. Edelman, Franz, "The Management of Information Resources—A Challenge for American Business." *MIS Quarterly* March 1981, pp. 17–27.

Index

Administration, data services, 16
Administrative process, 32
Administrative support, 104
AI/ES, 5
Application architecture, 23
Application development, 14
Application procurement, 56
Architecture, 23
Artificial intelligence/expert systems, 5

Behavioral feasibility, 20
Benefits, 90, 134, 143, 166, 179
Better relations, 145
Better requirements, 145
Better use of limited resources, 147
Building (or rebuilding) an information center, 198

Careers, 98, 161
Case studies, 9
    American Airlines, 231
    City of Dallas, Texas, The, 175
    EasTexas Industries, Inc., 115
    Electro-Tex Corporation, 152
    Federal Reserve Bank of Dallas, 233

FMC Corporation, 151
General Dynamics Corporation, 83
J. C. Penney Life Insurance Company, 154
Middle-Texas & Company, Inc., 137
MOSTEK-Thomson Components, 114
Otis Engineering Corporation, 85
Pier 1 Imports, Inc., 195
Potato-Tex, Inc., 214
Quick-Tex Corporation, 140
    Southland Royalty Company, 138
    Soutex Company, the, 253
    Texas Instruments, Inc., 171
    Zale Corporation, 193
Centralized resources, 244
Change in the nature of jobs, 166
Chargeback for services, 165
Charging, promotion, and marketing of the information center, 206
Charter, 89, 90, 94
Communications, 66
Computer efficiency, 132
Computer instructions, 66
Computer output, 108, 111
Computer programming, 66, 68
Consultation, 103
Control, 125, 206, 216

Cost accounting and chargeback, 129
Creating an information center, 199
    continuous review of the concept, 206
    IC creation checklist, 207
    management approval, 199
    organizing the team, 202
    planning for the IC, 203
Critical success factors, 243

Data, 181
Data access, 119, 163, 164
Data administration, 15, 119, 163
Data analysis, 66
Data architecture, 24
Data availability, 109, 162, 206
Data dictionaries, 120
Data integrity, 129
Data management, 119
Data processing, 5
Data proliferation, 128
Data query, 66, 70
Data search, 66
Data security, 128
Data services, 1, 11, 13, 14, 17, 39, 77, 78, 119, 134, 199, 236, 243, 245, 247
Data services support, 77

Data storage, 108
Database, 245
Database management, 66
Database management system
    (DBMS), 67, 108
Decentralized, 57
Decentralized resources, 244
Decision support systems, 4
Dedicated processor, 123
Departmental specialists, 105
Design, 7, 18, 24
DP contact point, 164
DP options, 90, 119, 162, 168
    data access, 119
    hardware options, 122
DSS, 4

Economic feasibility, 20
EIS, 4
End user, 61, 79
End user computing, 40, 54, 56, 61,
    63, 65, 71, 227
End user computing tasks, 65
End user development, 55, 226, 236
End user-developed project descrip-
    tion form, 219, 223
Evaluation of user projects, 223
Executive information systems, 4
Extract copy, 124

Feasibility analysis, 7, 18, 19
Firm (organization), 5
Formal development, 7, 8, 17, 37, 39,
    55, 226, 228, 236, 237, 243,
    245
Formal MIS development, 56
Formal request process, 32
Future of information centers, 167,
    223, 246

Graphics, 66, 69

Hackers, 41
Hammond, 88, 96, 111, 117, 130
Hardware options, 122

IBM, 88, 91, 92, 112
IBM-Hammond, 89, 90, 129

IC creation checklist, 208
IC documentation, 219
IC manager, 94, 95, 159, 201
IC mission statement, 218
IC staff, 95, 96, 97, 112, 160
Implementation, 7, 18, 27
Implementation of an information
    center, 157
Improved quality of information, 147
Increased productivity, 146
Informal end user computing, 56, 58
Informal end user development, 39,
    40
Information center, 84, 86, 88, 98,
    114, 116, 137, 138, 140, 151,
    153, 154, 171, 176, 193, 214,
    231, 233, 241, 253
Information center guidelines, 220
Information center manager (see IC
    manager)
Information center models, 216
Information center style, 159
Information resource management, 15
Initiation of an IC, 158

Languages, 105
Layout of a centralized information
    center, 209
Lunch time seminars, 186

Mainframe computers, 122
Maintenance and change, 7, 18, 29
Make-or-buy decision, 22, 49
Management characteristics that lead
    to a successful IC, 210
Management information systems, 3
Management issues, 90, 119, 124,
    164, 169
    benefits, 124
    computer efficiency, 124
    cost accounting and chargeback,
    124
    data integrity, 124
    data proliferation, 124
    marketing of the IC, 124
    promotion, 124
    user-data services relationships,
    124
Management support, 76
Manager of IC, 94, 95, 159, 201
Map of problem resolution, 74

Marketing and promoting of the IC,
    165
Microcomputers, 42, 122
MIS, 3
Mission statement, 219, 220

Network architecture, 24

OAS, 4
Office automation systems, 4
Outside procurement, 39, 49, 58
Outside timeshare, 39, 47, 56, 58

Personal computer, 39, 42, 56, 58,
    245
Physical IC facilities, 205
Pictorial display, 66
Premises, 88, 89, 90, 100, 112, 127,
    159, 168
Privacy, 127
Problems addressed by an information
    center, 179
Product specialization, 104
Programming, 7, 18, 25
Project evaluation form, 224
Promotion and marketing of the IC,
    131
Prototyping, 22, 39, 52, 56, 58
Purchased applications, 245

Quick reaction capability (QRC), 186

Read-only access, 121
Read-write access, 122
Records management, 66
Reduced cost of application creation
    and more timely results, 144
Reduction of the backlog, 143
Relations between end users and data
    services, 130
Reporting level of IC, 250
Rows and columns, 66

SDLC, 227
Security, 109, 125, 165, 206, 226
Security training, 225

Shared processor, 124
Signs of need for an IC, 157
Software and hardware evaluation, 190
Spreadsheet, 66
Staff, 88, 90, 94
Staff of IC, 95, 96, 97, 112, 160
Staffing, 242
Stages of growth, 247
Stages of IC growth, 249
Statistics, 66, 69
Support systems architecture, 24
Supported end user computing, 39, 54, 56, 58, 76
System, 3
System access, 110
Systems analysis, 7, 18, 21
Systems development, 15
Systems development life cycle (SDLC), 7, 18, 32

Technical feasibility, 19
Technical services, 16
Technical support, 103
Technology infusion, 190
Telecommunications, 66, 69
Telephone hotline service, 184
Test, 18
Testing, 7, 26
Texas Electric Service Company, 38
Tools, 105, 183
TPS, 3
Training, 100, 161, 190
    classroom training, 100
    computer-based training (CBT), 101
    one-on-one training, 101
    self-study training, 100
    Tutorial training, 100
    Vendor training, 101

Transaction processing systems, 3

Unique management considerations for an IC, 212
User development, 237, 239, 243, 245
User enthusiasm, 148
User group meetings, 185
User literacy, 147
User support, 16
User-developed projects, 229
User-friendly, 107
User's manual, 219, 220

Walk-in service in the IC, 185
Word processing, 66, 68
Written communications, 66